P9-DFX-336

The Gods Drink Whiskey

ALSO BY STEPHEN ASMA

Buddha for Beginners

Following Form and Function:
A Philosophical Archaeology of Life Science

Stuffed Animals and Pickled Heads:
The Culture and Evolution of Natural History Museums

The Gods Drink Whiskey

Stumbling Toward Enlightenment in the Land of the Tattered Buddha

STEPHEN T. ASMA

HarperSanFrancisco
A Division of HarperCollins*Publishers*

For further information on Stephen Asma and his work, try his Web site: www.stephenasma.com.

THE GODS DRINK WHISKEY: *Stumbling Toward Enlightenment in the Land of the Tattered Buddha.* Copyright © 2005 by Stephen T. Asma. All rights reserved. Printed in the United States of America. No part of this book may be used or reproduced in any manner whatsoever without written permission except in the case of brief quotations embodied in critical articles and reviews. For information address HarperCollins Publishers, Inc., 10 East 53rd Street, New York, NY 10022.

HarperCollins books may be purchased for educational, business, or sales promotional use. For information please write: Special Markets Department, HarperCollins Publishers, Inc., 10 East 53rd Street, New York, NY 10022.

HarperCollins Web site: http://www.harpercollins.com

HarperCollins®, ♣®, and HarperSanFrancisco™ are trademarks of HarperCollins Publishers, Inc.

FIRST EDITION

Library of Congress Cataloging-in-Publication Data
  Asma, Stephen T.
    The gods drink whiskey : stumbling toward enlightenment in the land of
  the tattered Buddha / Stephen T. Asma.—1st ed.
      p.   cm
    Includes bibliographical references.
    ISBN 0-06-072395-5
    1. Buddhism. I. Title.
  BQ4022.A83   2005
  294.3´4—dc   2004060864

05 06 07 08 09   RRD(H)   10 9 8 7 6 5 4 3 2 1

For my son Julien, who made my heart grow bigger than my head

CONTENTS

A Preface on Pop-Buddhists and Academics

It has become increasingly difficult for Westerners to understand Buddhism and other Eastern beliefs. I don't pretend to be an exception, but I do see some fixable problems. On the one hand, the popularity of Eastern ideas has done much to actually obscure Eastern ideas, by watering them down or forcing a Procrustean fit with Western values. On the other hand, the academic study of religious cultures has, since the days of Émile Durkheim, focused entirely on observable rituals and left the internal beliefs and philosophies of religious traditions out of the picture altogether. For one thing, those internal beliefs were not "observable" and thus fell outside the domain of positivist science. Furthermore, social science deemed that the most important thing about religion was its power to create social cohesion through us-them in-group mechanisms (ritual and myth, and so on). This is undoubtedly an important function, but it's not the whole picture.

After the founding fathers of sociology built the frame of inquiry, God fell out of the picture of religion altogether. And the pantheon of other spirits and beliefs also became relatively uninteresting to scientists of culture. You can't blame them really. I mean, you can't build a science unless you have some objects or behaviors to observe, measure, quantify, and so on. The problem is that internal religious beliefs are neither objects nor behaviors, and so, because of a methodological problem (left over from positivism), the very essence of religion (God, soul, immortality) has disappeared from the academic study of religious cultures. And don't hold your breath for the contemporary humanities to come to the rescue and return the gods to their central place in the study of cultures. Alas, they are too busy trying to deconstruct the representational discourses that gather together the *différence* of the fissures and marginalia of the horizon of being such that the "other" is met with, in its "othering" capacity, in order to manifest the hegemonic poststructuralist, postcolonial logo-phallo-centrism! And I guess they'll get back to us when that's all settled.

Contemporary academics have little interest in the actual beliefs of religious people, except as observable social rituals or as literary semiotic narratives. During the course of writing this preface, for example, I heard a long story on National Public Radio discussing the Parsee Zoroastrians living in India. The story detailed their difficulties and successes as a minority group in India and explained at length the difficulties of increasing their membership, the problems with young Parsees who are exposed to a plurality of spiritual options, the complex issues of marriage, the historical economic strength of the group, and so on. In a half-hour program, the journalists, editors, and producers never once thought it necessary to mention what Zoroastrians actually believe in. The whole story had no center. The Parsees' rich and exotic dualistic theology has an amazing history, but current intellectuals see those beliefs as entirely beside the point. They are decidedly *not* beside the point, however, for the people who hold those beliefs.

As I write this, God continues to loom large in the motivations of violent fundamentalist terrorists. Starting on 9/11, tens of thousands of Americans, Iraqis, and Afghanis have been killed. *Jihad* is a word that every American school kid now knows. It will do no good to keep dismissing these theologically motivated atrocities as the work of cranks and to go on blithely studying religions from the external social science perspective. American spiritual beliefs are so private (internal) and individualistic that, according to the religion scholar Martin Marty, they fail to have much impact or influence on wider social issues (although the last presidential election may put the lie to that generalization). Religion for many Americans is more like taste in music—I have my taste, you have yours, and none of it has to get in the way of our public lives. To my mind, there's nothing wrong with this. But make no mistake—other parts of the world do not share this privatized spirituality. And increasingly, parts of America are also no longer interested in a private spirituality. What they believe issues forth directly—sometimes beautifully, sometimes violently—into the public social world. If we do not try to enter into the theological beliefs of our neighbors, we will not understand them. And if we cannot understand them, we cannot find a lasting path to peace.

As negligent as contemporary scholars are regarding the metaphysical beings that populate the minds of believers, they are even less interested in the theological philosophical texts and arguments that surround certain religions. Buddhism is one of those religions that has an elaborate philosophical tradition. And unlike the Christian tradition, wherein church doctors like Aquinas muddied the waters a thousand years after the simple message of Jesus, the logical arguments of Buddhism come relatively straight from the Buddha's mouth. Unfortunately, I have met many social scientists studying Buddhists in the field who have never bothered to study any textual Buddhism.

Ultimately, there is no "real" Buddhism, only the various strands, sects, texts, schools, and cultural streams. However, studying cultural Buddhism only as an anthropologist does is not enough. There really was a Buddha, named Gotama, who lived at a particular time and place and had his ideas collected together (albeit imperfectly) into the Tripitika scriptures. What the Buddha actually taught should matter to people—

both the people who call themselves Buddhists and the people who study Buddhist cultures. Those in the former group at least admit this in principle (though less so in practice), but the latter group, the academic anthropologists, deny the importance of philosophical Buddhism in principle on the grounds that laypeople practice something else. This is historically understandable since early Western studies barely bothered to find out about the lived religion and preferred a more academic version. But those days are long over. Years ago, when it came to religious cultures, academia was all philosophy and no observation, but now it is all observation and no philosophy. My goal in this book is to steer a Middle Way.

Following the tradition that Stephen Toulmin traces back to the sixteenth-century philosopher Michel de Montaigne, I have tried to write "essays" in this book. The essay was a legitimate philosophical method that became relegated to the quaint non-epistemic realm of literature after Cartesian mathematical rationality became the model for all knowledge. But I agree with Toulmin, who thinks we need to reclaim this pre–Scientific Revolution model of reasoned argumentation. I have tried to write essays about my specific experiences in Southeast Asia. Contrary to the Cartesian model of rationality, which seeks timeless validity through rigorous deductive formal proofs, essays offer us a specific context of "where and when" and even "who." Following the essay method, I have generally avoided theories and tried instead to offer stories that may contain larger truths. I have tried to study simultaneously the ideas and beliefs of the people I met and the original ideas and arguments of the Buddha. My narrative here is personal, but it is also a narrative steeped in the wider issues of Buddhist philosophy. I hope that it has the detail to avoid the abstractions of pure theory while remaining theory-conscious enough to have some modest normative value as well.

I have made far too many value judgments in this book for contemporary scholarly taste, but I make no apologies. The current bloodless objectivism that passes for scholarship is as dangerous as the earlier judgmentalism. I've tried to take a Middle Way here too. I've tried, for example, to describe accurately some of the animistic spiritual beliefs of Southeast Asian culture, but I've made no secret of my hostility toward superstition. I would be doing a disservice to a culture and people I have come to love if I simply nodded my head in relativistic "wisdom" as they blamed themselves for Pol Pot or smeared animal blood on doors to ward off illnesses. I hope that my taking a stand on some of these issues will be received as goodwill rather than as superiority. I'm the first to admit that I'm an idiot on many matters, and I also admit that Western cultures can be as neurotic and confused as any, but those with real cross-cultural wisdom are as unafraid to give help as they are to receive it. The East has and will continue to teach us many things, and in return we shouldn't be so reticent and overly polite about encouraging things like science education. In 2003, for example, another developing country, Congo, reported Ebola virus outbreaks. The disease was interpreted by many locals as the result of sorcery and magic; as they grew increasingly suspicious of each other, the people ultimately killed four schoolteachers who were trying to educate the children about the biological nature of the disease and prevention methods. The superstitious murderers suspected that these teachers couldn't have known so much about the illness unless they were in fact the sorcerers who made the sickness. This is what happens when superstition goes unchecked. The sleep of reason still produces monsters, whether contemporary academia cares to acknowledge it or not. I hope that scholars both East and West will increase their efforts to study and teach the rationality of Buddhism and not simply indulge every superstitious belief on the grounds of some polite "tolerance."

A few comments up front about pop-Buddhists seem useful. It is my mission in life to take the "California" out of Buddhism. Maybe that's because I'm a Chicagoan—the son of a steelworker. Chicago Buddhism, if there is such a thing, is bound to be gritty, straightforward, and down to earth. My blunt style may occasionally jar the sensibilities of more delicate, cheerful, colonic types. But rest assured, it is not certainty but only geographic temperament that gives timbre to my voice.

At any social gathering, when Americans discover that I am a Buddhist, they frequently confide in me about a mishmash of their pseudo-Eastern-quantum-herbal beliefs. Their eyes widen and get watery at the prospect of some deep and meaningful sharing. I always smile carefully and back away slowly, looking desperately for the bar.

Often the stuff that passes for "Eastern" in the West would be unrecognized in the East. The reason why so many Westerners become hopelessly muddled about Eastern ideas is that they have little interest in them per se. Many Western searchers want the East on *their* terms. For Americans, Buddhist or Tantric or Taoist ideas have become like herbal remedies that one picks up at the local high-priced organic boutique-grocer. The ideas become like trendy alternative medicines that thrive because people feel disempowered by modern medicine. Consequently, Eastern ideas in the West float about like little self-esteem life-preservers—clung to desperately by disintegrating personalities. American Buddhists frequently go no further than, "This is what Buddhism means *to me*," never seeing the narcissism in this approach and never bothering to try to understand Buddhism on its own terms.

The result is that mainstream sensible Americans have a skewed perception of Buddhism because the local ambassadors of these ideas are notoriously spooky. Buddhism has become just one more self-improvement gimmick among the designer-water-drinking set. Perhaps this was inevitable when the form of Buddhism that entered America during the counterculture years was Zen. Zen, which I also love, is the hyper-puritan descendant of Buddhism—the neurotic cousin that's always disinfecting the furniture and showering off the impurities. It's so vigilant about eliminating dogma and anything outside of pristine meditation practice that it no longer bears any resemblance to Buddhism (except for its connection to the "mindfulness" discussion in the Buddha's Mahasatipatthana Sutta). This is not really a criticism of Zen. But my humble observation is that American dharma has evolved into its rather narcissistic form because Zen introduced Buddhism as a simple concentration practice and nothing more. Americans adopted the meditation idea but left behind the austere discipline of Zen and the cultural context. This neutered Zen Buddhism has no baggage whatsoever, so Americans felt that they could drape it over whatever beliefs they already enjoyed. That seems like a virtue at first ("Look, I'm a Christian *and* a Zen practitioner!"), but it lulled Americans into thinking that Buddhism is the Silly Putty of religions—infinitely malleable and conveniently fashionable. Buddhism becomes another accessory. Living in Southeast Asia, however, rids you of this confusion very quickly.

Theravada Buddhism is the whole enchilada. If Zen is the abstract, hygienic Felix Unger of Buddhism, then Theravada is the cluttered, messy Oscar Madison. It has its Vipassana meditation practice, but also its rich metaphysical and epistemological traditions (largely excised from Zen), its dynamic moral foundations (again, removed from Zen proper), and its dense (sometimes contradictory) cultural expressions. No one of these alone is the true dharma. Together they are all aspects of the dharma. I am not saying that we Americans should never borrow or pilfer ideas and practices from Buddhism. In the global village, fusion is inevitable. But before we just shave off a thin slice of Buddhism and then call ourselves "Buddhist" because it serves our conceit, we should first have the humility to appreciate its own inner logic and heritage. We should examine the roots carefully before we trim and collect the upper flora.

I say all this so that I can make a rather presumptuous request of the reader. I ask that you approach the story with an open mind and read it with an interest in *challenging* your views rather than just mirroring and confirming them. Traveling in the land of the tattered Buddha is an exotic and illuminating adventure—sometimes dark and sometimes joyful. I hope you enjoy the stumble . . . I mean, the ride.

GETTING MY HANDS DIRTY

My longboat cleaved through the dark gray water of a narrow river alley in Bangkok. My driver and I were the only ones on the water at midday, and the stink of fetid water and surrounding filth was overwhelming. We had entered this tributary of the Chao Praya River as a shortcut to find the giant golden Buddha near the temple of Wat Pho. (*Wat* is the word for temple throughout Southeast Asia.) It seemed poetic somehow that I should have to travel through an open sewer to get to the Buddha. At high noon the water was actually bubbling because the decaying mass of animal matter, excrement, and general rot releases nitrogen as it putrefies at the bottom of the riverbed. Countless shack homes and shanty shops back up against this polluted alley, and the poor people who live here are forced to use the river alternately as water source, transport system, and toilet. Naked kids waved to me as I passed. Pigs, dogs, cats, and chickens lazed about in the sweltering heat, seeking refuge in the open kitchens of the overcrowded stilt-homes. Women looked up momentarily from their labor over woks and bamboo steamers—some cooking, some cleaning. I covered my nose and mouth with my shirt in a pathetic attempt to screen out the river stench, and I recoiled when I saw an old man working neck-deep in the water to repair some dilapidated house-support beams. Just when I thought it couldn't get any worse, my driver yelled out to me, "Crocodile," and pointed excitedly to the nearby shore. Slithering out of the muck, onto a concrete slab, was a seven-foot-long prehistoric-looking Monitor lizard—some fugitive Komodo dragon escaped from the reptile farm we passed upstream. I'd seen these creatures on PBS nature shows before, but I wasn't exactly prepared for the firsthand nightmare. My driver steered toward it, of course, and I was gripped by the recollection that these reptiles have been known to eat small children. We got quite close to the little dinosaur before it slipped back into the murky water. I wondered what kind of havoc this thing wreaked in the black of night.

After docking, the giant Buddha brought me relative peace and tranquillity. Of course, after *that* boat trip, even a giant statue of Alfred E. Newman would have brought me peace and tranquillity. As I sat alone before the enormous archaic smile, joss sticks twisting their smoke around me, I felt very far from home but very close to my goal.

Philosophers are notorious for pontificating about principles without actually getting their hands dirty in the daily grime of lived experience. We've all been guilty of this to some degree. After all, in the arid realm of pure ideas, it is easier to universalize, dichotomize, and generally make sense of concepts. But down on the ground, so to speak, things are almost hopelessly, but beautifully, muddled together. Living in Southeast Asia, for example, gave me a keen sense of the slippage between Buddhist theory and practice. And it seemed embarrassing, to say the least, for me to articulate the *philosophy* of Buddhism back home and then discover real Buddhists acting and believing quite differently. My goal was clear— I had vowed to get my hands dirty, and now they were growing filthy.

In Cambodia, on the Gulf of Thailand, there is a little seaside town called Sihanoukville, named after the on-again-off-again king of Cambodia. Weeks before my Bangkok river expedition, I was in Sihanoukville, burning myself crimson red on the desolate pristine beaches. While I was there, an elephant and her calf did something very strange. Conservationists and ethologists are still mystified as to why this elephant, whom they nicknamed "Floaty," decided to leave her home in Botum Sakor National Park, walk into the ocean, and swim all the way to Koh Manoa, an island eight kilometers away. The Wildlife Protection Office claimed that this had never happened before—at least there was no record of an elephant swimming that far. The mother and calf apparently swallowed a great deal of saltwater, and naturalists were worried about their health. This mysterious migration apparently inspired two other elephants to swim from the national park to other small islands off the coast.

I'm not usually given to symbolic or metaphorical musing, but I couldn't help thinking of this elephant journey as a simile for Theravada Buddhism in Southeast Asia. Naturalists speculate that the dramatic change in elephant behavior was an adaptation response to increasing human encroachment on the mainland. Like an elephant nearly drowning to find refuge and ensure survival, Buddhism has been set upon by many threats in Southeast Asia, but it proves resilient, resourceful, and adaptive.

Actually, elephant metaphors abound in the original Buddhist scriptures (the Tripitika). The Buddha frequently analogized from pachyderms, often likening the difficulties of training the mind to those of training an elephant, and the much-loved Dhammapada is rife with elephant similes. But the story that resonates most, as I try to overcome my preconceptions in Southeast Asia, is the parable of the blind men.

The Buddha was confronted by a group of sectarian holy men who were quarreling over philosophical doctrines. One camp was vociferously championing the idea that the cosmos is eternal, and the other was equally convinced of the opposite. The Buddha tells a parable (Tittha Sutta, Udana VI.4) of a wise king who, when faced with similar doctrinal disputes, gathered together several blind men who had no previous experience with elephants. He asked one to feel the head of an elephant, another to feel the tusk, another the trunk, another the body, and another the end of the tail. Afterward the king gathered the men together and asked each of them to describe an elephant. The man who had felt the head reported to the group that an elephant is like a large water jar. The fellow who felt the tusk disagreed, saying that an elephant is more like an iron rod, and he who felt the trunk reported that the creature is more like a bent plow pole. The blind man who felt the end of the tail announced, with great conviction, that an elephant is like a broom's bristles, and so it went with all the other blind men, until they fell upon each other with quarrels and fighting.

The Buddha explained the two lessons of this parable. First, we see that human understanding is perspectival and subjective in the sense that our personal experiences shape the way we perceive reality. But reality and the truth are bigger than any one perspective. Second, we see how attached we are to our particular perspectives, even to the point of fighting over them. Our egos lead us to be more concerned with winning the debate than with actually knowing the truth.

People who travel, particularly those who spend time in exotically different cultures, tend to learn this lesson of the elephant almost automatically. When many of the things you fervently believe or practice are turned upside down by experiences in another country, you can't help but develop a little healthy skepticism toward your own beliefs. You start to feel like you've had your hand on the tail of the truth, but now you're getting some new acquaintance with its legs and trunk. This kind of immersion travel really cures national and personal smugness.

I was living in Southeast Asia because I had the great fortune of being invited to teach at the Buddhist Institute in Phnom Penh, Cambodia—a significant honor for a thirty-something Chicago philosophy professor. The academic calendar gave me occasional breaks, and I used them to journey all over the region, mining the indigenous wisdom. I came to this part of the world ostensibly to teach, but my deeper goal was to experience a place where Buddhism dominated the public and private psyche. I've studied Buddhism in an academic way for over twenty years now, and

I've been particularly fascinated by the philosophy—the metaphysical and ethical aspects of the religion. Like many other Westerners, I found these ideas to be exotic and yet reasonable alternatives to the Judeo-Christian worldview in which I was raised. At a time in my life when I was having grave doubts about the credibility of God the Father, the Son, and the Holy Ghost (around age fourteen), I began to learn about a "religion"—celebrated by millions on the other side of the planet—in which people didn't believe in the eternal soul, didn't believe in God per se, didn't believe in the divinity of their patriarch, and would rather have themselves extinguished (blown out) than have immortal life. If this doesn't strike you as strange, then you're either in a coma or you are yourself a Buddhist.

I spent many years studying the different schools and the history of Buddhism, trying to grasp a worldview in which all the fundamental girders of life are erected differently. But understanding a cultural framework like Buddhism—one that infuses every aspect of art and behavior—from the safety of one's own armchair is hardly sufficient. My recent travels in mainland China, Thailand, Cambodia, Laos, and Vietnam have helped me to really inhale Buddhism properly.

The first thing I learned was that there is no such thing as Buddhism, but instead there are Buddhisms. The different forms of Buddhism that exist in radically diverse geographic, economic, and ethnic regions all have a kind of family resemblance, but some of the distant cousins have almost no commonly recognizable features. The Theravada Buddhists of Southeast Asia would scarcely recognize Tibetan Tantric Buddhists, who in turn would be confused by Japanese Zen Buddhists, who would themselves find American Soka Gakkai Buddhists to be enigmatic, and so on. This is not surprising, and of course it is mirrored in the West by the widely diverse sects of Christianity—for example, Roman Catholicism, which at first blush looks relatively homogenous, is profoundly different in Ireland, Mexico, Italy, and the Caribbean. Still, something relates the disparate expressions—some Buddhist "DNA recipe" connects all the family cousins.

At the risk of oversimplifying things, let me suggest the following ingredients for that recipe. The first thing is the Buddha himself. Just as all Christians think a Jewish carpenter named Jesus revealed the deep spiritual truths, so too all Buddhists think an Indian prince named Gotama uncovered the big verities around the sixth century B.C.E. Perhaps the major metaphysical difference with the Jesus analogy is that J. is supposed to actually *be* God, whereas Gotama was just a smart human being who figured things out for himself.

The next ingredient in the essential Buddhist recipe is belief in the Four Noble Truths, which Gotama (the human) discovered while meditating under a tree. Whether in Thailand or Tibet or Japan, one finds commitment among all Buddhists to the Four Truths: (1) all life is *dukkha* (suffering, but more accurately translated as "unsatisfactory"); (2) all suffering is caused by attachment to *tanha* (desires); (3) if you cease to be attached to your desires, you will become free of *nibbana* (suffering); (4) by following *aryastangikamarga* (an eight-step program, or the Eightfold Path), you can detach yourself from your cravings by taking steps for *samadhi* (concentrating), *panna* (thinking), and *sila* (acting). The basic lesson of the Eightfold Path is that moderation in all things (the "Middle Way") will free you from the tyranny of your cravings. Lastly, Buddhists, wherever you find them, stress the impermanency of all things (including yourself) and the interdependence of all things because this perspective helps you rise above your own stubborn ego. These are the basic ingredients of Buddhist philosophy.

Back in Bangkok, Thailand, at the Grand Palace of Rama, my tour guide, Lek, explained the way this philosophy affects him on a day-to-day basis. After my disgusting riverboat ride, I made my way to the palace, where Lek and I sat in the temple of the beautiful Jade Buddha, trapped by a sudden rainstorm. The temple was dark, and a cool breeze from the downpour wafted in to give us a respite from the swelter. It also provided a welcome respite from the pat monologue that Lek had undoubtedly recited hundreds of times. We sat with our shoes off on the floor in front of the altar, and he occasionally jabbed me when my uncomfortable feet accidentally pointed disrespectfully toward the Buddha. He explained how every Thai man is expected to spend a few months in a monastery—every man is supposed to live as a monk for a little while. When a young man goes for even a temporary ordination, it brings great karma merit to his parents. Karma, which I'll explore in detail later, is the doctrine of ethical causality that links good actions to subsequent beneficial consequences, and bad actions to bad consequences. Karma means "action," and the consequences are called "fruits of karma." Karma is like the Western idea that "you reap what you sow," and cultural Buddhists believe that temporary ordination can sow seeds of happiness and peace for the whole family to eventually reap. The same tradition of temporary ordination is slowly reemerging in Cambodia and Laos, but Buddhists in the motherland of Theravada, Sri Lanka, do not believe in temporary ordination—once a monk, always a monk. Even this temporary ordination process is starting to disappear among contemporary Thais, but Lek did his three months when he was twenty years old. During his time as a monk he learned that the path to happiness or freedom was to gain control over his emotions—to learn to feel and express his passions in moderation. A tough task since the passions seem inherently immoderate.

"The Thai people," he explained, "seek to have a cool heart at all times. We don't always achieve this goal. Sometimes I have good days, for example, sometimes bad. But having a relaxed approach toward the goal is just one more aspect of the Buddha's lesson of moderation in all things. You Westerners have such hot hearts, it's not good."

This laid-back tolerant disposition is a very palpable aspect of Buddhist culture—it's part of the atmosphere in many communities. The greatest sin for Cambodians and Thais, for example, is to lose your temper, lose your head. Back in the States, being pushy and aggressive to get your way is often admired as a sign of strength. Such a person must be somebody who knows what he wants and goes for it. Here in Southeast Asia aggressiveness is a sure sign of weakness and lack of discipline.

I asked Lek about the monastic life followed by the orange-robed monks throughout Thailand. When I was visiting a rural monastery in southern Thailand called Wat Tham Sua, I entered a thick jungle area where monks lived in tiny cave homes. I climbed an ancient vine-covered stairway and discovered a giant, brightly painted Buddha statue. A lone monk kneeled in meditation before the Buddha, and sitting nearby on a bench was another saffron-robed monk. He appeared to be in his twenties, he was smoking a cigarette, and he had fantastic tattoos all over his body. He and I couldn't communicate very well, but he wanted me to photograph his tattoos, and then he offered me a cigarette and some much-needed drinking water. I don't smoke generally, but I indulged with him as a matter of courtesy. We exhausted our common vocabulary in about ten minutes, but then we sat quietly together for another fifteen, smoking and smiling at the carved Buddha. I coughed a lot.

Lek told me that, yes, smoking is permitted in the monastery now, but things used to be much stricter when he did his three-month stint. For centuries the monk's life has been consistently ascetic. Up in the morning around 5:00 A.M. for meditation, then a walkaround to get a little rice or leftover food from local laypeople. (The monks have always depended on the goodwill of laypeople, who donate food to the monks as a *punna*, or merit-making offering—a Theravada means of getting good karma points through acts of charity.) The monks meditate for a few more hours, then try to rustle up a little more grub, since they can't eat after 12:00 P.M. The rest of the day is spent learning scriptures and lessons from elder-monks about the *dhamma* (Buddha's teaching), followed by more meditation. The evenings, according to Lek, used to be for reading and having philosophical discussions with teachers.

"Now the monks can listen to the radio and even watch TV at night!" Lek explains, with some outrage in his voice. "Smoking in the evening is allowed too, but it is still unacceptable to eat. I disagree with these modernizations. It is not good for the monks to have these petty distractions. It is not good for the cooling of the heart."

Smoking, TV, and cell phones notwithstanding, the important personal and social ethics of the Thais trickle down from the philosophical principles, through the *sangha* (monastic community), and eventually to the laypeople. Since most of the monks return to lay status, they bring the philosophy back with them and impart it to their families. For example, Lek's practical wisdom about keeping a *jai yen* (cool heart) and the general Thai emphasis on nonconflict behavior is instigated, sanctioned, and continually reinforced by the formal teachings of Buddha's Four Noble Truths. And even the often misunderstood raison d'être of Buddhism, *nirvana* (which I'll explore later), literally means "cooling off" or "blowing out" the flames of aggression and craving.

But Buddhism is also a localized culture, and so countless beliefs and practices that have little or nothing to do with the philosophical center make up the outer layers of Buddhism. Living in Theravada countries opened my eyes to the "blooming, buzzing confusion" that the theoretical literature tidies up so neatly—and so falsely. For example, worshiping holy relics has little or nothing to do with the philosophy of Buddhism, but it's a wildly popular practice in Southeast Asia. So, given my resolve to grope the whole truth and not just its trunk or tail, I went to pay my respects, while in Cambodia, to the Buddha's tooth.

Exactly how Cambodia comes to have the Buddha's molar is still not clear to me. But before my pilgrimage, my Khmer students and I discussed the Maha-parinibbana Sutta—a scripture that famously details the Buddha's death and body-part disbursement. According to scripture, Gotama (the historical Buddha) ate some bad "pig's delight" (no kidding) at his friend's house. Realizing that it was tainted, he tastefully spared the other guests by telling his host to bury the other portions on the subterfuge pretense that such a magnificent dish should only be served to the Enlightened One. Then the eighty-year-old Buddha decided to use the food poisoning as a nice denouement to his illustrious career—riding the spoiled pig's delight into nirvana. I love this story. I mean, death doesn't get any more mundane than this. It's like saying that the Messiah passed away by slipping in the shower and breaking his neck. Even second-rate superheroes get nobler and more dramatic deaths than the Buddha. Certainly no selfless torture on the cross here, just terminal diarrhea. Anyway, after his followers cremated the Buddha's body, the bones remained, and scripture claims that they were divided eight ways—preserved throughout the Ganges Valley. Somehow his tooth ended up a very long way away, in Cambodia. Maybe it's not his real tooth, but who cares? After all, to paraphrase Erasmus, there was so much of the "true cross" floating around Europe in the Middle Ages that the original crucifix plank must have been the size of a football field.

One weekend while I was back teaching in Cambodia, my Khmer friend Kimvan agreed to meet me at Psar Thmei, the central market in Phnom Penh, and from there he would take me to Udong, about an hour north in yet another dusty, overcrowded bus. A few words about Kimvan, although a few words can hardly suffice. He's a real mensch. This is the kind of guy you want with you in a tough situation. He's half my size, married no kids, about forty years old, looks very much like a chipmunk, has a hilarious short-term memory problem and a very generous heart, and will totally go to the wall for you.

I started feeling nauseous on the bus ride to Udong, but I had no inkling of the nightmare to come. Udong Mountain (a big hill, really) could be seen from many miles away because the countryside is completely flat and used for rice farming. All along the roads are dilapidated stilt-homes, leaning and teetering on the verge of collapse, just waiting for the rains to flood the entire area and relieve them from their precarious elevation. On top of the mountain is a newly finished pagoda (the king of Cambodia brought the relic here on December 19, 2002), and we took *moto* taxis (motor scooters) to the foot of the site. At this point I was feeling very strange, like I was going to faint. My legs were starting to shake underneath me. I looked up at the half-mile of stairs above me and just resigned myself to a very unpleasant morning.

About halfway up the mountain, Kimvan started to realize that I was not myself. I should've been able to take these stairs no problem, but by the sixth flight he was holding me by the arm. I insisted that we press on. At the top, I was markedly worse, and profound nausea was setting in. I was also the only *barang* (foreigner) in a thirty-mile radius, and unlike in Phnom Penh, the locals here were not accustomed to seeing anyone who looked like me. I felt like I was about to pass out; meanwhile, crowds of curious Khmer were forming around me. Kimvan deflected some of this and steered me into a group of people chanting Pali scriptures. When I was safely camouflaged, he broke away to make offerings of incense and lotus flowers. You can't actually see the Buddha's tooth because it is installed in a high window of the pagoda, but you can pay your respects and make offerings from all sides of the structure. It was getting increasingly crowded at the shrine now, and I was starting to get tunnel vision. Kimvan returned, looking concerned, and practically carried me to a patch of grass at the side of the shrine, where he insisted that I stick my finger down my throat. Frankly, making myself throw up is not a skill I ordinarily possess, but the waves of pain and my increasing feebleness made me truly frightened. I proceeded to vomit profusely at the shrine of the Buddha's holy relic. A cadre of young monks watched with great interest. One can only wonder what effect this little stunt will have on my future rebirth.

Almost immediately after this, I was surrounded by an excited group of Khmer high school students, all of whom wanted to have their picture taken next to the big exotic barang. One jittery kid after another posed with me as his friends snapped away, passing around one camera. I did my best to smile but kept worrying that my food poisoning spasm would return and really give these kids a disquieting photo souvenir.

I made it home a few hours later, but that was only the beginning. I think my final count was thirteen wrenching purges, and I couldn't even keep a thimble of water down—dehydration became dangerous. Sometime after my eighth heave, I found myself reverting to Catholicism, having exhausted pleas to the Buddha (patron saint of food poisoning) somewhere around evacuation five. I thought, *Maybe these Western missionaries are right—I'll try to get a reprieve from a real God.* But since the Christian God allowed me to go another five rounds, I eventually retracted my fickle devotion. Not exactly the patience of Job, I know.

My landlord said that I appeared to be on death's door, and he offered to take me to get coined. Coining, a common folk remedy in Southeast

Asia, consists of a massage wherein one is oiled and then scraped with a large coin. The coin is dragged across the skin very firmly according to obscure meridian energy lines, and it leaves red bruises for days. Despite my coining, I eventually rallied over the next few days.

Almost all the expatriates I talked to said that Westerners always have this one really dramatic and awful microbe revolution when they've settled in the new bacterial environment of Southeast Asia. Afterward they're intestinally immunized and can eat almost anything, except of course the "pig's delight."

Acclimation, however, is more than simply biological. This book is about philosophical and spiritual acclimation. I started out with a paradigm shift in my gut but ended up with one in my head and in my heart. The Buddhists of Southeast Asia characterize this difficult perspective change as the movement from "me and mine" to "emptiness and no-self."

Naturally, this sort of spiritual awakening doesn't have to occur in Southeast Asia, but that's where it happened for me—in the surreal atmosphere of elephant taxis, saffron-robed monks, aggressive prostitutes, banyan trees that swallow ancient ruins, land-mine survivor beggars, marijuana pizza, giant praying mantises, gecko lizards and enormous cockroaches, teenage gangs fighting in the streets with sticks and knives, political assassinations, and quiet peaceful Buddhist meditations at dusk in the Wat Lanka.

This book, then, is my attempt to explain a progression of thinking and acting, a progression that's told in an idiosyncratic and personal narrative but that may reveal something of the universal in it. Perhaps this is too grandiose a goal for my meager talents. I'd be happy if I could effectively tell the story of a thirty-six-year-old agnostic philosophy professor from the United States who moved to Cambodia to teach Buddhism to post–Khmer Rouge college students—that's pretty idiosyncratic, I guess. But that's my story, and with a little luck I hope to simultaneously convey some bigger issues of cross-cultural spiritual yearning.

*   *   *

Buddhism is on the rise in America as part of a larger interest in spiritual matters. These days approximately two million Americans call themselves practicing Buddhists, and millions more are sympathetic and supportive toward the *dharma* (Buddha's teachings). Buddhism has enchanted the West in what seems like cycles of searching spiritualism. In the nineteenth century, American and Continental Transcendentalists recognized the wisdom of Buddhism and sought to integrate it in some fashion. In the Beat era of the 1950s, every bongo-playing poet had a copy of Buddhist scriptures in his pocket. And in the "New Age" of the 1990s, every occult thing from crystal healing to psychic spoon bending was spuriously linked with Buddhism or Eastern spirituality. In the past few years, we have had an onslaught of pop-Buddhaphiles, including Tina Turner, the Beastie Boys, Richard Gere, Steven Seagal, Lisa Simpson, and Phil Jackson. The bookshelves are flooded with inspirational pseudo-Buddhist primers, the Dalai Lama and Thich Nhat Hanh have popular new books out every five minutes, and meditation centers are cropping up all over the country. But ask the millions of American Buddhaphiles if they know anything about Theravada Buddhism, the oldest and purest form of Buddhism practiced by over 125 million people in Southeast Asia, and the answer is always, "Huh?"

In 1993 Columbia University researchers conducted a study that analyzed the presentation of Southeast Asia in twenty-seven major world history textbooks used in public middle and high schools; they discovered that the coverage was almost exclusively of the Philippines and the Vietnam War. Simply put, Americans don't know much about this part of the world. Americans have some shadowy sense of northern Buddhism because that Mahayana ("larger path") has had relatively good PR, with most of it centering on Tibet's Dalai Lama. Like Christianity's schism of Protestants and Catholics, the Buddhist world is carved into Mahayana and Hinayana ("smaller path"). The only surviving school of Hinayana Buddhism is Theravada, which is practiced all over Southeast Asia. But popular Tibetan Vajrayana ("diamond vehicle," an eccentric subspecies under the Mahayana genus) comprises a mere 6 percent of the worldwide Buddhist population (the remaining Mahayana comprise 56 percent and Theravada 38 percent), and so many Westerners have mistaken a highly idiosyncratic school of thought for the dharma itself. If they got a dose of the pure Theravada stuff, their minds would be blown. Among other things, I hope this book makes a modest start in repairing the huge hole in Western consciousness regarding Theravada Buddhism and culture.

Those of us in privileged countries have a yearning for the ancient spiritual (and exotic) traditions of developing countries, and we tend to romanticize them. But getting inside and living with that spiritual culture is truly eye-opening. Certainly, some of the romantic illusions are shattered; at the same time, the suspected "depths" are even deeper than you thought, though not necessarily *where* you expected them. Aldous Huxley said, in his travel journal *Jesting Pilate*, that when one is living in a developed secular country one longs to live in a spiritual country instead. One craves the deep meaningful connections of ancient tradition. "One is all for religion," he wrote, "until one visits a really religious country. Then one is all for drains, machinery, and the minimum wage." When Huxley was living in England and America, he read the Buddha regularly and took great inspiration, but when he lived in India and the Far East he read biographies of Henry Ford with admiration.

My own experience in Southeast Asia resonates with Huxley's insight about the ways different cultures romanticize each other. Many people in the West feel alienated and see the East as a cure for the woes of industrialization and development. But when you haven't had a really decent hot shower in months, you begin to see it differently. And when, as it did for me in Cambodia, it takes a month of meetings and government bribes to finally make a tiny change to one's passport visa status, then Western bureaucracy doesn't seem so Kafkaesque after all.

Still, there really is something profoundly important for us to learn from Buddhism and the Eastern way of life—something I call "transcendental everydayness." I try to bring it forth, slowly, in the course of my narrative. I don't pretend to have felt the whole elephant by any means, but perhaps I can convey a tusk or two.

One

THE RING OF GYGES

Living in Cambodia with Impunity and Hedonism

One of the main ways Khmers in Phnom Penh practice their Buddhism is by subjecting themselves to traffic. The constant near-misses, last-minute swerves, precarious balancing acts, and obstacle-course road conditions would put the average person into a stress seizure. Yet the locals remain unperturbed, which is why the no-system traffic system works. If you can get across town in full possession of your calm demeanor—your peaceful state of equilibrium—then you *are* the Buddha.

The "roads" can only be charitably described as ditches. The streets are dirt pathways with potholes big enough to lose whole cars, and almost all transport is done by *motos* (minibike scooters, the drivers of which are called moto-dups) or *cyclos* (bicycle rickshaws with the passenger seat in front). Everyone travels by moto, and it is not at all uncommon to see whole families precariously perched on a single bike. Walking down to the Foreign Correspondents' Club for a drink, I saw a little motor scooter, made for two, with a one-year-old baby balanced on his father's lap while the mother and two more children sat cramped together behind him on a ten-inch seat. The record number that I witnessed was six family members, but after a few months even this failed to register with my acclimated senses.

The good thing about traffic is that you can go from one end of town to another on a moto for about two thousand riel, or fifty cents. The bad news is that every time you get on one of these you get a serious I'm-not-fucking-around brush with your own mortality. The only time I ever enjoyed my moto adventures was when I was inebriated, which happened more than I should admit, but there it is. On those occasions, the paralyzing fright was transformed into exhilaration.

There are no traffic rules in Cambodia, and there can be hundreds of motos at any one time moving on one city block in the capital. If you have to turn left, you just drive straight into oncoming traffic and hope everyone sees you. If the oncoming traffic doesn't get you, the giant potholes and rubble will. There are some nasty accidents in Phnom Penh, but fewer than one would imagine. The dodging and weaving of the relaxed drivers, seemingly drugged on their own natural phenobarbital, makes for a successful rhythm of mutually accommodating motion.

I ordered a Mekong whiskey at the Foreign Correspondents' Club, and pulling up a seat at the balcony, I watched the action below me in Sisowath Quay. The view extends over the Tonle Sap River, and I watched the fishing boats troll downstream. A table of British reporters and photographers were attacking huge steaks next to me, seemingly relieved to be eating something besides rice and fish. Down below me, young saffron-robed monks meandered in a small group. A little girl who looked no more than four years old was begging unsuccessfully, and when she turned in my direction I saw that she had a newborn baby (undoubtedly her sister) strapped around her body with a wrap cloth. One baby carrying another baby. This kind of thing never ceased to affect me, and it was especially troubling because, as I came to understand later, this child's mother, and countless others like her, had put her child out on the street because the sight of a child's misery was more financially rewarding in these expatriate parts of town.

Having been to Cambodia once before, I naively thought that I was somehow "ready" for it this time. But you can never really be ready for Cambodia. It's sort of like seeing a really good punch coming at your face, bracing yourself as best you can, but getting knocked senseless anyway. The poverty in Phnom Penh is truly profound—it makes American urban ghettos like Cabrini Green in Chicago seem like plush utopias by comparison. Unlike America, where poor people suffer from obesity, poor Khmer people actually suffer from having no food.

I noticed a little Khmer boy, about five years old, who was causing mischief with every hapless passerby. This was Bunly, a kid I had met the week before when he asked me to buy an old copy of the *Phnom Penh Post* that he had fished out of a gutter. Bunly had acquired excellent English by simply living in the streets around the barang businesses on Sisowath Quay. The week before he had worked every grifter's angle on me, until I finally acquiesced and bought his tattered newspaper. I was sad that a kid this small already had the makings of a swindler, and I felt that dumb luck had put his birth in a place where childhood would be so short-lived.

On the northern side street, a sixty-something crippled man teetered across the street on a homemade cane that he'd fashioned from a kitchen mop handle. The poor guy's head was disfigured and partly covered too. One sees a lot of the land-mine survivors begging here, and it is truly heartbreaking. There are approximately five hundred land-mine injuries per month in Cambodia, the legacy of decades of civil war and conflicts with outside nations. My friend François, who fashions prosthetics for the Red Cross, assured me that all the land-mine victims near the Correspondents' Club have excellent artificial limbs that they deliberately leave home so as to garner more sympathy dollars, but that fact is still very cold comfort. When the man hobbled by, Bunly got in line behind him and began an elaborate impersonation, limping and tottering in melodramatic fashion. The kid was so delighted and amused by this, each step a more grotesque improvisation, that my moral indignation waned and I found myself smiling. This was followed by waves of guilt. And then more smiling.

About ten minutes later, this scene was followed by a stark contrast, a contrast that symbolically revealed the other side, the beautiful side, of Cambodia. At the river's edge, a young girl, about the same age as Bunly, was taking her ancient grandfather for what must have been his routine evening stroll. I say routine because it really looked like a carefully rehearsed choreography. The old man was so infirm that he could take only one small step every two or three seconds—he caught my attention because he and his granddaughter seemed to be moving in slow motion, while the riverside chaos careened all around them. The man had his right hand extended to the little girl's shoulder and his left hand cautiously manipulating a wooden cane. The girl moved ahead directly in front of him at exactly the right pace, and her devotion was visible. She seemed unfazed by the excruciating tempo, and the two of them just glided together in a weird ritual dance. It took them over half an hour to cover the short stretch of walkway in front of me. Not once did the little girl fidget or run off or otherwise break the patient parade.

This scene was shattered by a loud smashing sound in the street behind me. Then people were rushing to tend to the injured. The Buddhist traffic had suffered a glitch, but I consoled myself with a sop about the relatively harmless speeds of Cambodian vehicles. When I turned back, there emerged, from around the corner of the Riverstreet Bar and Restaurant, a gigantic elephant. I felt like I was tripping on LSD, a feeling that came frequently in Southeast Asia. The placid beast walked slowly in the street with all the traffic whirling past. A man with one leg was perched on top, giving gentle taps with a pointed metal stick. He led the huge beast onto the sidewalk, and a waitress met them with a bag of stale bread from the restaurant. The elephant ate about seven loaves of French bread. The one-legged man enjoyed one as well, and then they were off again down the street.

When I returned home that night I discovered that the eighty-year-old man who lived across the street from my guesthouse had died that afternoon. I didn't know the man personally, but I had seen him many times sitting on his front steps. I found the street filled with mourners—

I can't say they were mourning per se, but rather milling about like we do at wakes. Relatives had set up a makeshift kitchen on the sidewalk, and they were cooking furiously for the arriving mourners. A man was chanting Pali Buddhist scriptures into a microphone, and a cheap PA was croaking it into the street. The chants, astonishingly loud for so late in the evening, were about the impermanency of all things. Pali, which was contemporaneous with Sanskrit, is the original Indian language of Buddhism. Many Buddhist terms and even scriptures have two versions, reflecting the different ancient languages. The better-known term *nirvana*, for example, is Sanskrit, and its Pali version is *nibbana*. Likewise, the Sanskrit *dharma* is *dhamma* in Pali. This is worth noting because all of Southeast Asian Buddhism, Theravada, is based on the voluminous Pali scriptures, called the Tripitika in Sanskrit or Tipitika in Pali (three baskets). The three baskets of Pali scriptures are the Vinaya (rules for monks), the Suttas (teachings for laypeople), and the Abhidhamma (teachings for philosophers). I usually use the Pali terms throughout this book, unless I feel that the Sanskrit term is better known and more familiar to Westerners. I explore the scriptural traditions more later, but it was interesting here to see that funerals and other life-transition blessings were performed in the ancient language rather than the vernacular.

I sat with the moto drivers, who were taking a respectful break from their routine card game, and watched as the family organized round plastic tables and chairs for a funeral meal. They carefully placed blue tablecloths and hung a black-and-white mourners' banner across the open entry of the house. Inside the home (the first floors of most Khmer houses are wide open, like garages), they hung a large colorful painting of the Buddha on his lotus flower, and they built a makeshift shrine there. At the shrine, family members were dropping pieces of paper into a flaming pot, as a symbolic offering of money to the gods. The whole scene looked very modest to me, like the spread you see at a midsummer American block party. I was surprised when one of the Khmer maids from the guesthouse said to me, "You can tell zis family very rich. Eryzing is so nice and ezpensive."

The motorcycle traffic from nearby Sihanouk Boulevard drowned out the old man's chanting. People consoled each other. Two wild dogs got into a fight in the street, until a woman threw an empty coconut shell with contusional accuracy. A bold prostitute from the park approached: "Hey, mistah, you want boom-boom longtime?" "Aw kun, ah tay," I replied ("Thank you, no"). In theory, I had to admit to myself that I did indeed want boom-boom longtime, but my ethical and hygienic anxieties prevented me from accepting. She turned to the moto drivers and spoke in Khmer. I was the only big money in our little gathering, so she moved on. After a while the old man's throat gave out, and they started to play some very beautiful Khmer folk music over the loudspeaker. It was not like anything else I'd heard in Southeast Asia—very simple repetitions (like a drunken Philip Glass) on a marimba dulcimer.

Samnom, one of the neighborhood moto drivers with whom I had made friends, gestured for me to sit on his bike while we stared at the funeral developments. The mourners closed off the street and lit a bonfire in the dirt road. I noticed, from my new vantage point, that the perfectly full moon could be seen just over the dead man's house. I thought about my own son who was growing rapidly inside his mother back in Chicago. I thought about the babies who were being conceived at that very moment, and I wondered about reincarnation. Even though their Buddhism rejects the idea, many Khmers cling to the animistic belief that the soul of the deceased will wander for a week before it transmigrates.

I was about to drag myself off to bed when a moto headlight came speeding up from the darkness of Kapko Market.

"Steef, Steef! *There* you are," the excited voice exclaimed from behind the blinding light. I recognized Heng Joli's voice right away—his mispronunciation of my name was singular (but probably more accurate than my version of his name). "Li," as his friends referred to him, had quickly become an important ally in Phnom Penh. I chanced to meet him one day while wandering about the side streets near Psar Kapko. He leapt out of a darkened first-floor room, emerging into the dry dust-brown street from between the half-closed gates that lock most streetside homes.

"You speak Khmer, boss?" he asked on that first day, coming close and smiling wide under his baseball cap.

"Very little, I'm afraid."

"That's okay, boss, I teach you some. And maybe I practice some English with you, no?"

"No," I responded, tired, surly, and wary from all the grifters and anglers one encounters every day in Phnom Penh. This guy, I thought, is like all the rest of the vultures vying for dollars. But he wasn't.

"Heng Joli is my name, but you call me Li," he offered, unperturbed by my coolness. Thus started an eventual friendship that built up over several months, slowly overcoming the cycle of opportunism and suspicion that marks many such relationships. I came to know his story well, and he came to know mine—helping me gain the access and insight into Theravada Buddhism that no merely academic study can provide.

But right now he was shining his moto headlight in my face and excitedly shouting something about Wat Lanka.

"A monk has been shot, Steef!" he blurted at me. "I look erywhere for you, boss. Come now! I take you to Wat Lanka."

Li was a reliable source, so I got on the moto immediately, and we peeled away from the funeral fire. Looking back over my shoulder, the late-night festivities seemed dreamlike—chanting mourners cast dramatic shadows away from the conflagration, making my familiar neighborhood seem strange and ominous. The Khmer death music, still audible under Li's bike, evaporated slowly as we sped down Sihanouk Boulevard.

When we arrived at Wat Lanka, only a short distance from my neighborhood, we discovered a small group of monks gathered at the entrance gate, together with police and laypeople. There was a nervous tension here, a palpable sense that something terrible was hanging in the air. In this fearful atmosphere, people talked rapidly at each other and gestured in frustration.

With Li's help, I managed to gather some facts. The very popular monk Sam Bunthoeun was shot twice in the chest by mysterious gunmen inside the walls of the *wat* (temple). This was truly unprecedented. Even in a place as violent and lawless as Cambodia, no monk had ever been shot *inside* the temple while wearing his *robes*. Even criminals have a deep respect for the sacred space of the wats. And the saffron robe is so revered in Theravada countries as a potent spiritual symbol that even the Khmer Rouge (the violent Communist army of the 1970s Democratic Kampuchea Party, DK) would disrobe monks before killing them. Additional evidence of the robe's power can be seen in the recent practice of Thai environmentalists who have saved many trees from logging by wrapping them in the orange robes for protection.

Sam Bunthoeun, who was forty-seven years old, lingered in the hospital for two days after being shot in the chest, but then passed away. Bunthoeun was the popular and respected president of the Buddhist Meditation Center of Udong, and he had built up an important Vipassana community in this village north of Phnom Penh.

Venerable Sam Bunthoeun had come to Wat Lanka on a visit from his home temple in Udong, a former capital city about fifty kilometers north of Phnom Penh. He had a good reputation in the Khmer sangha (monastic community) because he had constructed the spiritual center, but he was particularly popular with younger monks because he had progressive views regarding politics. There was some disagreement among the monks whom I talked to in early February and the months that followed about whether Venerable Bunthoeun had explicitly opposed Supreme Patriarch Tep Vong's edict prohibiting monks from voting in the upcoming elections. Tep Vong, the highest-ranking monk in Cambodia and a supporter of Prime Minister Hun Sen's ruling party, the Cambodian People's Party (CPP), had publicly forbidden monks to register to vote in the July 2003 elections. Many Cambodians believed that the CPP, the soft-core Communist party, was frightened by the monk vote (which could be fifty thousand strong) because many monks were critical of current corruption, and their obvious detachment from material gain always leaves the monks free to voice a purely moral position. Some of the monks I spoke with said that Bunthoeun was encouraging monks to violate Tep Vong's edict and that his death (according to their interpretation) was retaliation and a warning sent by CPP thugs. Other monks were less sure, offering up claims that Venerable Bunthoeun always kept himself above political partisan fighting.

Li and I informally interviewed a number of monks, and I continued to press the issue for months after, but things only got murkier as time passed. No one was arrested for the shooting, no one was held as a suspect, no one had any clues in the case. Fury grew toward the police and the ruling party in the months that followed. Even American senator Mitch McConnell criticized Hun Sen's government for failing to make any progress on the case and suggested a political cover-up.

Amid all this uncertainty, one thing was clear. A sacred line had been crossed in this Theravada country. On that night, when Li and I stood shocked in front of the decaying gold and white gates of Wat Lanka, we experienced, along with the rest of Cambodia, a breach of sacred trust. Obviously, monks had come under vicious attack before in Cambodia, but since the insanity of the Khmer Rouge's ideological elimination (1975 to 1979), the sangha had been slowly emerging again as a sacred community—as the heart and soul of Khmer identity. Since the reestablishment of a legitimate Cambodian government in 1993, the sangha and wat structures have played their traditional roles: providing moral education; adjudicating village disputes; blessing the life transitions of birth, marriage, death, and so on; serving as a place of Pali scriptural study; sometimes acting as a bank, an orphanage, or a nursing home; and generally serving as a source of ethnic pride and identity. In short, the Theravada sangha is the most important social structure in Cambodia next to the family. Now someone, possibly with crass political motives, had fired two gunshots into the heart of Theravada spirituality.

It's hard for an American to understand this entirely. Sure, we know what it's like, as individuals, to have a domain of life that's above politics. Despite the international caricature of us, many Americans are spiritually minded and have devotional feelings toward something above the vagaries of political values and debates. But Theravadans feel this higher devotion *together*, they feel it *collectively*, and that is something we don't have. For Americans, in contrast, spirituality is primarily a private matter. Of course, this is a natural outgrowth of the Establishment Clause of our First Amendment, but an attraction to private spirituality is also being felt more keenly today by young people who are dissatisfied with institutional religion. A large number of Americans under thirty describe themselves as religiously "unaffiliated." My generation is turned off by hypocritical money-grubbing televangelists, buggering priests, fundamentalist mosques, antiquated rabbis, and effete ecumenical theater churches. But for all that, people in their twenties and thirties are not bereft of spiritual values—they have simply gone the route of deeper internalization. In fact, it's this subjectification or privatization of spirituality that has made the enlightenment paradigm of Buddhism so intriguing for younger Americans, myself included. But living in a Theravada country really opens your eyes to the missed dimension of public spirituality.

When Venerable Bunthoeun was killed inside a wat, wearing his sacred robe, it sent a chill through Khmers. Most Khmers over thirty still remember the last time a secular political movement, Pol Pot's Democratic Kampuchea Party, disastrously tried to eliminate their collective spiritual and cultural identity by killing monks and intellectuals, razing wats, and abolishing families, money, traditional education, and art. Pol Pot's hyper-communism made Chairman Mao look like a moderate; he pressed the persecution of Buddhism on the grounds that it was, like all religions, an opiate of the masses—a social hierarchy that privileged monks and kept laypeople docile and deluded. All through the 1980s, even after Pol Pot had been removed, Cambodians struggled with civil war and with the Vietnamese. Things normalized only slightly in the 1990s, and since the early part of that decade Khmers have worked hard to revitalize their supra-political Buddhist traditions. Now, with the death of Sam Bunthoeun, the threat of a government that would violently force the sangha to stay under its thumb had a frighteningly familiar resonance.

*   *   *

A month before this horrific murder, I didn't know much about the con-
troversies surrounding monk voting. Actually, in hindsight, I didn't know
much about anything. I was sitting in a Chicago airport with a backpack,
a large suitcase filled with books, and a beat-up guitar. I stretched out at
the gate of my Singapore Airlines flight, relaxing with my airport-priced
ten-dollar bag of pretzels, zoning out to CNN on the airport TV. I
couldn't really hear the television over the hum of airport noise, but I
wasn't paying much attention anyway—it was one of those moments
when the medium itself gives comfort regardless of content. The board-
ing attendant had called my row, and I glanced up at the television
monitor while I gathered my bags. Suddenly there were images of riots
on the screen—buildings burning, people being beaten, and a headline
caption at the bottom of the screen: "Violence Tonight in Phnom Penh."
What? I think pretzel crumbs actually flew out of my mouth. I strained
to hear the low-volume speaker above me but couldn't make out the
story. Something about the Thai embassy in Phnom Penh being torched,
hundreds airlifted out of danger, the Thai-Cambodia border closed,
people killed, and the Thai ambassador narrowly escaping the angry mob
by crawling to the river. The indecipherable story was over in twenty seconds. I instinctively clutched at my ticket, my ticket for Phnom Penh.
None of the people around me seemed to care. After all, they were only
going as far as Singapore. I was the idiot on his way to Cambodia.

In 2001 I first went to the mysterious Angkor Wat site to study the influence of Buddhist ideas on the artwork of those ancient temples. I had
been fascinated by photos of the ruins ever since I was a kid, and I simply
took the summer vacation from my teaching gig at Columbia College to
explore them firsthand. While there, I made connections with the Center
for Khmer Studies and a small NGO (nongovernmental organization)
called the Khmer Education Assistance Program (KEAP). I had written
and illustrated a popular primer on Buddhist philosophy called *Buddha
for Beginners* in the mid-nineties, and after negotiations with the director of KEAP, Dr. Peter Gyallay-Pap, I was invited to teach a graduate

seminar on Buddhist philosophy to Cambodian students at the Buddhist Institute in Phnom Penh.

This was a very great honor for me. From its founding in 1930, the Buddhist Institute was the leading research and publications institution in Cambodia until its closure in 1975. Most of its library and the entire documentary collection were lost in the chaos of the Khmer Rouge regime. In 1992 the commissions of the institute were finally reopened, but since that time they had been largely inactive owing to a lack of qualified personnel and financial support. Starting in 2001, a steering committee comprising representatives from the Buddhist Institute, the Center for Advanced Study, and the Royal University of Phnom Penh was trying to repair the sorry state of Buddhist studies in Cambodia. They invited me to teach a graduate seminar on philosophy to the pilot class of twelve Cambodian students. I was privileged to be part of a small team of Cambodian and international scholars who were endeavoring to reconnect young Khmer with their own lost culture. So this was the reason I found myself at O'Hare Airport in early 2003, spraying pretzels in disbelief.

When I arrived in Phnom Penh, the embassy and dozens of Thai businesses were still burning and smoldering and the rioting was still erupting in small pockets throughout the capital. It all started when a newspaper editor at *Rasmei Angkor* reported a bogus story asserting that the Thai actress Suwanan Kongyin (also known as "Morning Star") had expressed her desire for the Angkor Wat temples to be "returned" to the Thai people. This is like having the Italians ask the Egyptians for their pyramids back. Cambodian prime minister Hun Sen was opening a school for blind and deaf children in Kampong Cham when he responded by saying that Morning Star wasn't worth a blade of grass at Angkor. Cambodians started burning her photo and throwing bricks that night. The next day, January 28, the Thai actress denied ever making such a remark, but things only heated up instead when, on January 29, a radio call-in show announced that the Cambodian embassy in Thailand had been looted and twenty Cambodians killed. This falsehood led

Phnom Penh protesters to burn down the Thai embassy and many other Thai businesses. The army was called in, but things spun out of control throughout the night.

The Thai ambassador, Chatchawed Chartsuwan, called everyone he knew in the Cambodian Foreign Ministry for help because his own residence, located behind the embassy, was set ablaze. Help failed to arrive, so Chatchawed was forced to scale a back fence and race to the Bassac River, where he was rescued by boat.

Many Cambodians smelled something fishy in the series of misunderstandings and the mysterious lack of police control during the riots. Sam Rainsey, the head of the oppositional Sam Rainsey Party, accused the regime (the CPP) of fostering the violence for political reasons. Rainsey said publicly that the riot "was very distinctive of the politics of dictators who want to distract public attention from internal problems they cannot solve. They try to create an external problem."

Shortly after making these comments, Rainsey had to go into hiding. Six years before, Rainsey had organized a demonstration against the CPP-biased judiciary outside the National Assembly building. Though it was never officially proven, most Cambodians believe that Prime Minister Hun Sen sent CPP thugs to grenade the demonstration, leaving twenty-five victims dead and many more wounded. Then Hun Sen publicly blamed Sam Rainsey for failing to protect his supporters, even threatening to prosecute Rainsey.

In the 1998 elections, an amazing 90 percent of Cambodians voted. Hun Sen's CPP gained the most seats in Parliament. But they failed to get the two-thirds majority to form a government, so an uneasy coalition was formed by King Sihanouk between Sihanouk's son, Prince Norodom Ranariddh, and Hun Sen. I say uneasy because earlier, in July 1997, the CPP and the prince's soldiers had fought each other in a bloody attempted coup by the prince. After 1998, Ranariddh, whose royalist party is called FUNCINPEC, was given the position of speaker of Parliament, and Hun Sen was placed as prime minister. Hun Sen, who controls the Royal Cambodian Armed Forces, is the unequivocal "strong man" leader of Cambodia, while Ranariddh has very minimal power and the king plays only a ceremonial role.

At the time of the anti-Thai riots, the CPP was getting increasingly nervous because the 2003 elections were fast approaching. Many Khmers were not entirely happy with the job that the CPP was doing. Government corruption had reached ridiculous extremes. For example, government workers make around fifteen dollars a month officially, but somehow manage to drive sixty-thousand-dollar cars. Some local pundits argue that Cambodians, despite their voting habits, never really liked the CPP—their vote was more about ensuring some stability in an otherwise unstable region by simply agreeing to stay with the entrenched powers. One expat told me that if the crew of Gilligan's Island had promised stability, Khmers would have voted Gilligan into the prime minister's chair. The CPP's position is not a reflection of the people's interest or belief in communism per se; in fact, the vast majority of provinces (where 85 percent of Khmer live) would relish a return to the monarchy—one infused by Buddhist values (*dhammaraja*). Secularism, whether it be communism or liberal democracy, makes little sense to Cambodians.

In light of all this, many people think that the anti-Thai riots were secretly fostered by the CPP because the threat of instability is the best card that Hun Sen and the CPP can play. The politics of xenophobia helps to keep the CPP strong and attractive. But here's the soap-opera bit. Many Cambodians actually connected this weird xenophobic outbreak to the recent publication of a controversial booklet on the life and times of the most famous Khmer actress-dancer Piseth Pilika. What everyone knows, but is too afraid to voice publicly, is that Pilith was Prime Minister Hun Sen's mistress. And in 1999 she was murdered, shot three times in the back. Cambodians believe that Pilika was killed by Hun Sen's wife, but all of this is covered up and shrouded in mystery. It's not good for one's personal health to even raise such issues in the wrong company. The published booklet details some of the relationship between Pilith and the prime minister, including damning letters and poems. The same day that the underground booklet appeared at bookstands, roving thugs showed up and confiscated all copies of it. As a result, many Cambodians suggested that Hun Sen simply capitalized on and encouraged the Thai xenophobia to distract people from his own improprieties.

To be perfectly honest, American politics seems boring by comparison. In the States, you always know what everyone is going to say, you know precisely how they will behave, *you* know that *they* know that *you* are watching them through a media lens and that they are working hard to pose without too much self-consciousness. The soap-opera quality of Southeast Asian politics, by contrast, appealed to my prurient nature and I followed it religiously. In the States, the president gets a blow job from a chubby clerk, then sheepishly confesses it all, and even his wife tours Oprah-style talk shows, best-seller under arm, stoically fielding questions about the tepid tryst. Everyone involved sets their jaw hard and acts very grown-up and restrained. In Cambodian politics, you just kill the people who cross you.

The riots caused bad press all over Asia and even made a tiny splash in the Western press. The small shop owners and guesthouse proprietors groaned at the prospect of an even more pathetic tourist season to come. To speak of a tourist industry in Cambodia is sort of absurd, but there are a handful of mom-and-pop businesses in Phnom Penh, Siem Reap, and Sihanoukville, poised ever ready to blossom. Cambodia is a relatively frightening place to most outsiders, however, so tourism is quite low. Street rioting is not high on the list of "things to see" in most guidebooks. But when I had settled into my modest digs in Psar Kapko and slowly started acclimating to this new world, I began to see that there was very little *random* violence. Khmer violence, while profoundly creepy and abundant, is usually focused political violence or long-standing domestic and neighbor vengeance. There is much more random violence in my hometown of Chicago. Very few people get killed accidentally in Cambodia, so rest easy in the knowledge that if you get killed in Cambodia, somebody really wanted you dead.

The truly frightening thing about Cambodia is that the murderers regularly get away with it. Khmer people do not have much faith in justice. They are still waiting for the coalition government and the United Nations to bring the Khmer Rouge murderers and torturers to justice some twenty-five years later. Many of the most brutal DK criminals live quietly and comfortably throughout Cambodia, unpursued and unpunished. Combine this with the fact that political killings continue to multiply unchecked and almost always go "unsolved" and it is easy to understand the levels of skepticism and mistrust among the unprivileged classes. The murder of the monk Sam Bunthoeun was unsolved, and in the few months that followed there were seventeen suspected political killings and thirteen attempted political murders—all dismissed by the ruling party as nonpolitical personal violence. Even after the 2003 elections, murders continued while the CPP, FUNCINPEC, and the Sam Rainsey Party were slowly corralled by the king into a functional coalition. In October, two FUNCINPEC members were shot dead, and the famous Khmer singer and actress Touch Srey Nich was shot twice in the face in broad daylight by several men in front of the InterContinental Hotel. Nich's politically tinged songs were played frequently by the FUNCINPEC campaign, so many people suspect some CPP involvement in the crime.

Living in Phnom Penh made me think of Plato's famous Ring of Gyges. The corrupt ruling class seemed out of control here, but really *anyone* in Cambodia who had a little money felt the ring's power. In the *Republic*, Plato tells this story of a simple man named Gyges who discovers a mystical ring that makes him invisible when he turns it on his finger. The ring removes the possibility of any detection and punishment, so the ring bearer degenerates into a life of indulgent vice. He sets about sleeping with the queen, murdering the king, and taking over the kingdom. It's a melodramatic thought experiment, but the prediction that "power corrupts" can be readily tested while living in Cambodia. Living here is like having the ring, in the sense that very few laws constrain the prosperous residents. This goes for police, military, and politicians, but the average expatriate resident can also, if he desires, float above the usual legal and ethical constraints of civilization. If one should be unfortunate enough to cross over a legal line somewhere and have someone notice or care, the offense is easily remedied by a small bribe. A general culture of impunity allows the powerful, the modestly rich, and the criminal elements to act in any way they wish, with no real danger of being brought to justice. My own relatively innocent antinomian behavior pales when compared with the much more sinister events in Phnom Penh, but everyone experiences the lure of temptations in a world where desires and cravings (the chief enemies of enlightenment) are easily indulged. Buddhism has its work cut out for it in Cambodia. Hedonism is readily available, so overcoming one's cravings can be like trying to *nibbana* (cool off) in the middle of a firestorm.

On a particularly sticky Saturday morning, Li and I explored the region south of Mao Tse-tung Boulevard in search of a good amulet. Amulets are extremely important throughout Southeast Asia because the necklace figures (frequently the Buddha, but also figures from the Hindu Ramayana and animistic totems) can be imbued with powers when blessed by a spiritually potent monk or a *kru* (sorcerer).

After a morning of intense haggling with merchants, we ended up on a tiny dirt road near Psar Toul Tom Poung, or the Russian Market, so-called because of its popularity among Russian expatriates in the 1980s. Here an angry dog met us at a large wrought-iron gate surrounding a modest two-story home. Barbed wire circled at the top of the gate, as it did for almost every building in Phnom Penh—the entire city feels like a military outpost. No one really trusts anybody in Cambodia. We were at the home of Greg, a British expatriate who had been living in Southeast Asia for many years; based on crumbs of information from his almost constant narration, I got the impression that he had left England for legal reasons. I didn't really want to know too much about Greg anyway. We were here to buy pot. That's all.

Marijuana is plentiful in Phnom Penh, but not like it used to be. A few years ago, one could walk through the Russian Market, a huge shantytown of sales booths and produce stands all covered with a low claustrophobic ceiling, and buy pounds of high-grade weed that just hung from the rafters. Nowadays you had to look for it . . . well, for at least a few hours.

We sat on the veranda of Greg's modest home, shaded by a large red tarp, guzzling bottled water and passing around a cigar-sized spliff. His beautiful Khmer girlfriend hovered inside the house, occasionally appearing in the doorway. We discussed the alarming situation in neighboring Thailand, where Prime Minister Thaksin Shinawatra was flexing his muscles. Thaksin, perhaps swept up by antiterrorist policymaking strategies, had begun a relentless assault on drug users and dealers. He had also implemented a series of formal and informal policies intended to align Thailand more closely with the United States, including allowing the CIA to bring suspected Al Qaeda members to Thailand for interrogation and permitting the U.S. military to use Thai air bases in its efforts in Afghanistan and Iraq. Greg argued that Thaksin's recent crackdown on drugs was just kowtowing to George W. Bush, because towing the hard line on drugs would bring future economic trade benefits to Thailand. Perhaps. But one thing was certain: Thailand wasn't approaching the issue with a "just say no" slogan or even a stiff jail sentence. It was simply shooting people dead.

In a few short months in early 2003, over two thousand "suspected" drug dealers were killed by police. The press in Southeast Asia dubbed this the "shoot to kill" drug policy. You don't have to be a mathematician to see that many innocent people must have perished. This shotgun-spray style of social "justice" seemed frightening to me, and it highlighted something that often struck me while I lived in Southeast Asia. The idea of human rights is not really a foundational building block in these countries. The individual's rights are not sacrosanct. This is the creepy underbelly of cultures that are oriented more toward the collective than the individual. This same orientation can be a beautiful thing when it means that an individual gives up his selfish desires for the good of his family, but it's unsettling when it means that the individual is very easily expendable if the putative good of the state is at issue. Buddhism, as a philosophy, demands respect and compassion for all people, but this egalitarian message is frequently eclipsed by even older cultural traditions of imbalanced power.

When I inarticulately voiced these addled views, Li turned to me with an amused look.

"Steef," he said laughing, "life is cheap in this part of the world." Greg, a sort of honorary local, shook his head in agreement.

Greg was huge, twice my size but built very solid. He sat like some giant mufti wedged into his chair. He was broad everywhere—even his head looked like some blocky Communist propaganda statue of the noble worker—and the heat was merciless with him.

"Can you throw a good punch?" Greg asked me suddenly.

"What?"

"Can you throw a good punch?" he repeated. And thinking this was a hypothetical stoner question, I nodded slowly and offered my subjective assessment.

"I think I can, although I haven't had a fistfight since high school."

"Well, that's excellent," he smiled. "You see, my problem is this shoulder." He extended his right arm and slowly rotated it over his head, producing a distinct clicking sound.

"Hear that? That's what's left of my rotator cuff—I totally ruined it with weight lifting. I can't throw a decent punch to save my life." He paused for a minute and looked carefully at Li, who was leaning over the veranda to see the furious dog below.

"How about your friend?" Greg asked. "Can he handle himself in a scrape?" The dog got louder, and Greg's girlfriend appeared in the doorway.

"Shit, they're here," Greg said as he pried himself out of his chair. "Look," he confided, "this may get ugly in a minute, and you may need to do some fighting, so be on your toes, mate. These blokes coming in are very upset about one of my little business transactions, so I'm hoping to smooth things over, but you never know. These Khmers are inscrutable, eh?" A wide smile stretched across his face, and a quick jump of his eyebrows tried to punctuate his use of the old "inscrutable Oriental" stereotype. An instantaneous wave of fear rose up in me, followed by anger that Greg had carefully kept us from leaving earlier.

I rolled my eyes at Li when Greg stepped into the house. I explained to my friend that we'd landed in the middle of some dispute and he should be ready for trouble. Khmers don't panic easily. Maybe the oppressive heat of the tropics naturally discourages overreacting behavior, or maybe the unpredictably violent political climate keeps one detached. Or maybe it was just the gun lodged in Li's pants that he then revealed to me for the first time. He showed no fear at all, so I doubled my own anxiety just to make up for his lack.

The sweat was pouring off me, and I felt way too high to punch anybody. Besides, the fact that many young Khmer men carry guns seemed to cancel out Greg's query about quaint gentlemen's fisticuffs. Li and I quickly debated whether an expatriate drug dealer with a bad rotator cuff would also own a gun.

Greg stepped back out onto the veranda, followed by two tense-looking characters. The two Khmer ne'er-do-wells were each half my size, but I instinctively puffed myself up to appear larger and more intimidating. I felt my shirt sticking to my chest, and I could hear my blood pumping in my temples. Suddenly Li exploded with a laugh.

"Niak sohk sabaay te?" Li addressed the man in front, who instantly recognized Li and smiled broadly, revealing a paucity of teeth.

"Kh'nyohm sohk sabaay," he replied. They knew each other. The rapid-fire Khmer exchange that followed was too fast for my skills, but I could tell from their body language that they were, if not friends, at least friendly acquaintances. Suddenly I felt terrible thirst, and I tried to keep my cool while my momentary adrenaline rush subsided. Greg too looked profoundly relieved as he laughed nervously and gestured for us to sit down. Together with Li's diplomatic skills, Greg managed to defuse the tension entirely and made amends for his earlier infraction by producing a significant gift bag of weed. But Li told me later that these guys, one of whom was a distant relation of his, were definitely carrying weapons and had a mind to teach Greg a lesson. It turns out that Greg had sold them some dud methamphetamine, a large quantity in fact. Greg's girlfriend was strung out on *yama*, the Khmer word for speed, so Greg had strayed into trafficking. Yama was a major problem in Southeast Asia, particularly in Cambodia, where young kids were bingeing on it for about two thousand riel (fifty cents) a pill and hardworking sweatshop laborers were dosing regularly just to stay awake in order to work ridiculous hours. The head of the UN Office on Drugs and Crime estimated that at least thirty thousand tablets of yama were being consumed each day in Phnom Penh alone.

Greg was much obliged to Li's diplomacy and insisted on taking us out that evening for a night on the town. I would have been very happy to never see Greg again, but Li was so happy to get the rare offer of Western hospitality that I acquiesced and quickly found myself in a string of bars along Sixty-third Street. Our group grew and shrank throughout the evening, with an even mixture of expats and locals. Greg began the night by shelling out for our drinks, but the later half of the evening was dominated by the generosity of our hard-drinking Khmer brethren. National pride and genuine Cambodian warmth led them to introduce us to brainbending local spirits and also to insist on paying the tab.

Invariably, as often happened in the wee hours of such carousing, the local boys demanded that we hit the brothels. This was just one of those illusions that were shattered for me by living in Southeast Asia. The sex industry, despite propaganda to the contrary, is not built around the patronage of foreign men (although there are some twisted sex tourists). It is overwhelmingly dominated by local patronage. This is certainly the case in Cambodia, but it is true in Thailand as well, where a significantly larger sex tourism industry exists. In a 2002 report on human rights and trafficking, for example, it was estimated that in Bangkok only 9 percent of sex work is attributable to tourism. The same study pointed out that in Phnom Penh 48 percent of sex customers were Khmer, 42 percent were other Asian ethnicities, and only 10 percent were Western. It is unquestionably the indigenous men who sustain the flesh trade in Southeast Asia.

One of the blitzed Khmer in our group wanted to go to Svay Pak, otherwise known as the notorious K11 (located eleven kilometers outside Phnom Penh). My neck tightened with dread at the very mention of it, and I began to mentally try out excuses for why I couldn't go. Svay Pak is a creepy brothel village where both sides of the dirt road are lined with prostitutes. Svay Pak is a pimper's paradise, where between three and four hundred sex workers live, but it is also well known as a site of child sex exploitation—the kind of place that keeps the human trafficking trade in business. For ten dollars, scumbags can buy sex with children. The thought of it was making me nauseous, and I was relieved to hear one of the Khmer women in our group, Phroung, announce that Svay Pak had just been closed down again.

Some of the young men groaned with disappointment and began strategizing an alternative, but Phroung expressed disappointment for very different reasons. I discovered that she had worked as a beer girl for a while before she got her current job in an upscale hotel. She was upset at the government crackdown because it would only hurt the working girls (including some of her friends) and not address the real criminals, the traffickers of children.

Under Cambodian law, it is legal for individuals to engage in prostitution voluntarily, but operating a brothel or pimping is illegal. Police and corrupt politicians rarely crack down on brothels unless it serves their immediate interests, and when they do, it's usually heavy-handed harassment of the girls themselves rather than the owners. This time the temporary closing of Svay Pak coincided perfectly with Cambodia's hosting of the ASEAN Tourism Forum. It was a short-term attempt to clean up the country's image for this meeting of the influential Association of Southeast Asian Nations.

Phroung's argument—and as I discovered upon further research, the argument of many NGOs—is that prostitution in Southeast Asia requires a fresh approach. We should think, she said, in terms of harm reduction rather than prohibition. The usual moralistic condemnation is being opposed primarily by women's groups, who are seeking to remind us that the world's oldest profession is indeed a profession. Subsequently, sex workers should have the rights and protections of any other laborers. It's the usual pious moralizing and the resulting policies, they claim, that keep the women themselves in vulnerable situations—at the mercy of the pimps and sharks who negotiate the minefield of police corruption and black-market thuggery. Closing brothels does not decrease demand—it only imperils women by sending them back into the shadows.

Phroung told me about her friend Samon, who became a sex worker in the mid-1990s. Samon's father had been a moto driver, and her mother sold jackfruit at a roadside stand. When her father fell ill, the family, which included two younger sisters, could neither sustain themselves nor pay the medical expenses. At eighteen years old, Samon, unbeknownst to her family, agreed to sell her virginity for three hundred and fifty dollars. The money helped her family pay their debts and survive another year. Samon continued to work in the sex industry to help her family, but for every dollar she made her madam took half. Eventually she joined a sex workers' union, an organized labor group founded by the Cambodian Women's Development Agency (CWDA). In the late 1990s, the group swelled to several hundred members, many of whom were Vietnamese girls trafficked in from over the border. With the help of the union, Samon broke away from her madam and set herself up as an independent sex worker, even renting an apartment for meeting with clients. The growing union also made regular rounds to brothels to explain workers' rights to owners and employees and started education programs for the women that dealt with everything from how to handle difficult clients to basic literacy and, most important, HIV/AIDS prevention. (As of 2002, 29 percent of commercial sex workers in Cambodia were HIV-positive.)

Such rudimentary labor organizations, out to protect workers, are largely responsible for condom distribution and STD education in Cambodia. But corrupt police regularly raid the brothels like Svay Pak to shake down the girls and the owners for bribes and fines, all the while

adopting the posture of high moral ground while they pocket the workers' profits. Occasionally they close brothels like Svay Pak temporarily
(sometimes motivated by threats from developed nations attaching
strings to their aid money), and consequently the women are forced to
separate and work in unsafe areas without union or peer protection. The
old mechanisms rise up again: pimps start to control the business with
violence; women become increasingly victimized by clients; and the relatively protective community of women who provided education, support,
and condoms disappears, leaving poor women disempowered and increasingly vulnerable to deadly disease.

Pimps, madams, police, and the corrupt elements of government all
want to break these unions and labor organizations because their work
cuts out the profits for the middlemen and gatekeepers and undercuts
the raison d'être of the black market. According to the 2000 Cambodian
Human Development Report, there are between 80,000 and 100,000 sex
workers in Cambodia. (Some social scientists put the figure much lower.)
Many women's groups in Southeast Asia argue that if those workers
united (taking greater ownership over their profits), and if sex work
became fully legalized, then women's economic and political power
would quantum-leap forward.

I felt very surprised by all this information and quietly drank my beer.
I guess I had expected Phroung, one of the only women left in our group
at this hour, to viciously denounce prostitution and cry exploitation. But
instead she was arguing for better prostitution. Back home, prostitution
is denounced on the right because Judeo-Christian values characterize it
as sinful promiscuity, but it is also denounced on the left by feminist intellectuals who see it as yet another example of male power politics played
out against long-suffering women. I discovered later that Phroung's position, while relatively unfamiliar in the West, is rather popular in Southeast
Asia. And in Bangkok, a place so notorious that even the Microsoft
CD-ROM encyclopedia refers to it as a flesh trade center, a press release
was issued by the Asia Pacific Women's Council in 1997 supporting "the
recognition of prostitution as work and the promotion and protection of

the human rights and dignity of women in prostitution." The group of fifty participants from twenty Asian and Pacific countries went on to deny that sex work is exploitation and pointed out that sex work is not the problem, but rather abuse, violence, and trafficking. These women are disentangling the amoral sex work of consenting older prostitutes, which they want to decriminalize, from the morally disgusting phenomenon of child exploitation, which they want prosecuted to a greater extent. Even Janet Ashby, the regional consultant with the UN Interagency Project Against Trafficking in Women and Children in the Mekong Sub-Region (try fitting that on a business card), says that governments should not crack down on places like Svay Pak but rather "should work with local authorities, brothel owners, sex workers, and service providers to regulate conditions and prevent exploitation—in particular to ensure there are no underage sex workers."

Thailand and Cambodia have different legal and enforcement frameworks for handling prostitution, but in the end they both financially cripple the women and reward management (pimps, brothel owners, madams). In Cambodia the law allows consenting individuals to sell sex, but it forbids brothels. In reality, however, the government allows brothels and penalizes individual prostitutes. In Thailand prostitution became illegal with the Prostitution Suppression Act of 1960, but in 1966 new legislation created greater protections for the "entertainment" industry. These entertainment businesses (bars, clubs, karaoke halls, show theaters) include women offering "special services." These are just brothels by a different name, and since prostitution is formally illegal, the "special service girls" depend on the pimping owners to protect them from police crackdowns (employers bail them out of jail, pay bribes, and so forth). Both the Thai and Cambodian systems function in a manner that removes at least half the profits from the pockets of the women.

While living in Southeast Asia, I gradually came to appreciate the incredible complexity of this issue. For example, while prostitutes suffer some of the predictable stigma, many young women who move from a

rural province to an urban center and support their family on prostitution money become local heroes and celebrities. They are often seen as
worldly and sophisticated by their native neighbors, and when they
return to their provincial homelands the locals "kill the fatted calf," so to
speak. Judge not lest ye be judged, I guess.

Phroung left our drunken company, and eventually we all staggered
out into the street and meandered a few blocks, the group dispersing as
we went. By the time we reached Sihanouk Boulevard, it was only Greg,
Li, Li's cousin, and myself. Greg insisted on steering us toward a nearby
massage parlor, and it took little convincing to persuade us. Some parlors
function as informal prostitution sites (Li's cousin was vocally anticipat-
ing his "happy finish"), but most of them also offer real honest-to-God
massages by trained women who will knead you into pap for about three
dollars. Since this was about the same cost as my daily coffee fix back
home, I began a regimen of massages every other day and lived life as a
slack, relaxed, centered version of my usual uptight self.

We entered the dim lobby of a small obscure hotel and were led up-
stairs to a series of couches opposite a giant curtained plate-glass window.
This was not a swanky place. There are very few swanky places in Phnom
Penh. The atmosphere was slightly ominous, like you might lose your
money and possibly your life here. But after living in Cambodia for a while,
you just get used to it. The creepiness slowly dissipates, and you grow accustomed to a dingy patina of sordidness on everything—it looks sordid at
first, but it's really just the ubiquitous corrosion of poverty. We sat comfortably and ordered some drinks, palavering with the manager. He
signaled an older woman sitting across from us, and she disappeared for a
few minutes. Then the window curtain slowly opened, revealing a dozen or
so beautiful Khmer and Vietnamese women positioned on raised bleacher
seats. Each was dressed in a bright yellow shirt and white shorts, and each
wore a large white button with a black printed number displayed promi-
nently. It took me a few months to get used to window-shopping for my
masseuse, but it's done this same weird way all over Southeast Asia.

Li's cousin was in a hurry and asked the manager for number 7. The moment of choice is usually the same: all the young women laugh and display some playful protest of neglect, and the chosen girl is ecstatic because she will get her one-dollar cut of the three-dollar price. Number 7 appeared quickly, and she and Li's cousin disappeared to one of the private massage rooms. The rest of us were not in a hurry, and we bantered a while over our drinks.

"I always feel a little guilty about this," I said, "even though it's just a massage."

"Why is that?" Greg asked.

"Well, I feel like I'm exploiting these young women somehow." I gestured at the shopping window in front of us. "I mean, look at how objectified these girls are."

Greg smacked his forehead loudly, exasperated. He sometimes adopted an irritated and condescending tone, the tone of the seasoned veteran impatiently instructing the neophyte.

"Christ, mate, your head is filled with that sanctimonious twaddle. You're just getting a massage. But even if you were gonna shag one of these lovely ladies, like I am, what the hell is so wrong with objectification? Ninety-five percent of sex is objectification as far as I can tell, and I assure you that women also treat men as sex objects. You might be overcome by piety suddenly and walk out of here feeling righteous, but all you're doing is denying one of these girls their badly needed wage, not to mention that you're going home with a stiff back. Stop wringing your hands with that Victorian morality and pick a girl!"

"Oh, I'm not Victorian here, man." I might be a moral hand-wringer, but I wanted to be in the right century. "I'm offering up a twenty-first-century feminist critique."

"Listen, my simple friend." Greg smiled magnanimous condescension. "The Western women's lib movement was great for securing political and economic power, but the movement remained totally Victorian in its views of the bedroom."

"What do you mean?" I asked. "What about the sexual revolution of the 1960s and '70s?"

"Oh, please." He rolled his eyes. "Look at these girls here," he said, gesturing to the window. "And look at most Southeast Asian women. They don't have the hang-ups and head trips about sex. Western women have mistakenly held on to the antiquated idea that shagging is somehow a concession to men, an act of submission. Even your enlightened postliberation women feel threatened by sexuality—they're taught to feel that it's a tool of male aggression. They believe that pleasing a man in bed, even if they are reciprocally pleased, is to give up something to a man, to be dominated and made weak. And the more recent feminists—you know, the ones raised in politically correct "women's studies" programs— are so uptight they think that even a man's "gaze" is an act of aggressive domination! Christ almighty, there's all this suspicion, psychological negotiating, manipulation, and power jockeying surrounding sex in the West. You can fuckin' keep that lot, I'm staying with Asian women, my friend. I have the Yellow Fever."

"Well, maybe that's the fun of it all for some people," I offered halfheartedly. "Perhaps all that drama gives greater weight to the actual sex."

"Maybe," Greg said, pondering for just a moment. "But I'd rather just have the sex, thank you. Spare me all those head trips, old man."

I could muster no real counterargument to this frank admission and decided to study the ladies for a bit. Soon Greg and number 12 were off to the back rooms, and Li picked up the discussion.

"The Buddha's teachings about womens and sex are compricated . . . complicated," Li offered. He had spent a year as a monk and knew more than the average Khmer about Buddhist orthodoxy.

"Sex is not considers a sin in Buddhism," he continued. "It is only probrem if it become . . . how you say, obsession. If tanha [craving or thirst] is too strong, then sex become like slavery inside you. You must get freedom. According to Buddha's philosophy, mens and women is equal, but in zis culture zhere is very old beliefs of woman as too tempting. Monks cannot be oscillating with women so much.

"In beginning," Li explained, "Buddha say that women is equal to mens, and they can have the ordination—they can have the nuns . . . they can *be* the nuns. But then, over many years, the old ways come back, and women lose place in sangha."

Li drew a distinction between the egalitarian dhamma of Gotama and the folk attitudes toward women in Theravadan countries. Women held high places in early Buddhism, and it was believed that they had equal access to enlightenment (the *bhikkhuni* order of nuns existed in India until the fifth century C.E.), but men eventually demonized women on the grounds that they caused so much craving in men. In a classic patriarchal move, men blamed women for the sins of male lust.

Technically speaking, of course, there are no sins in Buddhism, not in the sense of divine prohibitions. Partly this is because there is no God or Brahman to dispense binding rules, but more interestingly this is because ethics is couched within the wider framework of the pursuit of freedom or nibbana. Activities and life choices are always weighed pragmatically as to whether they contribute to or detract from *dukkha* (suffering), and the answer to that evaluation largely depends on who is asking. Activities themselves, whether they be helping old ladies across the street or selling your body for money, are neither good nor bad. They are inherently value-neutral—they just *are*. The activity becomes "bad" only if you become attached to it—if you find yourself "needing" it and obsessing about it and not being able to be content without it. Even helping old ladies across the street can become bad if you become sanctimoniously righteous about it and stake out crosswalks to get your pious "fix." So too sex for money is problematic when either the sex or the money becomes an addiction, but not before that. This means that there is no commandment list of *absolutely* wrong things in Buddhism, and while sexual desire and drugs and greed might trap you in this world of suffering, so might rigid religiosity and nationalism and moral righteousness. So philosophically speaking, one could both *be* a prostitute and *employ* a prostitute, and as long as one remained egoless and detached about the whole business, one could continue as a good Buddhist. (This example also assumes that no deceptions are being engineered, like husbands lying to wives.)

The point is that, in Buddhism, nothing has inherent evil or inherent goodness, but some things are harder to rise above than others, and the dhamma warns us of potential enslavements. The Buddha Gotama, being liberated from craving and ego, would have no problem engaging in a heroin-tinged orgy down at the local brothel. It would not enslave him. But the Buddha is a pro, and the rest us should not try this at home. Unlike the Buddha, if I indulge this behavior, I will certainly get a taste for it, and then I will not be able to put it down again. But the "sin" is not in the behavior—it is in my attachment to the behavior. Buddhist sexual moderation is not premised on an argument from divine authority but rather from a consequentialist argument about the self-defeating potential of unrestrained craving. Consequentialist ethics pragmatically assesses the value of an action in terms of that action's effectiveness for bringing about a stipulated good, and for Buddhism that stipulated good is personal peaceful equanimity (minimizing dukkha) and social compassion. So, unlike in Western religions, I will not be punished *for* my sins (this doesn't even make sense in Buddhism); I will be punished *by* my sins, in the sense that I will be enslaved by my own tanha.

The Buddha understood that we are biological animals and that we are all composed of five *khandas* (aggregates): *rupa* (body), *vedana* (feeling), *sanna* (perception), *sankhar* (dispositions or volitional tendencies), and *vinnana* (consciousness). Having this human biological composition means that we are susceptible to drives and instincts as well as to desire, craving, and suffering. I have a drive or instinct to eat because I have a body and feelings and volition, and so on, but when this same drive is indulged repeatedly in a mistaken attempt to possess the pleasures of eating, then it transitions into a case of craving (for example, one becomes obese) and thereby a case of suffering. Li explained that Buddhism is not strict asceticism—Gotama tried this for a while before his enlightenment, but he rejected it. Buddhism does not promote repression of our natural tendencies. When you're hungry, eat. When you are tired, sleep. When you want sex, have sex. That's not the same as hedonism. In Buddhism, you are not trying to become a robot, immune from feelings, inspirations, and impulses. Having a body means that you naturally encounter attractions and repulsions—that is the first step of experience. But Gotama teaches that we must stop the second step of experience—ego consciousness, or the egoistic attempt to possess that which cannot be possessed. This second step is where the discipline must come into play.

"When you have nize ezperience," Li said, "you want very much to hold on to zis ezperience, you want to keep it inside you and not to be letting go of it. When zis happening then you are becoming ego-consciousness. The ezperience itself, like all ezperience, is only temporary—it come and go, it always disappear. But ego want good feeling to stay and stay, but it cannot!" Li drew his hands together tight and then broke them apart with fingers waving. "Everyzing impermanent, boss."

This is a major misunderstanding of Buddhism in the West. People think that the Buddha wants us to lose our feelings and become detached from the world altogether. This is not true. Gotama himself lived for almost fifty more years after his enlightenment, and during that time he got hungry, enjoyed food, got sick and grew well, felt disappointments, had tremendous joy, probably got laid, became tired and slept, and experienced every other range of emotion and feeling. His liberation was not freedom from these experiences but freedom from the ego-consciousness that jumps in after these feelings and tries to hold on to them. Human experiences and behaviors are neither good nor bad in themselves. It is the ego attachment that causes tanha and dukkha.

As Li pointed out to me, however, not everyone has the education or the leisure to do philosophical analysis of human behaviors, carefully evaluating one's subjective tanha responses to inherently neutral phenomena. So the Buddha gives the people a simple road map for negotiating the lures and pitfalls. These are referred to as the Five Precepts. Theravada lay Buddhists refrain from killing, stealing, lying, consuming intoxicants, and committing adultery. Theravadan people take these seriously, and the precepts contribute to the creation of a socially conservative, virtuous, rural culture, with strong family values. The ethically conservative Khmer majority in Cambodia is still in shock after half a century of fighting and chaos, but they yearn for peace and traditional Buddhist culture. Just because some urban thugs can get away with murder in Cambodia, we should not be blinded from seeing the vast numbers of deeply ethical Buddhists.

Still, Cambodia really is a dangerous place—many people seem to have the Ring of Gyges. But if properly reclaimed, the rich Theravadan culture can begin to provide solutions. The Buddha was not a utopian or a naively idealistic philosopher. His ultimate teachings of nibbana (through the cessation of craving) can certainly heal Cambodia's heart of darkness, but he does not place the burden of peacemaking entirely on the individual. In the Kutadanta Sutta and the Cakkavatti Sutta (both found in the Digha Nikaya), Gotama explains how a good ruler must ameliorate crime rates through economic reforms. Following his general view of *paticca samuppada* (the causal interdependence of all things), the Buddha reminds us that crime is usually dependent on social inequities and poverty. He tells the myth of King Wide-Realm, who finds his country awash in violence and crime. The king seeks to quell the violence and deviance by making a ritual sacrifice, so he turns to a sage for advice. The sage, however, informs the king that justice will never come through religious sacrifices, nor will it come from increased fines, punishments, death penalties, and the like. The sage says,

> Now there is one method to adopt to put a thorough end to this disorder. Whosoever there be in the king's realm who devote themselves to keeping cattle and the farm, to them let his majesty give food and seed corn. Whosoever there be in the king's realm who devote themselves to trade, to them let his majesty give capital. Whosoever there be in the king's realm who devote themselves to government service, to them let his majesty give wages and food. Then those men, following each his own business, will no longer harass the realm; the king's revenue will go up; the country will be quiet and at peace; and the populace, pleased with one another and happy, dancing with their children in their arms, will dwell with open doors.

So, while there are individual psychological roots of violence and law-lessness, the Buddha also recognizes the more systemic causal matrix of poverty. Perhaps if Cambodia's leaders were more attentive to sustainable economic development, then there would be less need for assassination of alternative voices and intimidation at the polls, less need for young girls to prostitute themselves to save their families, less need for guns and barbed wire everywhere, and less need for black markets and burning embassies.

By now the window girls were no longer interested in Li and me, and they had resumed their lax downtime postures. The manager was dozing in a chair nearby, and we'd emptied our drinks.

"I think I'll take number 9," I resolved suddenly.

"No, no, boss, I was wanting number 9!" Li feigned outrage.

"But I'm a guest in your country, Li. I think I'm entitled to some of your renowned Khmer hospitality. Besides, number 3 has been eyeing you for a while now."

Li quickly scanned the bleachers and laughed when he discovered number 3 fast asleep on the bench.

"Steef," he said, "you should practice your Buddhist non-attachment and give up number 9."

He was right. I ended up in the capable hands of number 10, but was effectively passed out before she even reached my calves.

Life in Southeast Asia presents one with many opportunities for hedonism, and it frequently removes the threats of punishment that keep us in check. For approximately sixty dollars, one can, in Cambodia, buy an ounce of marijuana, a half-gram of heroin, a handgun, and a full day at the brothel, finished off by a relatively decadent meal. After that full day, you can, for just a little more money, kill one of your enemies and bribe your way to safety. This is a dodgy world where passions can easily consume you, but Buddhism is powerful medicine. After all, what good is your Buddhism if it's never put to the test—if it's never tempted? If you can only be spiritual when women are covering themselves up, or when you're living in a monastery or a nunnery, or when you're prosperous, or when you're otherwise "protected" from the myriad causes of craving, then it's a pretty flimsy spirituality. There is nothing flimsy about Theravadan Buddhism, a spirituality that acts like an eye of tranquillity in a hurricane of vice and suffering.

Two

REASON FOR THE FEW, MAGIC FOR THE MANY?

Monkey Gods and Penis Worship

The Buddhist Institute sits like a giant golden spirit house at the end of Sihanouk Boulevard, overlooking a long strip of nighttime food stands and the curve of Sisowath Quay. Two giant green cobra bodies form the ascending balustrade, and the architectural spandrels feature carved *garudas* (mythical bird-men warriors that serve as mounts for Vishnu). The institute is quite close to the Naga Floating Casino, which is more humble and depressing than glitzy. The casino is a dirty, modest-sized boat with Japanese tourists chain-smoking and playing blackjack. While I was teaching at the Buddhist Institute, two gigantic towers were slowly rising up behind the institute, dwarfing us and forming a barrier to the river. The incongruous structures will eventually be new casinos. The juxtaposition is bizarre. The Buddhist Institute, arguably the fulcrum of Khmer Theravada Buddhism, being overshadowed, literally, by gigantic, looming casinos. The shrunken symbol of moderation next to the massive incarnation of craving.

Every day I walked from my home in Kapko Market to the institute, where, before I taught, I briefed and debriefed with my colleague Kimvan. Kimvan, who you'll recall took me on that fateful Udong vomit pilgrimage, was teaching a course in Khmer folklore and literature. He grew up in Cambodia but also studied for a while in Laos. One day, almost in passing, he mentioned that an American bomb had dropped on his home in 1970 and killed his mother. I shuddered at the prospect of something like this happening to me and couldn't quite take it in. It was horrible, but it was abstract and remote. It even seemed abstract for him, given his matter-of-fact way, but of course it was not. I asked him if he hated Americans, and he said that Cambodians hated my stupid government but not American people.

In 1969 the United States began a secret bombing campaign in Cambodia. As early as 1965, Viet Cong had begun using Cambodia as a covert base of operations in their attempts to overthrow South Vietnam. Using a ham-fisted method and a profoundly irresponsible logic, the United States carpet-bombed Cambodia, trying to wipe out these Communist enclaves. B-52s unloaded ton after ton of horror for four years until the U.S. Congress stopped it in 1973, leaving tremendous civilian casualties and countless refugees.

Kimvan explained to me that his large family lived in a rural village outside Phnom Penh. His mother believed that the bombing was getting closer and that they would all be safer in the capital. So she began moving the children in shifts, first taking little Kimvan and his sister to the city, where they stayed with older siblings who were already established. She went back for the rest of the family, but Kimvan's father was hesitant to leave his home. While they were still organizing their departure, a bomb landed directly on their house, killing Kimvan's mother, his sister, and two more brothers. The father survived but was badly burned. In this state of shock and injury, he alone buried his family under cover of darkness. Eventually an older brother made the dangerous journey back to the village and discovered the tragedy, finally rescuing the devastated father. Most Khmer people have similar stories of unfathomable suffering.

The next day Kimvan brought me a photo of his whole family. It was a weathered black-and-white, and he held it carefully. The picture was a treasure for him, and he beamed with quiet pride. There were fourteen people, dressed in fine Khmer and Western clothing, grouped around a central figure—Kimvan's mother. She sat on a high stool, bouncing baby Kimvan on her knee. He carefully pointed out his mother and father. Then he showed me the two brothers who had also died in the American bomb blast and indicated which sister had perished. They all looked so vital and proud. They weren't abstract at all.

We quietly looked at the photo for a while. Then Kimvan pointed to the right of his mother at another young couple holding their baby—an older brother's family. He told me that they were all killed by the Khmer Rouge in the late 1970s. I reeled at the thought of so much misery visited upon a single family. Then he pointed to yet another brother and sister and told me that they had been killed in the 1980s during the Vietnamese occupation of Cambodia. I was speechless. We sat together and just looked at the picture for a very long time.

A few days later Kimvan picked me up at my guesthouse, and he drove me down to the Tonle Sap riverside on his moto. This riverside area of Phnom Penh is bustling with new development (little hotels and restaurants), but just behind it to the west are city blocks of very poor locals who are living on the street, in medieval markets, and in leftover, crumbling, colonial-era buildings. Between those two cultural territories one finds Wat Ounolom, a beautiful temple complex. Kimvan wanted to show me another holy relic of the Buddha. We seemed to be touring the Buddha's remnant body parts—the last time it had been the tooth in Udong, and this time it was the Buddha's eyebrow.

Just inside the gates of the wat were four sculpted figures in sequential order. They were dramatic symbols of Prince Gotama's awakening to the problem of dukkha. Buddhist lore has it that when Gotama was born

(Theravadans place the date at 563 B.C.E.), his father, King Suddhodana, was warned that the boy would eventually become a wandering holy man. Suddhodana, however, wanted his son to follow in his footsteps and become a powerful ruler, so he tried to shelter his son from the outside world. Gotama was provided with every luxury imaginable so that he would have no reason to leave home and fulfill the disappointing prophesy. Despite his overprotective father's plans, Gotama made a chariot expedition outside the palace walls, and there encountered three deeply powerful sights. First, he saw a very old man, struggling and laboring with infirm limbs, hunched back, and downturned head. (A life-sized stone statue portrayed this character at Wat Ounolom.) The young prince was shocked by this experience, and when the chariot driver explained to him that all people eventually end up in this decaying condition, he grew despondent. Next he happened to catch sight of a maimed person, and again he was surprised and depressed. Lastly, Gotama came across a corpse lying in the street. In an attempt to undercut human vanity and demonstrate the impermanence of all things, Buddhist scriptures are filled with nauseating details about rotting carcasses and putrid flesh. In the Anguttara Nikaya, for example, the scripture asks, "Did you never see in the world the corpse of a man or a woman, one or two or three days after death, swollen up, blue-black in color, and full of corruption? And did the thought never come to you that you also are subject to death, that you cannot escape it?" (III.35). Thankfully, the statue depicting the corpse was more restrained and toned down, though it did represent a cadaver with a carrion bird perched on its belly, picking the entrails out.

It was these three experiences—age, injury, and death—that wrenched Gotama out of his sheltered existence and forced him to renounce luxury and leave the palace to find a cure for suffering. In the courtyard of Wat Ounolom, the three statues are followed by one more, an image of the enlightened Buddha. The stylized Buddha is portrayed as a young man (Gotama became "awake" in his early thirties) with arms pressed to his sides and a beatific smile on his visage. Fragrant frangipani shrubs circle the statues, and tamarind trees gently shade them.

Kimvan and I sauntered around the gardens, and he explained to me, pointing to a tattered gold and white building, that this was the original home of the Buddhist Institute in the 1930s. The fancy new Buddhist Institute that I taught in, at the foot of the casinos, was moved from Ounolom in the late 1990s. We continued past the elaborate *stupa* (or *chet dai*, burial monument) of Venerable Chuon Nath, famous monk and Khmer dictionary compiler, and made our way behind the central *vihara* (ceremony hall). Here a smaller temple contained the Buddha's eyebrow. In the same way that I couldn't really see the actual tooth in Udong, I had to take it on faith that the eyebrow was indeed buried below the altar area. A life-sized black Buddha figure sat in lotus position inside a small tabernacle niche, and the eyebrow was thought to be buried underneath. Fresh-cut lotus flowers, still closed tightly, framed the statue, and a little tree of gold leaves sat perched in the corner. After our respectful three prostrations, we lit some incense offerings and returned to the gardens. It is customary in Southeast Asia to kneel before the central Buddha image in a pagoda, raise prayerful hands to the forehead, and bend low, almost touching the face to the ground. This prostration is often abbreviated to one bow in the presence of other religious paraphernalia and imagery, but before the Buddha it is to be repeated three times. Kimvan claimed that three gestures correspond to the "three gems" of Buddhist belief—the Buddha, the dharma (teachings), and the sangha (monastic community)—but he couldn't be sure, and he admitted that everyone just did three because they'd always done three. Here we chatted with a couple of monks, and they seemed to disagree about whether the eyebrow really was in Ounolom at all; one monk felt quite certain that the holy hairs had been moved to Udong sometime in the first decade of the 1900s.

The importance of relics in Southeast Asian Buddhism is more a reflection of cultural folk beliefs than Theravadan orthodoxy. The folk cultures of Buddhism have frequently deified Gotama, and this tradition attributes special metaphysical spiritual powers to the Buddha's physical remains. The Buddha himself would have been amused, and possibly irritated, by the idea of people worshiping his bones and hairs. For one thing, in the metaphysical scheme of things, the body is impermanent and momentary, and the attempt to preserve it is futile clinging. Second, the Buddha wouldn't let anybody worship him when he was alive, so it seems dubious that he'd approve of the posthumous practice. He always insisted that he was only an awakened man, not deity, and he was fond of saying that *he* was not nearly as important as his *message*, the dhamma (dharma).

Still, holy relics are important to practicing Theravadans. For example, about the same time that Kimvan and I were paying our respects to the sacred eyebrow, the Thais were making a mad rush, in Bangkok, to see the only other *phra khieo kaeo* (tooth relic), on loan temporarily from China. The tooth was brought in honor of the seventy-fifth birthday of Thai king Bhumibol Adulyadej, and in March 2003 the tour was over and a Chinese envoy was returning it home. Supposedly, this tooth surfaced in Nanjing around 500 C.E. and then made its way to Beijing, where it has been housed since 1071.

Reaching back further, we find that after the Buddha's cremation his leftovers were sent to eight provinces. Legend has it that King Asoka of India (269–32 B.C.E.) consolidated the relics by plundering those provinces, but then further divided the remains into thousands of bits and sent them out with emissaries to spread the dhamma throughout Asia. Some body parts went north, eventually becoming important to Mahayana Buddhists (for example, the Chinese tooth), and some went south to Sri Lanka, eventually becoming important to Theravadan Buddhists (the Cambodian tooth in Udong, for instance).

In an unprecedented attempt to rejoin a little bit of Buddha body, Thailand, Sri Lanka, and Myanmar have all volunteered to combine a total of twelve relics for installation at the United Nations headquarters in New York City for permanent exhibition starting in 2005. This gesture is a response to the UN General Assembly's 2000 announcement of an International Vesak Day—the holiest of Buddhist holidays. Vesak Day (the word stems from the Sanskrit and Pali words for May) is celebrated on the full moon of May and recognizes the day of Gotama's enlightenment.

I was raised Catholic, so the idea of holy relics makes perfect sense to me. That is to say, I understand it as much as I understand the other things in Catholicism, which is to say that I don't understand it as much as I recognize it. And when I say I recognize it, I guess I mean that I remember it. Come to think of it, I'm not really clear on this. On the one hand, you can interpret relics as supernatural entities charged with some mystical power—a power that you can tap into and use in your life. Or you can interpret relics as natural objects that possess no inherent supernatural vibes but are great *reminders* of important values and ideal persons. The first interpretation is really thrilling but kind of hard to believe when living in a scientific culture. The second is smoothly reconciled with science and common sense but lacks the verve and panache. Theravadans interpret relics both ways and don't see a conflict.

Kimvan and I walked across the street from the wat to the Tonle Sap riverside because he wanted to show me another example of Theravadan folk culture. In the twilight now, the wide promenade was filling with its usual bevy of vendors—men, women, and children with horizontal broom handles across their shoulders, weighted on either side with durians, pineapples, plums, and coconuts. A small group of people surrounded a *chapei* (musician), who was sitting cross-legged on the ground, playing his two-stringed guitar-type instrument and singing folk songs. This music was banned during the Khmer Rouge period between 1975 and 1979 on the pseudo-Communist grounds that such frivolities as music and art should be replaced with manual labor; subsequently, many skills and songs disappeared. The musician was blind, and while he sang a little dust-covered toddler kept walking up to him, trying to strum the instrument. The poor guy seemed very confused because he could feel the close presence and interference of the child but couldn't grasp what was going on. He kept pulling his tip jar closer and generally stressing out in between verses.

We studied two altars that Kimvan pointed out. Each altar was composed of a small building, no bigger than the average kitchen, and a surrounding array of large clay jars for offerings of lotus flowers, or garlands, or joss sticks. Khmers lined up to enter through one open doorway, laid offerings at the inner shrine, and then exited out a side doorway. But the figures inside were not Buddhas. One of them contained a fierce blue Vishnu, and the other altar contained an ancient military figure dressed in battle armor with sword raised. These two small altars, and countless similar ones all over the country, revealed the other central spiritual traditions that intertwine with Theravada Buddhism in Southeast Asia, namely Brahmanism and animism. ("Hinduism" is a more recent term that tries to capture the entire body of loosely related Indian beliefs; "Brahmanism" falls inside that larger category but is a devotional tradition that existed in India and traveled to Southeast Asia during the Upanishad scriptural era, roughly 900 B.C.E. to 200 B.C.E.)

Kimvan explained that the warrior depicted at the altar was the most famous of the spiritual beings collectively referred to as *neak ta*. Neak ta are spirits that inhabit specific regions or even specific natural entities, like trees, rivers, or mountains. These animistic forces can be appealed to for favors and for protection, but they can also be quite mischievous, and people all over Southeast Asia make offerings in order to keep the peace with these supernatural antagonists. The warrior neak ta, however, is definitely one of the good guys.

Ghlamn Mioen, Kimvan explained, is the protective spirit who lived as an army general under King Ang Chan (1516–66), and he is a hero to Khmer people because he defeated the invading Thai (Siamese) army. His method was singular. Ghlamn Mioen, his wife, and his sons threw themselves into a pit of sharpened stakes, thus killing themselves in order to secure the help of the ghost world. Some say that he returned with an army of supernatural beings to fight the Thais; others claim that he returned bringing a devastating outbreak of cholera to his enemies. His self-sacrifice and profound dedication make him a widely acknowledged spirit hero, one who continues to help Khmer people in their everyday struggles.

I struggled to understand the relationship between the rational philosophy of Buddhism and the more widespread religious superstitions. Religion in Southeast Asia has the same tension between its poetic and rational dimensions that one finds in Western monotheisms. I kept thinking of Dostoyevsky's famous "Grand Inquisitor" scene in which Christ comes back to the modern world and is arrested by the Church. Dostoyevsky, a devout Orthodox Christian, unfolds a story in which the Church captures Christ and the chief Inquisitor asks Him to go away because the challenge of righteousness that He brings is way too difficult for weak human nature to accomplish. The Inquisitor explains to Christ that "the Church" is much better than Jesus at giving humans what they want and what they need: "miracle, mystery, and authority." What's great about this little chapter of *The Brothers Karamazov* is that you can't just oversimplify the protagonists with some "Christ good, Inquisitor bad" interpretation. When the Inquisitor is finished with his rant, he really seems like a person who loves humanity more than Christ does, because he (the Church) can give average people the comfort and ease that their daily suffering requires. Sure, it comes to the people as a distracting tonic of "bread and circuses," but at least their lives are made relatively happy. The cost is that people have to hand over their freedom and responsibility to the authority of the Church, but according to the Inquisitor (and the psychologist Erich Fromm, for that matter), most people will gladly lay down the "burden" of moral responsibility if they could just have a holy man (or some other authority) tell them what to do. The real teachings of Christianity, the Inquisitor argues, are just too difficult for such weak beings to live up to.

I really have no idea if this is true or not, and I'm sure Dostoyevsky didn't know either. It's a pessimistic view, that much is clear. But it also points out the fact that for every big idea, there're always two versions: a pop version for the masses and a gnostic version for the cognoscenti. In ancient Greece, the teat for the Western mind, they used to say, "Rationality for the few, magic for the many." A similar tension exists here in Theravada Buddhism throughout Cambodia, Thailand, Laos, Sri Lanka, and Myanmar.

I interviewed two young *bhikkhus* (monks), Venerables Amnann and Sovanrattana, about the current tensions between Buddhism's philosophical principles and its superstitious culture. They arrived at my guesthouse on the back of motos, and we greeted each other with the traditional *wai*—hands raised in prayer. I held my hands high to my forehead, which is a sign of deep respect reserved for monks. They brushed this off and adopted a casual manner.

"Zhank-you, Steef, but not necessary," said Venerable Sovanrattana.

On the rooftop of my building, we drank iced tea and talked shop. Both of these monks had just finished an eight-year intensive program in Buddhist philosophy in Sri Lanka—they were Khmer, but they had to go to Sri Lanka to study philosophy because after Pol Pot, no higher-level Buddhist education remained in Cambodia. (I'm actually part of the fortunate first group to help re-create a Buddhist studies program here.) These monks, unlike the cultural Buddhists I meet every day, are very well versed in the philosophical concepts. Within the first fifteen minutes of our lengthy discussion, we delved into the phenomenological perception theory of the Abhidhamma, and in the full course of things we discussed the main topics of Buddhist philosophy: (1) *anatta*, the theory that we have no permanent soul or lasting personal essence; (2) *anicca*, the theory that all things, including ultimate reality, are impermanent; and (3) *paticca samuppada*, the theory of "dependent arising"—all beings are dependent on other beings in an ecological "web" of relations. More on this stuff later.

When asked whether the average Khmer Buddhist is familiar with these philosophical concepts, Venerable Sovanrattana laughed and told me that if he actually taught real Buddhism to the people, he would go hungry! Remember, every monk depends on the daily donations of food made by the local devotees, who give as merit-making behavior.

"Honestly," he explained, "ze laypeople would have no part of it. Real Buddhism is too rational, not magical enough, for most practicing Buddhists." And Venerable Amnann confirmed what we at the Buddhist Institute have also concluded when he stated flatly, "Cambodians say they are Buddhists, but they don't know anything about Buddhism." If the Buddha came back today, one wonders if the laypeople would ask him to go away so they could return to their own version of miracle, mystery, and authority.

For the sake of clarity, let me call the more magical beliefs and practices "cultural" Buddhism and the scripture-based teaching (virtually unknown to practicing Buddhists in Southeast Asia) "philosophical" Buddhism. So what exactly is the miracle, mystery, and authority? Let me sketch some Brahmanic influences, totem worship, penis worship, neak ta cults, and deification of the Buddha. First, the Indianization of Southeast Asia.

Originally, Buddhism grew out of Hinduism (or Brahmanism), in a way similar to Christianity's evolution out of Judaism—many continuities, together with a few revolutionary innovations. Just as Jesus was a Jew steeped in the traditions around him, Gotama imbibed the Brahmanic traditions with his mother's milk. Then both these revolutionaries transformed their theological inheritance significantly. In the Buddha's case, he argued against the emphasis on caste and ritual that he encountered in Brahmanism, but he also philosophically argued against the Hindu beliefs in a *Brahman* (permanent God) and an *atman* (permanent soul).

In Southeast Asia the religious climate has been heavily influenced by the pre-Buddhist Hinduism—Brahmanic ideas arrived in the Cambodian region first, mixing with the indigenous animism; then Buddhism followed. (Indian emperor Asoka sent Buddhist teachers, along with those relics, south to Sri Lanka in the third century B.C.E., and from there

Buddhism spread to the areas now known as Thailand, Myanmar, Cambodia, and Laos.) In Cambodia, Buddhism and Hinduism intermingled and coexisted with relative tolerance for each other—Hindu gods, like Vishnu and Shiva, dominated in the first millennium, but Buddhism started to wash over the Khmer psyche in the thirteenth century C.E. (first the Mahayana Buddhism of King Jayavarman VII [1181–1219]— builder of many of the Angkor temples—and then the Theravada Buddhism that dominated all the way until the Pol Pot era). But Buddhism all over Southeast Asia never really disentangled itself from Hinduism, and the evidence of this religious gumbo is everywhere.

At the famous Angkor temples, for example, one searches in vain for Buddhist imagery. In countries like Cambodia and Thailand, the sculptures, bas-relief carvings, and paintings are overwhelmingly Hindu, predominantly traditional Shiva and Vishnu representations. Most people have seen the classic sculpture of Shiva dancing (one leg up) in a ring of fire, stretching his many arms to the side. But in Southeast Asia, Shiva is represented as a giant penis statue, called the *lingam*. Khmers and Thais engage in a very ancient cult of penis worship. Why anyone would worship the penis is, of course, plain as day and needs no explanation (spoken like a man), but to find out why Shiva is represented this way is an adventure in itself.

On a break from teaching, I was fortunate enough to find myself beachcombing in southern Thailand during the early rainy season. Most people agree that Thai beaches, like Phi Phi, Phuket, and Krabi, win the picture-perfect-postcard competition hands down. The islands are unparalleled for their lush and exotic character, but tourist culture is quickly encroaching. The Leonardo DiCaprio film *The Beach* was filmed here, and every guide lets you know it on a regular basis. Couple this pop-culture lure with the reality TV show *Survivor: Thailand*, and you have a recipe for turning the pristine beaches into a Florida spring-break frat party. But like every other tourist trap, there are always things to discover if you get off the beaten path a little, which is what I did one afternoon in a kayak off Raileh Peninsula.

After cruising around in the emerald-green water and gawking at the massive stalactites hanging off the mountain cliffs, I came to a desolate little beach tucked into the bottom crease of a tall precipice. I struggled in the strong tide to ground my kayak, and two Thai women emerged from a mysterious cave to lend their expert help. One girl kept offering me a "massah" over and over again, and eventually I figured out that she was an ersatz masseuse. Over her shoulder I glimpsed the small shallow cave and some brilliant-colored altar inside. The strong smell of incense hung like a trapped fog in this acute geologic corner. When we entered the well-worn ancient temple cave, I could hardly believe my eyes. A small altar table, covered with brightly colored garlands of flowers and dyed cloth, was surrounded by hundreds of penises. Big ones, small ones, red ones, white ones, black, purple, orange—all carved of wood. Some of the penises were as large as a man and others as small as a real penis. One of the women standing next to me brought forth a small carved phallus from under her batik wrap and placed it on the altar, following this with an incense offering and a bow and prayer. Well, you don't need to know anything about Freud to know that the sight of a severed penis, even if it's made of wood, dredges up some primordial anxieties for every man. Here was a grotto of hundreds of castration scenarios. My anxiety was wholly transformed, however, when I discovered that this was no temple of emasculation, but instead an altar of penis worship. I surveyed the whole scene with fresh eyes.

Like most people raised in the Christian West, I grew up with some fairly neurotic attitudes toward sex and the body. I'm not alone when I remember wrestling with Catholic guilt and shamefully confessing to a man of the cloth that I'd been "pleasuring myself" as of late. Western guilt is aggressive and legislates over not only your impious actions but also your "impure thoughts." Some of this puritanism is simply a by-product of parents telling their kids scary scenarios to keep them from genital manipulation in public—a remarkably tempting impulse among children. Everyone knows a few of these cruel warnings: you'll go blind if you keep masturbating, or hair will grow on your palms if you keep "spanking the monkey," and so on. And remember, God can see what you're up to even when no one else can. All relatively harmless, I guess, but then most parents forget to "unscare" their kids later on when they are finally well disciplined, thereby leaving a healthy residue of self-loathing. Of course, we can't blame our parents really, because nobody remembered to unscare them either. But some of this hostility we have toward our bodies is built into the religion at more foundational levels. Sometimes the sexual anxieties are cultivated to protect the social cohesion of the nuclear family system. For example, you'll burn in hell for all eternity if you have premarital sex, and this same fate awaits you if you merely fantasize about your neighbor's wife. Harsh stuff really, but it probably worked well in maintaining fidelity bonds. However, even more foundational levels of sexual angst exist in Western theology itself. The flesh is inherently bad, the spirit is good.

Western theology is rife with this denigration of the flesh, and Nietzsche referred to its adherents as "despisers of the body." When I was growing up, nobody ever said it to me directly, but I was given the distinct impression that sexual desires were obstacles to, rather than vehicles for, spiritual enlightenment. Asceticism seeks to mortify the flesh so that the spiritual dimension of the devotee will be purified or freed, even if only temporarily. Do a little digging and you can find explicit expressions of this in Saint Augustine—a guy who asked God, "Please make me chaste, but not just yet." It's this basic assumption of the human being divided against himself that leads the Eastern yogi to starve himself and deprive himself of sleep and the Western priest and nun to refuse themselves erotic pleasures. To indulge the body, according to this tradition, is to give in to the "dark side." The early Christian presbyter Origen (184–254 C.E.) not only pronounced that his own body was alien to him but also had himself castrated as a young man so that he could, without scandal, become a scriptural teacher for young women.

Imagine my amazement and pleasant surprise when I discovered the Southeast Asian theology of penis worship. As I said before, however, this is no ordinary penis, but rather the lingam, a phallic representation of the Hindu god Shiva. And as you might guess, the lingam is a manifestation of "generative power," the male version of a fertility totem. Lingam worship, while originally Indian, is still practiced in Thailand and Cambodia and in pockets all around Southeast Asia, even though the official religion is Buddhism.

The Thai women I met at the grotto were making offerings to the lingam in order to secure good healthy pregnancies, and if at all possible they wanted to have boys. This is one of the most common uses of the lingam's power, as is the occasional plea from fishermen and farmers for prosperity. What else can the lingam do? Why should one cozy up to the divine rod? Well, according to Shiva in the Vamana Purana scripture, "Those who worship my lingam in a spirit of complete devotion will find nothing hard to achieve, ever. Anyone who commits sins, even knowingly, is purified by worshiping my lingam."

The original story of the lingam can be found in the sacred Hindu writings called the Puranas, a diverse body of texts composed between the fourth and twelfth centuries C.E. But this text, the Brahmanda Purana, merely codifies a much older folk tradition of penis worship, the origins of which are shrouded in mystery. The penis god, Shiva, is one of the divine trinity that also includes Vishnu and Brahma. In addition to Shiva's more familiar images as a multi-armed humanoid, he can shapeshift and materialize in myriad ways, one of which is this impressive phallus. The scripture explains that before the beginning of earthly time, Vishnu was reclining in the divine darkness, looking around with his thousand heads and thousand eyes and feet, holding inside his belly all the creatures not yet born. Suddenly another creature appeared who announced himself as Brahma, the maker of the worlds. To this unexpected interruption Vishnu responded that *he* was the maker of worlds, and the preserver and the destroyer to boot. As they were arguing about who was more potent, a flame began to grow in a distant region, and it approached them at lightning speed and with blinding intensity. The powerful shaft of light forced Vishnu and Brahma to bow in reverence; it was the awesome manifestation of Shiva. The humbled gods came close to the column of flame and discovered that it was a garland of fire that spiraled around a luminous penis that was growing larger and larger. Then Brahma told Vishnu to fly down to the bottom of this growing phallus, while Brahma ascended toward the top. In this way they would discover the true dimensions of the behemoth. But each of them traveled in their respective directions for a thousand years without discovering the beginning or end of the divine prick. Becoming afraid of the sublime size, the gods returned to their point of origin and got on their knees to placate this superior being. After a deluge of compliments and tributes from Vishnu and Brahma, Shiva finally transformed from a phallus into a humanoid shape. He laughed at the underling gods but, being impressed by their devotion, granted them protection and blessings.

Your average penis devotees today are probably not acquainted with this scriptural passage, but they employ the totem in a variety of religious rituals that have been passed down through oral culture. It is believed that water that passes over a lingam sculpture becomes holy and has the power to grant wishes and give fertility to the soil itself, as well as to humans. In Cambodia an ancient king actually built an irrigation channel that had hundreds of penises sculpted into its floor so that all the water passing over them, intended for crops, would carry potent generative power. I hiked to this River of a Thousand Linga when I was in the jungles of northern Cambodia. Outside Siem Reap, my moto driver and I braved Khmer Rouge country and malarial mosquitoes to find the obscure river at Kbal Spear. I felt like Martin Sheen in *Apocalypse Now*, clawing my way deep into the nightmarish jungle to confront the horrible Kurtz. But when I got there, I was embarrassed to find a handful of Hong Kong high school students and their tour guide laughing and eating lunch on the shores of the penis river. Apparently there was a much easier route on the other side of the mountain, and the kids had pranced up effortlessly.

Anyway, a religion in which the genitals are not only tolerated but actually celebrated strikes me as refreshingly healthy. The puritanical religions of the West encourage people to see part of their own body, and its attendant pleasure, as a necessary evil—you gotta have this equipment in order to make a baby, but otherwise it's nothing but trouble. Western spirituality is not completely devoid of a penis-friendly attitude, I guess, but you have to go back a long way to find it. The ancient Greek god Priapus, for example, was an important male fertility character. Son of Aphrodite and Dionysius (party animal extraordinaire), Priapus was often represented as a little man with a huge erection, or sometimes he was simply carved as a giant phallic statue. Most representations of Priapus were, quite predictably, destroyed by uptight Christians, but for one brief moment we had our own lingam god.

Now don't get me wrong. I don't want to give some overly macho impression here. What I'm noting is easily transferred to women's bodies as well. The same puritanical impulses that make men feel ambivalent toward their libidinal tool equally lead women into self-estrangement. And thankfully, women have a good pagan antidote in the West, named the Venus of Willendorf. The Venus is a prehistoric female fertility goddess (dating from around 23,000 B.C.E.), whose buxom image includes extremely exaggerated breasts and vagina. And to assure women that Eastern lingam culture is not just another phallocentric ego trip, I must point out that wherever one finds a lingam statue, one usually also finds a *yoni*. The yoni is a female phallic symbol shaped like a square vessel with an opening at one side—a very abstract vagina and uterus. Like most men, I would happily agree to worship women's privates, if *they* would only agree to get on board with this whole lingam thing.

If Westerners thought differently about sexual ecstasy and spirituality, then they might see the wisdom of genital religions. If you think about it, sexual ecstasy is a transcendental moment in which your individual ego disappears and merges with something greater than yourself. And that's precisely how most religious mystics define the truly spiritual experience, the divine communion. This same perspective can be found in the Tantric traditions that developed later.

Many of the Angkor temples in Cambodia have a lingam and yoni as the centerpiece of their altar. And these "deities" can be found throughout contemporary society as well, often carved as small amulets to be worn around the neck for protection. It is not at all uncommon to find Buddhist images and rituals right alongside lingam worship. In Southeast Asia you are not *either* a Buddhist *or* a Lingaist, you are *both* at once. No problem.

In addition to Shiva worship, Hindu epic stories like the Mahabarata, Puranas, and Ramayana are dominant cultural expressions of spirituality. The Ramayana, known here as the Reamker, is everywhere—even traditional Khmer and Thai dance is mostly about the Reamker story. My little pet theory (for what it's worth) is that the Ramayana is wildly popular throughout Southeast Asia because it is really, really cool. A team of Hollywood writers and special-effects geniuses could never invent anything as fantastic as this Indian story (composed between 200 B.C.E. and 200 C.E.). The basic plot line has all the right stuff, as far as I'm concerned. Through kidnapping, Rama (an incarnation of Vishnu) loses his beautiful wife, Sita, to the evil god Ravana (who has ten heads). What follows is a weird story in which Rama enlists the monkey god, Hanuman, and the king of monkeys, Sugriva, to fight evil Ravana and his monster allies. Hanuman has the ability to jump from one side of the planet to the other, which he uses to great effect—grabbing a whole mountain in the Himalayas, for example, to bring back medicinal herbs. After fourteen years of warfare, Rama wins back Sita by shooting Ravana's multiple heads with arrows. But Rama's unfounded suspicions about his wife's fidelity cause her to be swallowed up by the earth (burned up, in some versions), and then Sita and Rama (who truly love each other) are tragically separated forever.

As if the Ramayana was not surreal enough, the Khmers have also mixed the characters together with another Hindu story from the Puranas, and the resulting scene can be found throughout Cambodia. The popular scene has Vishnu transformed into a giant turtle who is helping Hanuman (monkey god) and Ravana use a huge *naga* (cobra) to churn up an ocean of milk. By twisting the naga through the milky sea (a semen metaphor), they create a foam that spits forth beautiful dancing maidens called *apsaras*, and the overall motive for this monumental effort is to froth up the elixir of life itself. In Cambodia and Thailand this amazing image exists right alongside Buddha statues, and the fusion runs very deep.

Hindu images and stories abound throughout officially Buddhist countries like Cambodia, Thailand, and Laos. And who can blame them? Ask yourself which images and stories are more exciting: a guy named Gotama sitting in the lotus position in a quiet trance, *or* two superhero-styled gods and their mutant minions kicking supreme ass over a trippy landscape in which chaotic seas of milk churn forth beautiful apsaras? Oh, and let's not forget a giant penis in the center of the altar. Somebody was doing some serious *soma* drinking. Soma is the hallucinogenic drink (made from a plant) that inspired the Hindu spiritual teachers of the Vedic Indian culture. One suspects that soma helped to create the surrealism that one finds in the Indian folk traditions that migrated to Southeast Asia.

In addition to all the Brahmanism that infuses and colors Theravada Buddhism, the animistic beliefs in neak ta are truly dominant in the everyday lives of Southeast Asians. Besides the well-known spirit of the general Ghlamn Mioen, which Kimvan explained, there are local spirits inhabiting almost every farm, home, river, road, and large tree. The Thais usually refer to these local spirits as *phii*, the people of Laos call them *phi*, and the Burmese refer to them as *nats*. Even the shortest visit to this part of the world will make one familiar with the ever-present *saan phra phum* (spirit houses) that serve these tutelary spirits. When people build a home or open a business, for example, they must make offerings to the local spirits; otherwise, these beings may cause them misfortunes. Everywhere in Cambodia and Thailand you find these miniature wooden houses with offerings dutifully placed inside them. The spirit houses are usually colored according to which day the owner was born, and they often contain miniature carved people who act as servants to the spirits who take up residence there. The offerings can be incense, or flowers, or fruit, or anything valuable and precious, but the spirits are particularly pleased by shot glasses of whiskey or other liquors. A Lao friend of mine always places whiskey in his spirit house on full moon evenings, otherwise the spirits will trouble his children's dreams. In Southeast Asia the gods drink whiskey.

The offerings are designed to please neak ta and phii, but also to distract and pull mischievous spirits into the mini-homes, thereby sparing the real homes from malady and misfortune. Every business and every home that I went to in Cambodia, Laos, and Thailand had these shrines. The mix with Buddhism is so complete that monks frequently make offerings to these spirits, and the Buddhist pagodas actually have little spirit shrines built into one corner of the structure. Even the national celebration of *loen neak ta* (raising up the ancestors), which takes place in January or February, blends Buddhist rituals (monks reciting protective scriptures) with animistic offerings—the Buddhist part of the ceremony winds down just before the neak ta are offered their much-loved alcohol.

Technically, Buddhists are not supposed to consume intoxicants. In the last chapter, we encountered the universal ethical code of Buddhism—the Five Precepts. Recall that laypeople are to refrain from killing, stealing, lying, consuming intoxicants, and sexual misconduct (read adultery). When I lived in Southeast Asia, however, I drank booze regularly with Buddhists, and as for the prohibition against adultery— well, it runs counter to a long-standing cultural machismo that only recently abandoned polygamy. Hypocrisy, however, is the stuff of every religion, and Buddhists are no worse than Christians on this front. Still, the way that pure Buddhism compromises with the cultural quotidian is interesting. How do people survive, for example, if they're not supposed to kill anything? In a Vajrayana Buddhist country like Tibet, the problem is profound, since meat makes up most of their diet. In urban areas, Buddhists in both Tibet and Cambodia employ Muslims to butcher animals. (Cambodian Muslims called *cham* do this in the cities.) But in the rural areas where nomadic Tibetans live, the herders occasionally stuff the mouth and nose of a yak or sheep with mud and then leave while the animal suffocates to death, returning sometime later to feign surprise and then flay and eat the animal. This practice seems to ease the tension between hunger and philosophy.

During a lunch at my friend Li's home, I asked him how we were able to eat the tasty chicken in our hands, and he explained that, in addition to cham butchers, Khmer people employ pubescent boys to do the killing because it is believed that they are old enough to do the job but not old enough to accumulate bad karma from such deeds. At that same meal, Li poured us out a shot each of moonshine whiskey, but not before he poured one out for his neak ta altar.

In addition to neak ta spirits, many Cambodian Buddhists also believe in *khmoc* (ghosts), *arak* (evil spirits), and *mneang phteah* (guardians), to name a few. Relatives of a deceased loved one must provide food offerings to the dead person's spirit; otherwise, the spirit will cause misfortune to the family. If supernatural problems begin to arise for the family, a shaman called a *kru* can be called in to negotiate a resolution. Some of these sorcerer krus are actually men who have spent time as Buddhist monks. And many Buddhist wats will have a *haor teay*, or fortune-teller, living on the premises to help local families plan for important decisions like marriage dates and good times for traveling.

People who die violently or painfully, like women in childbirth, produce very dangerous and powerful spirits called *bray*. Their tragic death is understood differently than it would be in the West. Here, with *kamma* (karma) looming in the conceptual background, people associate this tragedy with the idea that the person contains impurity, and this makes bray very dangerous. The Khmer scholar Ang Choulean explains that belief in bray exists "symbiotically" with Theravada Buddhism. For example, almost every wat has its own river racing canoe, and there is a very popular yearly race that Khmer celebrate in which monks and parishioners compete against other wat communities. Both monks and laypeople believe that a bray spirit can be coaxed to live inside the canoe and thereby give the craft great strength and aid in the competition. But more interesting is the case of a bray being transformed to live inside the pedestal of the Buddha statue inside the vihara of a temple. In this case, the bray converts from a malevolent being to a protector of Buddhism and takes on Buddha's *parami*—literally "perfection," but informally "superhuman power." When people seek supernatural help for mundane problems, they usually appeal to this converted bray living inside the Buddha statue, not the Buddha himself.

The confusing thing for me is that the imagery of Buddhism, animism, and Hinduism is not just mixed up in the artwork and the cultural practices but also in people's heads. Eventually, with work and patience, you can untangle some of this and understand how things are related. As an analogy for this Gordian tangle, imagine a Cambodian person transplanted to America during the Christmas season. She would be met with a sea of interconnected images and ideas. Even if she knew something about Christian theological beliefs, she would certainly encounter many strange connections. And the logic of those cultural connections would be opaque, to say the least. There would be images and stories of baby Jesus mixed with Santa, Rudolph, Frosty, the Three Magi, the Grinch, a virgin, elves, the Star of Bethlehem, the Bailey Building and Loan, and swaddling clothes. This would be found together with practices like stuffing stockings, going to church, making cookies for Santa, lighting menorahs, burning Yule logs, decorating trees, going to confession, and so on. There's enough here to make a semiotics professor shoot himself. And things are no less confusing in Southeast Asia, where many crossfertilizing traditions fall under the umbrella of Buddhism.

The key to understanding the Theravada-animism tangle is in the unique way people understand deities, spirits, and ghosts. Obviously, the spiritual culture of Theravada countries does not reject the realm of supernatural beings, but here's the part that's a little confusing for Westerners. These spirits have absolutely nothing to do with salvation. Buddhism is first about freeing oneself from suffering by detaching from craving (attaining *nibbana*), and second about getting off the wheel of becoming (*samsara*) altogether (*parinibbana*). Getting off the wheel of becoming means that one is able to attain freedom from rebirth. Enlightenment is a goal and a process that stands above and beyond the metaphysics of ghosts, spirits, and deities. Technically speaking, the two are unrelated. Spirit beings like neak ta or bray are considered more like another species of animal, possessing different traits and powers that can be negotiated for gain or protection, but ultimately they are also engaged in the larger project of freeing themselves from samsara. Spirits cannot intervene in a human's ultimate emancipation—they can only help or hinder in mundane matters. Unlike in the West, spirits are not closer to God or closer to heaven, because, technically speaking, there is neither God nor heaven in Buddhism. There are images of heaven and hell in Buddhist culture, but if they are believed in literally it must be remembered that these regions too are simply other dimensions of reality wherein other beings are trying to work out their own enlightenment with diligence; these realms are not privileged over the human realm. The Western idea of spirits is inapplicable in Southeast Asia. (The Mahayana traditions, wherein *bodhisattvas* can aid humans in their quest for enlightenment, are quite different.)

In the end, the Buddhism that I found in Southeast Asia was multidimensional because human beings are multidimensional. The dhamma is adapted to our rational natures, and the imaginative, magical spiritualism speaks to our emotional needs.

Perhaps all of this Brahmanic and animistic tradition is at the forefront of the Khmer spiritual psyche in part because it gives people a gateway to negotiate with and manipulate the fates that are otherwise beyond their control. Ever since the late 1980s, when it became acceptable to practice Buddhism again in Cambodia, this more magical form of Buddhism, called *boran*, has been spreading rapidly. Boran, which is heavily Brahmanistic and esoteric, can be contrasted with Thammayut Buddhism—a rationalist form of Theravada originating in Thailand in the nineteenth century. Thammayut sought to strip away the corrupt accretions of magic and return to the simple demythologized dharma of the Buddha. The famous Thai king Mongkut, better known as Rama IV (repeatedly and patronizingly re-created for us by stage and film productions of *The King and I*), founded the Thammayut sect in the 1840s, during his pre-king days as a monk (1824–51). Thammayut literally means "those adhering to the dharma," and it emerged out of Mongkut's unique blend of Sri Lankan influences, his own strict forest monasticism, and his unprecedented cultural dialogue with Western intellectuals.

Under encroaching threats from Christian missionaries, Mongkut distilled an essential, rational Buddhism that would have universal appeal and stand on a strong intellectual footing against competing paradigms. For example, Mongkut and the Thammayuts purged many of the age-old magical beliefs and metaphysical speculations from Buddhist orthodoxy, including the very popular cosmology of the Three Worlds. The Traibhumikatha, a treatise on the Three Worlds, was a fourteenth-century book of cosmology that articulated the existence of different worlds or dimensions. The World of Desire included eleven different kinds of beings, including hungry ghosts, demons, animals, and human beings, while the World with Partial Form included sixteen different species, including Brahmas with infinite luster, Brahmas with finite luster, and Brahmas with limited auras. Lastly, The World Without Form contained four realities: absolute nothingness, nothingness, infinite mentality, and infinite space. This speculative cosmology, rife with supernaturalism, became extremely popular in Southeast Asia and effectively worked its way into Theravada doctrine. Many of these cosmological dimensions appear to be reifications of the traditional Buddhist *jhanas* (trance-states), so people erroneously came to associate different stages of meditational consciousness with different cosmic "places." An analogy would be having a dream about your dead relatives and then, upon waking, erroneously thinking that you'd actually been to another world to hang out with your relatives. The Thammayut argued that this kind of cosmology is purely speculative and without empirical weight, is not from the true scriptural canon, and does not help in the detachment from craving and liberation from samsara. In short, it isn't real Buddhism. This metaphysical housecleaning of the Thammayut reminds me of Thomas

Jefferson's personally edited Bible, from which he cut every miracle and supernatural passage, leaving a thin, purified, but ethically profound edition. In fact, Gotama himself was deeply antimetaphysical and gathered all such questions of cosmology into a category that he called *avyakata*, or unanswerable.

The modernist rational Buddhism of Thailand had a large influence on a group of Khmer monks in the 1920s and '30s, eventually leading to a more progressive branch of the mainstream Buddhist order of Mahanikay. This Thammuyut-influenced version of the Cambodian Mahanikay order came to be known as Thammakay, and eventually as Samay. These Khmer modernists appreciated the nonsuperstitious strain of Thai Theravada, and they also believed in the scripture-based approach. Seeking to nationalize the movement, they translated the Tripitika (the Pali canon scriptures) into the local Khmer language, a project successfully completed after forty years of labor. The most famous of these spiritual leaders is Venerable Chuon Nath (1883–1969), the monk whose funeral monument Kimvan and I saw at Wat Ounalom. Every day, on my way to teach, I passed beneath Chuon Nath's portrait (which can be seen all over Cambodia) as I entered the Buddhist Institute. He sits sullen in his orange robe, with thick, black-rimmed glasses—himself a symbol of ancient and modern fusion. I guess I am very, very remotely connected (remotely indeed, since I'm a white boy from Chicago) to the educational mission started by Chuon Nath and his Buddhist Institute brethren. But I'm not just connected by institutional affiliation. After living in Southeast Asia, I came to believe in a "modernized" Theravada Buddhism—one that can be respectful of the animistic and magical traditions of boran while also standing independent of those traditions. Let me explain.

The psychological attraction of boran, or magical Buddhism, is not hard to see. Let's say a loved one in your family becomes terminally ill. According to Buddhist philosophy, you and the doctor do your best to heal that person and try to make him or her comfortable, but in the end you must come to the realization that you're powerless against a reality in which all things are impermanent (and that's a tough pill to swallow and

takes years of dharma discipline). But in the more esoteric boran traditions, there are many more "weapons" in your "arsenal": you can pour
water over a lingam statue (thereby charging the water with holy power)
and then sprinkle your sick family member with it; you can pray and
make offerings to neak ta to chase away evil forces and grant your relative
peace; you can ask Vishnu, Ganesh, and Brahman to heal your loved one;
you can have a monk come and chant over your relative in order to undo
the damage; you can negotiate with a fortune-teller; you can have holy
mendicants bless totems and amulets and lay the energized objects on
the body; and so on and so forth. I'm not saying all this in a condescending way. I suppose all this magic, mystery, and authority helps ease
people's grief and sense of helplessness. Of course, on balance, I suspect
that the intervention of a good medical doctor is in the patient's best interest. But it's not the victim who's interesting in this scenario—it's the
relatively helpless family.

The world is a tough place (dukkha, First Noble Truth), if only in the
sense that you can't control most of what happens to you. The most
prevalent response to this is to find ways to negotiate with the uncontrol-
lable forces in your life through prayers, offerings, sacrifices, rituals, and
so on. The road less traveled, however, is to give up trying to control the
fates and instead just learn to control your mind and your desires (which
is much easier said than done). The human psyche seems built in such a
way that it always prefers the first path—boran is the first path, Thammayut is the second. According to the Buddha, it is not really possible for
me to control the external course of things, but if I can control my own
mind, then there is no need to control the external world.

Personally, I feel split down the middle on this, and I'm not the only
one who's conflicted. My aesthetic sensibility (my sense of art) prefers the
magic and the mystery and the esoteric. The intoxicating imagery and the
ecstatic consciousness, communicating with gods, demons, giant genitals—come on, who doesn't feel the lure? But my sensibility for what is
socially, politically, and psychologically healthy makes me insist on rationality. It makes me prefer Thammayut Buddhism.

The present moment in history is pivotal for Cambodian Theravada Buddhism. The vacuous spiritual hole that Pol Pot left in his wake is slowly being filled again with Buddhism, but which Buddhism? Proponents of boran not only look to the cosmology of the Three Worlds (the Khmer version is the *Trai Phumi*) but also blend dharma with magic and supernaturalism of every kind. The problem with this, as I see it, can be appreciated if we look at the way this stuff plays out in people's daily lives.

While I was living in Cambodia, a frightening epidemic struck the remote northeastern province of Ratanakiri, near the Vietnamese border. A SARS-like disease overtook the villages of Ping and Bornhok, spreading horrible respiratory breakdown, fever, diarrhea, and death. This region is part of the notorious Ho Chi Minh Trail, so it's haunted by the violence and death of relentless U.S. bombing campaigns and jungle warfare. (The famous trail was a network of roads and jungle pathways that carried North Vietnamese Communists down toward Saigon in the south, passing through parts of Laos and Cambodia and making those neutral countries "legitimate" targets of American anti-Communist military strategy.) But in addition to its bloody, war-torn history, the trail is also considered by locals to be haunted by the many animistic spirits and ghosts of Khmer folk religion.

The villagers of the region were convinced that a local spirit was angry with them and the disease outbreak was a punishment. Various local shaman debated the cause of their misery. One theory held that Arak Chantoo, a mountain spirit, and Arak Bree, a forest spirit, were angry because local men had cut down sacred trees. Another shaman explained that a sixteen-year-old girl named Mel had been killed by the disease as a punishment for a sexual affair. In response to the onslaught of supernatural wrath, the locals organized a large sacrifice ceremony in which chickens and pigs were eaten and shared with the spirits. Blood from the animals was mixed with rice wine and smeared on homes for protection, and creepy-looking scarecrow effigies were placed around the village as guardians.

The World Health Organization and doctors of Western medicine descended on the villages and controlled the growing epidemic with antibiotics, eventually stopping the deaths altogether. But village leaders were convinced that their sacrifices and ceremonies had quelled the angry spirits. The chief of the village of Bonhok, Meou Vang, said, "I know the disease was caused by spirits because after we held a big ceremony with all the villagers, people stopped dying and didn't get sick anymore." Here then is a concrete example of rival worldviews: one paradigm is metaphysically obese with trickster ghosts and obstreperous spirits, while the other is metaphysically lean and deals with another sort of "invisible" reality—microscopic bacteria and viruses. Is this a case of reason for the few, magic for the many?

The current trend in anthropology, and academia generally, is simply to note these different paradigms but pass no value judgment on them. Still wincing and embarrassed about the prejudice of the old "manifest destiny" of Eurocentric anthropology, most Western intellectuals are nervous about judging between supernatural and rationalistic paradigms. I'm not so nervous. I suspect that a bacteria caused the outbreak, not a spirit, and that the disease was not a punishment directed at "immoral" people but rather a purposeless microscopic organism trying to do what organisms do—namely, survive and reproduce. And I'll go out on a limb here and say that modern medical remedies, not shamanism, contained the disease. In this health-related example, supernatural spirituality seems neither quaint nor enchanting. It seems dark, witless, and infantile.

One more story is relevant. Just five days before the 2003 national elections in Cambodia, a grisly triple homicide occurred in Poul Commune, north of the capital. At first the murders were thought to be the usual political assassinations, but on closer examination they revealed a superstitious nature. Axes and machetes were used to hack to death eighty-four-year-old Ray Mong Kuch, together with his son and daughter-in-law. The attack was especially vicious, and the first reporters to see the carnage described a horrible scene in which fingers were hacked off, mouths were slashed wide open, and entrails were spilled out of carved bellies. The son's throat was slashed outside their stilt-home, and his screams first drew the other villagers to the site. The three Meas brothers, who lived next door, were arrested and charged with the murders.

The father of the Meas brothers corroborated the strange story that the brothers themselves proffered. Several months before the murders their mother's belly swelled, and she became extremely ill. The symptoms repeated those of an earlier illness of the father's brother, who eventually died of the sickness. When a traditional Khmer doctor was called in to examine the ailing mother, he examined her feces and discovered hairy buffalo skin in the excrement. They concluded that the mother was being killed by black magic, and the three sons became convinced, goaded on by the suggestions from their shaman, that the evil perpetrators were in fact their own neighbors. When their mother died, the oldest brother, Meas Nhoeun, came to believe that the neighbor, Ray Mong Kuch, had created a magic cow in his house and was using this creature to inflict the deadly maladies.

When you mix together gullible superstition and magic with ingredients like crushing poverty (the house of the three victims was salvaged to get the wood needed to build their coffins), profound illiteracy, and pathetic health care, you have a recipe for tremendous suffering. Real Theravada Buddhism, however, is a firm vine that can pull people out of this quagmire of fear and anger. But if magical boran Buddhism wins out and becomes mainstream in Cambodia, then the quagmire may only grow wider and deeper.

Belief in supernatural Buddhism is not confined to the backwater provinces. Venerable Daung Phang, for example, is the very popular abbot of Wat Prek Prang, near Udong. He is considered a major proponent of magical boran Buddhism, and he has been celebrated by both King Sihanouk and Prime Minister Hun Sen. Venerable Daung Phang is renowned throughout Cambodia for his magical abilities, being able to bestow great powers on holy water and also possessing the gift of prophecy. Indeed, magical monks and their respective wats are receiving greater patronage these days from high-ranking Cambodian officials.

Some historians and anthropologists of Cambodia, most notably the famous French scholar François Bizot, have argued that the true Buddhism of the rural people is extremely magical (even referring to it as Tantric Theravada), and the more rational and demystified forms of Thammayut or Samay Buddhism are not as "authentic." But the rational modern Buddhists, who dominated the twentieth century in Southeast Asia, stressed the universal and egalitarian aspects of the dhamma and the power of non-attachment to overcome craving and reduce suffering; and they drew on Gotama's general agnosticism toward metaphysics to justify their own elimination of supra-empirical realities. Like the Protestant Reformation, this Buddhist reformation placed greater weight on the scriptures themselves and sought to disseminate dhamma with translations and publications in lay languages. Magical Buddhists, however, associated these modern purifications with the French colonialism that ruled at the same time as the reforms—a bogus association, as far as I can tell, since reform Buddhism was also a wellspring of early nationalist movements. Nonetheless, apologists for magical Buddhism tend to associate reform Buddhism with Western influence and thereby question its authenticity, painting it as somehow "outsider."

Which Buddhism is the "pure" Buddhism? Which is the more authentic? These questions have been percolating in Southeast Asia for centuries, and the relatively recent interface of ancient tradition with Western modernization has only been the latest staging ground for the debate. Some contemporary Western intellectuals like to celebrate and romanticize supernatural paradigms, partly because they've bought into the trendy view that rationalism and science are cultural impositions— hegemonic absolutes that seem vestigial in the contemporary reigning mood of cultural relativism. Magic and myth, they claim, are just as "true" as science, because science is just another culture-bound social construction anyway. Suffice it to say that neither the educated nor the uneducated Buddhists in Southeast Asia share this postmodern terminal suspicion of truth. I guess I don't either, and here I offer three reasons— in full knowledge of the fact that "reasons" won't impress irrationalists very much—why rational Buddhism is better than magical Buddhism.

One reason why a rational Buddhism is preferable to a magical one is that Gotama, the historical Buddha, preached it. Anyone who thinks that the East had to wait for Westerners to bring rational philosophy to them has never read the Buddha's Suttas or the Abhidhamma. Even before Socrates famously called Athenians to answer only to the authority of their own universal rationality, Gotama repeatedly told his followers to stop having "faith" in him (or anybody else) and simply to test the dhamma for themselves. Like a scientist asking colleagues to run their own experiments to corroborate his findings, the Buddha believed in the importance of do-it-yourself investigation. Don't take my word for it, he said, just try the Middle Way, or try mindfulness, or try to meditate on impermanence, and so on, and you will discover for yourself whether it is a fruitful path. The Buddha is so careful to avoid the deadening effect of blind faith and devotion to authority that even if you find the dhamma to be helpful, he warns you against holding on to it too tightly. In the Majjhima-Nikaya (22.113), for example, he tells a parable of a man who, on an important journey, needs to cross a vast and violent river. So he constructs a large raft made of grass, wood, leaves, and branches. The raft works splendidly to get him across the dangerous waters, but when he reaches the other side, he is so impressed with his new and useful raft that he vows to strap the burdensome barge onto his back and carry it around with him forever. This man, the Buddha says, is confused. Buddhism is like the raft, he says. It is for crossing over, not for carrying. The Khmer, Thai, and Sri Lankan monks who reformed Theravada in the twentieth century saw themselves as returning to this purer and more original humanistic Buddhism—one that was self-reliant rather than reliant upon magical forces and the priestly class that conjured them. The reformers never saw themselves as accommodating Western ideas—indeed, how could they be if Buddhist empirical rationalism predates the West's?

In addition to noting Gotama's own empiricism, it's absolutely crucial to see that rational Buddhism, unlike magical Buddhism, preserves the most important feature of Buddhism, namely, its emancipatory mission.

This is my second reason for arguing the superiority of rational Buddhism. Buddhism is one of the earliest causal theories of human experience, explaining how human responses to sensual stimuli can cause suffering. As the Buddha says, "If you speak or act with a corrupted heart, then suffering follows you—as the wheel of the cart, the track of the ox that pulls it" (Dhammapada, 1). The best way to free yourself from the world of dukkha (suffering) is to shear off the craving part (ego-consciousness) of your natural human response to stimuli. "When a person lives heedlessly," the Buddha says, "his craving grows like a creeping vine. He runs now here and now there, as if looking for fruit: a monkey in the forest" (Dhammapada, 334). This monkey-mind is not just the result of simple sensual pleasures, though it certainly flourishes there. The monkey-mind is also an affliction in the realm of our beliefs, and superstitious belief in troublesome spirits and ghosts only doubles the already bulging mundane world of troublesome afflictions. David Hume nicely summarizes the tortures of supernatural metaphysics:

> Man, it is true, can, by combination, surmount all his real enemies, and become master of the whole animal creation: but does he not immediately raise up to himself imaginary enemies, the demons of his fancy, who haunt him with superstitious terrors, and blast every enjoyment of life? His pleasure, as he imagines, becomes, in their eyes, a crime: his food and repose give them umbrage and offence: his very sleep and dreams furnish new materials to anxious fear: and even death, his refuge from every other ill, presents only the dread of endless and innumerable woes. Nor does the wolf molest more the timid flock, than superstition does the anxious breast of wretched mortals. (*Dialogues Concerning Natural Religion*, pt. 10)

The goal of Buddhism is to free yourself, and superstition does not help. If you cannot overcome your superstitious fears and cravings, then your sorrows will grow, the Buddha says, "like wild grass after rain." But if you can overcome craving and fear, then "sorrows roll off you, like water beads off a lotus" (Dhammapada, 336).

My third and final argument for preferring rational Buddhism over magic is that it is the only version that will be able to coexist effectively with the sciences (hard sciences, soft sciences, and medicine). This may seem like an odd point, but I think it's absolutely crucial. Simply put, science is the very best paradigm that we have for understanding *nature*, and anyone who thinks otherwise has not bothered to study any science. Religions that decide to set themselves against science cannot survive long, unless of course they sustain themselves by totalitarian measures. This is as true for Taliban lunacy and American creationism, for example, as it is in Southeast Asia, where the science-faith clash is more recent.

Religion in Southeast Asia and other parts of the developing world is unquestionably superstitious. But these religions also emerge from a profoundly rich cultural imagination—something once active in religions of the West but now atrophied. More precisely, the imaginative force has been ripped away from its parent, religion, and now goes it alone in the West under the name "art." But this disconnect, this schism between imagination and religion, has not happened in Southeast Asia to the same degree.

The imagination is not interested in being logically consistent, nor is it interested in corroborating its claims with empirical, double-blind peer testing. It simply spews forth like some élan vital of cultural meaning—a fountain of dramatic, interconnecting, sometimes contradictory, and intoxicating images and stories. I'm reminded of Walt Whitman's stanza, "Do I contradict myself? / Very well, then I contradict myself, / (I am large, I contain multitudes)." In religion, which is a work of the imagination, it is easier for mutually exclusive ideas to coexist. To demand that devotees either accept the soul (atman) or reject it (anatta), or that they accept the tutelary spirits (neak ta) or reject them, or that they accept God (Brahman) or reject it (paticca samuppada), or that they accept either Shiva or Buddha—to demand any of this is to import a criterion of logic into a domain where it has traditionally had little traction. Having said that, however, it must be remembered that while logic and evidence can learn to keep their place when it comes to religious claims, so too the imagination (the engine of religiosity) needs to learn how to get out of the way and let science do its thing when the stakes involve human rights and human health.

Antiscience New Agers, postmodern theorists, Luddites, and dogmatic religious fanatics—all take heed: science and its favorite son, technology, are not going to go away. Time to deal with it. In the same way that it is irresponsible to teach your American child that Darwin was evil and Jesus made the dinosaurs, so too it does a great disservice to young Khmer children to offer superstition as a valid competitor to science and medicine. Asking Khmer children, for example, to turn their backs on rational Buddhism because magical beliefs are more "authentically Khmer" is not much different from modern Greeks telling their kids that they should believe that the earth is at the center of the universe because the great Greek Aristotle believed it. (Heliocentrism, then, would be just the ravings of a foreign Pole and an Italian.) You cannot go back to believing that the earth is the center of the cosmos just because it's better for your ethnic vanity. In our current climate, wherein identity politics and cultural self-affirmation have been made sacrosanct, it's hard to remember that some things—like the truth, for example—are actually more important than pride.

I've just articulated a rather unpopular view among the vanguard Western liberal elites, who tend to romanticize indigenous paradigms, but I suspect that very few of them have actually lived in developing countries—countries where a simple wisdom tooth infection can kill you, where infant and mother mortality rates are through the roof, where bat hearts are eaten for asthma, where smearing blood on doors is considered good strategy for fighting off bacterial epidemics, and where magic cows can cause death to your enemies and machete-justice can right the wrong.

The original ideas of Gotama are largely consistent with contemporary science. For example, not only did Gotama employ Ockham's razor, long before Ockham was even born, to cut away superfluous metaphysical speculations, but in paticca samuppada he also invented the most holistic ecology theory imaginable. Ockham's razor is the scientific principle, originally set forth by William of Ockham (c. 1287–1347), that simpler explanations are preferable to metaphysically complex explanations of phenomena. This law of parsimony is expressed by the Buddha's reluctance to enter into metaphysical speculations regarding the afterlife, the infinity of the universe, and other experientially unresolvable issues. And we can see this same attitude in his rejection of an elaborate caste system and his preference for the simple, observable explanation that good people are created by their good actions, not their caste membership.

I discuss the theory of paticca samuppada (dependent arising) later, but it's worth pointing out now that it is the Buddha's view that all of nature is woven together in a sequence of complex interdependencies. This view, which can be seen as an early ecology theory that pushes us to see all life in holistic terms, led Buddha to reject the idea of a miracle-working personal God that creates and sustains the world in favor of a self-contained matrix of causal connections that condition each other and compose reality.

It is no wonder that Albert Einstein perceived the unique compatibility of science and Buddhism when he said,

> The religion of the future will be a cosmic religion. It should transcend a personal God and avoid dogmas and theology. Covering both natural and spiritual, it should be based on a religious sense arising from the experience of all things, natural and spiritual and a meaningful unity. Buddhism answers this description. If there is any religion that would cope with modern scientific needs, it would be Buddhism.

All of this is already there in the core ideas of Theravada, and it would be a shame for the twenty-first-century cultural leaders of Southeast Asia to fall back on the overly familiar formula of "reason for the few, magic for the many."

Three

"My God Can Beat Up Your God"

Missionaries

When I arrived at the little Internet station down the street from my apartment in Phnom Penh, I could barely get inside the tiny place. This was a family storefront business that contained a handful of slow computers. The two teenage brothers patched parts together and resuscitated processors while their father usually dozed on the couch in the middle of the small store. On this afternoon, it was uncharacteristically crowded with some huge Americans, speaking in loud voices and dwarfing the Khmer teenagers around them. The Cambodians looked frightened and tense. The three Americans were massive guys in their thirties, sweaty, with shaved heads, wearing T-shirts and shorts. When I walked in, the owners, who were used to me coming in there, looked at me plaintively— like they needed help.

"Jesus will enter into this heart of yours," one of the giants shouted as he poked a Khmer kid's chest, "and His presence will set you aflame, my brother." He spoke with the melodrama of someone who's watched *The*

Lord of the Rings many times. "Please come with us tomorrow. You must do whatever you can to be there because you will be delivered, brother, and then you will thank me for the rest of your life!"

This, and everything else they said, was at a shouting volume for some reason. And the contrast was jarring because Khmer are very soft-spoken. The Americans also did a lot of the "laying on of hands"—pressing their palms onto various Cambodians' foreheads, passing pious vibes onto their unregenerate brethren. After they left, I talked to the Cambodians there, asking what it was all about. The kid who had his chest poked told me that the Christian missionaries were inviting them to a healing session tomorrow at the swanky Hotel Cambodiana.

"They have the special powers," he informed me, "and they will take away sickness. They will cure polio and malaria and the cancer tomorrow at the Jesus meeting."

The older sister, who "managed" the store by occasionally kicking her brother when a customer entered, must have read the skepticism on my horrified face, because she turned toward me and said, "I don't believe it." I was relieved to find a kindred spirit. Then she followed up with, "I mean, maybe they can cure polio, but not cancer!"

Every day Cambodians approached me and engaged me in conversation. Oftentimes, it was because they wanted to practice their English skills, sometimes it was because they were bored and sought to prattle with the exotic barang, and sometimes it was just because Khmer are very friendly people. Invariably they would ask how long I'd been in Cambodia, and when they found out I'd been there a couple of months, they assumed that I worked for one of the many NGOs. When they discovered that I was a teacher from the USA, they always said, "Oh, you teach English, you are Christian." It always blew their minds when I told them that I taught Buddhism at the Buddhist Institute—they became totally confused by this turn in the conversation. It was an understandable confusion. But besides the obvious surrealism of a white guy teaching Cambodians about Buddhism, it was even harder for them to understand because

99 percent of all the other white American "teachers" they'd ever met were in fact Christian missionaries. "English teacher" is frequently code here for "missionary."

Evangelical Christian groups like Kampuchea for Christ International and the International Christian Mission go into the poor provinces of Cambodia's countryside, where recent drought has left farmer families literally starving, and they build churches and schools. The schools are populated by American teachers of English, many of whom have done their homework and can speak Khmer. The teachers convince the local parents to send their children to the school to learn English, but the actual subject matter is the Bible. These American fundamentalist Protestants start to teach the children that Buddhism is stupid and Jesus is a better, more powerful God. They also invite the starving families to Sunday services at the newly built church, and as an incentive they offer a container of rice to the families that attend.

This phenomenon, which is happening all over Cambodia, is producing what are called "rice Christians"—people who convert, become baptized, and go through the motions in order to get the lifesaving rice supply every Sunday. Many of the Khmer people become "Christian" in name only. When your family is starving, you'll jump through any hoops they give you. But missionaries are turning up the volume on their "good news" campaign. They have started to proselytize with bullhorns in the countryside, telling locals not to feed their Buddhist monks and telling them that their misery will end if they just convert. Failing to feed the monks is doubly damaging for Theravadans. Obviously the monks start to go hungry (and they're already on a pathetic ration of leftovers from poor villagers), but the villagers themselves lose an important means of building spiritual merit, *punna kamma*. Merit-making actions, like giving alms or presenting monks with new robes after the monsoons, are crucial means by which Theravadans attain good kamma and thereby secure good futures. The Christian missionaries are trying to undercut the spiritual foundations of Theravadan culture.

Some of this stuff is actually working on younger people, and it's not hard to see why. Between 1975 and 1979, the Khmer Rouge wiped out an entire generation of educated people—in fact, they targeted intellectuals in particular, torturing and killing them, because they were considered "too corrupted" by non-Communist ideas. You could be shot (or worse, sent to torture chamber S-21, Tuol Sleng) just for wearing reading glasses or being able to do mathematics. Pol Pot's insane goal for "Year Zero" was a clean slate on which to inscribe his own twisted ideology, and to that end he tried to wipe out religion, money, cities, and families. Taking advantage of a chaotic government situation in which the traditional monarch, Sihanouk, had been overthrown by the U.S.-backed general Lon Nol, the Khmer Rouge garnered widespread rural support during the early seventies and eventually invaded the capital in 1975. Prior to the fall of Phnom Penh in 1975 to the Khmer Rouge, it is estimated that there were 88,000 Buddhist monks in Cambodia and 3,500 monasteries, serving a total population of just over 7 million people. It is estimated that 30,000 monks were executed, and most others died of starvation and disease, while over half of the temples were destroyed or desecrated. The total loss of life is estimated at around 2 million—almost 30 percent of all Cambodian people.

The Khmer Rouge ideology was an attempt to remake Cambodia into a peasant-dominated agrarian cooperative. Following Maoist ideals of a leveled society, and with the limited help of Chinese economic and military support, the Khmer Communists tried to eliminate the "parasite" classes of people. But unlike Mao, Pol Pot's regime skipped "reeducation" and simply executed dissenters and nonproletarians. Anyone who did not earn their meals, clothing, and shelter by the sweat of their own brow (manual labor) was considered parasitic. For this reason, the Khmer Rouge sought to eliminate the traditional values placed upon royals (although they spared King Sihanouk), spiritual leaders (Buddhist monks), educators, and the bourgeoisie generally.

On the one hand, the twisted experiment failed when, in 1979, the Vietnamese army, fed up with Khmer invasions into southern Vietnam, eventually swept into Phnom Penh, conquering the Khmer Rouge and sending Pol Pot packing to the jungles of the Thai-Cambodia border. On the other hand, the elimination of a generation who had served as torch-bearers of Khmer culture did indeed clear the slate. The young Cambodian today is a tabula rasa and has little understanding of her own traditions. This makes her ripe for conversion and manipulation. Many young Cambodians become Christians because it's the only spiritual structure they have to make sense out of the dramas of their lives. The repeated crises of the past twenty years have all but eliminated intact families. (Most of the people I've talked to who are over thirty years old have literally "lost" family members—they assume that the missing family members are dead, though they don't have the psychological closure of knowing for sure.) In many cases, younger people do not have elders to provide them with remembered spiritual traditions.

Religious tension is definitely growing in Cambodia. Groups like the International Christian Mission are unabashedly competitive and say that they are "winning souls to Christ," but some Cambodians have had enough of it. In October 2002 there were anti-Christian protests in four villages of Prey Veng Province. Near the end of 2002, a series of letters began to circulate written by a Buddhist group calling itself the Committee of Twenty Pagodas, stating that "in the upcoming days there will definitely be a religious war." It goes on to say, "We, the Khmer citizens throughout the Kingdom of Cambodia, propose to reject Christianity." The letters compare the "Jesus People" to Pol Pot—in the sense that they are a dangerous underground force deceiving Cambodian people. These circulated letters, asking Cambodians to overthrow "Pol Pot Number Two" (the Christians), actually bore the stamp of the Buddhist Institute, but the BI says the stamp is a forgery, and everyone I talked to at the institute was genuinely mystified about their origin.

What, if anything, is wrong with missionary work? Buddhists don't really proselytize in the way that "Jesus People" do, but maybe they're just not "ambitious" enough about saving souls. I suppose the thing that rubs me the wrong way about missionaries is that they lack basic respect for other people's views. There's a little missionary inside all of us, frankly, when we feel like we've seen our way to some truth and want to share it. I'm definitely guilty. But the domain of religion is not like the domain of science. Persuading people, for example, that unseen viruses cause diseases is called education, but persuading people that my god is better than your god is called indoctrination. Missionaries do not recognize the subjective nature of their taste in gods and see their own religion as just another example—indeed, a better example—of the objective truth that science attempts to discover. I think this is a category mistake that conflates faith-based values with facts and confuses deep yearnings with certainties. It is the category mistake of the fundamentalist (found in all religions), and it leads many people with originally good motives to end up in religious warfare.

Most proselytizers, of course, will be thoroughly unmoved by my argument here because, understandably, they cannot suddenly convert their deep convictions about "objective" spiritual reality into subjective matters of taste and custom. So I'm compelled to point out another reason why missionary work is problematic. I'm compelled to point out the hypocrisy of mainstream missionary logic. Christian ethics has long denounced the idea that "the end justifies the means." Good intentions and pure motives are considered by most Christians to be more important than consequences. Successful outcomes are not supposed to justify prior manipulations, and rice briberies seem to qualify as ulterior rather than pure motives. To be more consistent with Christian ethics, a Christian should give rice to a starving Khmer because it is a pure-intentioned act of charity, not as a coercive means to bring about the end goal of conversion. Rice bribery missionary work is an age-old bait-and-switch tactic that seems rather polluted when held up to Christian ethical ideals.

Late one afternoon I left work at the Buddhist Institute and wandered down, along Sisowath Quay, to the riverside. The sun was still aggressively blasting away, and the locals had not yet made their nightly pilgrimage to picnic near the waterfront and the Royal Palace. I sought refuge in the Riverstreet Bar, where I ordered my usual lemon soda and tried to peel my sweat-soaked shirt from my skin. I was always profoundly thirsty in Cambodia and tried to drink anything safe I could get my hands on. Seltzer water and fresh-squeezed lime or lemon seemed especially effective in staving off my ever-approaching desiccation. I felt like I was continually on the verge of dehydration, and I marveled daily at just how dark my scarce piss could become. My big Dutch-American body had definitely evolved for a radically different climate, and it didn't help that I felt obliged to wear the more formal clothing that is expected of a teacher in Cambodian culture. The petite and perfectly comfortable-looking Khmer waitress, whose name was Dary, took pity and flipped on the overhead fan above my table.

Dary and I talked casually, since there was no real business in the al fresco bar. She was nineteen years old, and she carried herself like a high-quality piece of porcelain. It is striking just how elegant the poor young women of Southeast Asia are, and the same can be said of the young men. They carry themselves with tremendous dignity and self-respect, while never straying from the cultural humility that is well known in Asia. They make Americans look obese, disheveled, and vulgar by comparison. Maybe self-possession becomes paramount in a world where you have no other possessions. Like most other legitimate waitresses, as opposed to bar girls (who dress in short skirts and tight shirts), she wore an immaculate white cotton blouse with a long black skirt.

I asked her about the elephant that came to the bar every evening, and she got very excited, saying that she usually got to feed the elephant the leftover baguettes. We made small talk. Her English was good, and she had that charming innocence that one finds readily in Cambodia—innocence that's harder to find in neighboring Bangkok and Saigon. Actually, there was frequently something a little coquettish in the young women I met throughout Southeast Asia. And while I'd like to think it had something to do with me specifically, the truth is that it had much more to do with what I represented. Many barang, or *farang* (Thai for "foreigner"), appear to some young local women as potential tickets to prosperity. This is not a value judgment, or a judgment of any kind really. It is simply an acknowledgment that the expatriate foreigners in this part of the world (even the hippie backpackers) enjoy more prosperity and more opportunity than the local people living in a depressed economy. In Cambodia, for example, approximately half the population lives below the poverty line, and the poverty line is calculated at around fifty cents per day. Consequently, in urban centers one routinely finds middle-aged, paunchy, aesthetically challenged, expat white guys with stunning native beauties on their arms. An expat living in Thailand once told me that he couldn't get a date living in the States, but in Thailand he was a hot property. The women are not selfish opportunists by any means. They cannot be compared with the species of narcissistic gold-diggers that one occasionally encounters in the West. In Southeast Asia, young women pursue such liaisons for themselves but also for their families: a sick brother, a little sister who needs to finish school, a dead father who needs grave maintenance, a mother whose house is disintegrating, and so forth. And correspondingly, the expat men are not just pigs who are exploiting young women; many of them are good-hearted guys who take pride and satisfaction from helping the entire extended family. It is a cross-cultural system that works in ways that can surprise and explode your Western categories of gender dynamics.

"Do you have a why?" Dary asked me during a lull in the conversation.

"I'm sorry," I said. "Do I have a 'why'? I don't quite understand."

"I am meaning," she clarified, "do you have a why live here in Cambodge, or she live in American?"

I got it. She was asking if I had a wife. This turned out to be a fairly regular question during my time in Southeast Asia. If I was alone, then it would take only a few minutes of conversation for a young woman to query me on my availability. It turns out that many negotiations occur between barang and local girls. Legitimate marriage, with the financial security it brings, is of course the holy grail of arrangements, but many women become "minor wives" or even seasonal "monsoon wives," in addition to the more standard boyfriend-girlfriend relation. Dary was simply testing to see if she should allow herself to take the lid off her own jar of dreams. With her fortunate job in a popular expat part of town, she could perform this test with regularity, and her chances of eventual success were high. But not this time, not this barang. She relaxed when she realized that we were just having a conversation.

"I want to go America very much, one day," she confessed.

Oddly, this is not as prevalent a desire as one might expect. Very few people in Cambodia show interest in going to America. Partly this is because they see it as a dangerous and shallow place, but it is also because they know they will never ever be rich enough to afford the plane fare to America or anywhere else. Most Cambodians are so poor that they can only dream about their own beloved Angkor Wat, knowing they will never be able to afford the boat or train ride to see it. So if you ask them if they would like to go to America, it's like asking them if they would like to be reborn in their next life as a king. They look at you quizzically as if to say, *Of course I would, now stop asking me meaningless questions.*

"My brother and I are orphans," Dary explained, "and we want to go to study at Brigham Young University."

Okay, I thought, *that explains things.*

"Are you a Mormon?" I ventured.

"Yes, I am member of Church of Jesus Christ of Latter-Day Saints," she said, carefully enunciating the words. "My brother and I learn English from Mormon people. Zhey come at first to orphan home and speak good Khmer. They bring us to church, and we learn about Jesus. Jesus have many power, and he save everybody. I very much want to go BYU to continue English and Jesus study."

"So you believe that men can have many wives?" I said, laughing.

"No, no," she cried, delivering a playful fake punch to my arm. "We don't believe this anymore. This very old idea, from time when everything different."

Mormons are the fastest-growing Christian sect in Cambodia, and according to some stats, they are making great strides all over the international front—some predict 50 million members worldwide by 2040. They follow the Book of Mormon, discovered in the 1820s by Joseph

Smith. Smith, working on a tip from an angel, claimed to have discovered golden plates buried in rural New York. The plates were etched with symbols that Smith called "reformed Egyptian," and he translated them, dictating to his wife, who sat dutifully behind a curtain in their home. When Smith finished decrypting the sacred plates, he returned them to the angels. Mark Twain, in *Roughing It*, calls the Book of Mormon a "prosy detail of imaginary history, with the Old Testament for a model; followed by a tedious plagiarism of the New Testament. The author labored to give his words and phrases the quaint, old-fashioned sound and structure of our King James's translation of the Scriptures; and the result is a mongrel—half modern glibness and half ancient simplicity and gravity." Nonetheless, Smith won converts with this new theology, which among other things interpreted the Native Americans as mysterious descendants of the lost tribes of Israel. In the 1840s, after the increasingly horny Smith proposed what he called "celestial marriage" to several already married women, a mob of angry husbands and fathers shot him to death. Fellow polygamist Brigham Young then took up the torch and led the Mormons out to Utah in 1847.

Alas, this fast-growing religion already claims six thousand new converts since 1997 in Phnom Penh. They are part of a recent boom in Christian conversions in Cambodia that may total, according to a U.S. State Department report, upward of one hundred thousand people. Dary, of course, didn't know any of the odd theological aspects or historical events of her religion. She just knew that they were nice Jesus people who taught her English and seemed to open up a world of new and exciting opportunities for her and her brother. One day the Mormons might actually help her get to the United States. To younger Khmers, Christianity is useful, just like English is useful, just like barang are useful.

Dary told me that she was Buddhist until the elders came and taught her that Buddha was *only* a man, but Jesus was a god. In Cambodia, Protestant missionaries celebrate this difference like it's some rhetorical checkmate in the competition of religions. Of course, the missionaries don't seem to understand that whether Jesus is God or not doesn't bear in the slightest on the worth of his moral advice. What does it matter whether God told me to love my neighbor or I read it on the back of a soup can I found in a Dumpster? It's not the messenger that matters, as far as I can tell; it's the message. And the ethical message has to be evaluated in terms of whether it works—whether it creates the people and the society that we value. And why do we *value* ideas like "do unto others as you would have them do unto you"? I suspect it's because we've *experienced* the opposite (hurtful behavior) and would like to avoid it in the future.

The missionaries here also don't seem to grasp the hollowness of their superiority complex. Let's just concede, for a moment, that Jesus really was God. Contrary to missionary logic, I think this may actually deflate rather than inflate appreciation for Jesus. Big deal, after all, if God Himself figures out some deep spiritual truths or overcomes some devilish temptations. Come on. He's *God*, for chrissakes—of course he can access the important information and beat back the enemy. To my mind, being impressed that God gave us the Golden Rule is like being impressed that Babe Ruth got a hit. Other Christians, like Nikos Kazantzakis in his book *The Last Temptation of Christ*, have understood that Christ's power as a moral ideal comes from his human struggle rather than his divine status. That is why Kazantzakis famously portrays Jesus as vulnerable to temptations, as more human than godly. And as far as I can tell (and I know the evangelists won't agree with me), this portrayal of Jesus makes him even more impressive as a spiritual hero. If Jesus is all-knowing, all-powerful, and all-good (the general qualities for the Western God), then he can't really *overcome* temptation because he can't really *be* tempted.

"We go this weekend to have new baptisms." Dary smiled. "Maybe you come with?"

"Maybe."

"We will baptize my parents this weekend," she elaborated.

"But I thought you were an orphan," I said.

"Yes, my parents killed by Khmer Roo in late 1980s," she explained. "Thai government keep giving Khmer Roo weapons to fight with Vietnamese forces in Cambodge. My father killed in fighting. My mother killed by the land mine."

"I'm very sorry to hear that," I offered pathetically. "But your parents were probably Buddhist then, no?"

"Yes, they Buddhist," she replied. "But Christian elder in my church tell us that no one can get to paradise without the baptizing, so we can baptize the dead people and that can make them go to the paradise."

I so desperately wanted to roll my eyes at this, but I stopped myself. Instead, I smiled politely and ordered a Mekong whiskey. I felt that there was no substantial difference between this Mormon nonsense and the Khmer superstition of smearing animal blood on doors to fend off malicious spirit diseases. But I also felt a strong sense of compassion and respect for this girl, who yearned to honor her parents in whatever fumbling way she could.

Later that evening I went to Wat Lanka to practice some sitting meditation. Meditating after drinking whiskey is probably a big Buddhist no-no, but I shrugged it off and forgave myself quickly—I was becoming adept at the local practice of self-charity. I made my way inside the temple walls and meandered about the tiny Vatican-type city of monks. The sun was setting, and the wat was bubbling with post-siesta activity. A group of monks were planting orchids in clay pots, and another group was fortifying a thatched roof. I climbed the stairs of the vihara and watched from the balcony as my tall, lanky friend Peter entered the temple gates.

Dr. Peter Gyallay-Pap was my attaché in Cambodia. It was largely through his efforts that I came to teach at the Buddhist Institute, where he himself served as technical adviser to the Buddhist studies master's program. More important, he showed me the ropes in Cambodia, and we became good friends. I would have been lost without his tireless help.

Peter was Hungarian by birth but grew up speaking Finnish while living in Germany; his family eventually ended up in the States. Every few weeks he would shock me by speaking yet another language to someone we accidentally met in the streets. Peter first came to Asia as a young American soldier to fight the Communist threat in Vietnam, but he quickly discovered the lunacy of that conflict. He was shocked by the heartless manner in which his fellow soldiers stereotyped all Vietnamese people as "gooks," utterly failing to notice both the deep culture and the beautiful character of the people of Vietnam. Some years later, he made his way back to Southeast Asia to work with Khmer refugees who were trapped in miserable conditions along the Thailand border. Since the 1980s, Peter had been splitting his time between Southeast Asia and the States, and he knew everyone even remotely connected to Cambodian research.

We had arranged to meet for meditation at the wat and afterwards take our grub at a South Indian restaurant across the street. Only eight people collected inside the vihara. Offering respectful wais to the monk and the giant Buddha statue, we each walked to the front and ritualistically chose a small thin pillow. Then we silently carved out our own turf on the floor and stretched into lotus positions. Every Thursday evening and Saturday morning the wat offered these public meditations.

I closed my eyes halfway and concentrated first on my surroundings. For a moment or two, I stared at the platform of the giant Buddha statue and wondered if a bray spirit inhabited it. Perhaps the ghost of a woman who died in childbirth now rested under the pacific backside of the enlightened one. How could I know? How does anyone really know? I mean, at some point in this rather common scenario one of the respected monks must turn and say something like, "I think we have a bray in the vihara," and other monks "corroborate" that idea by comparing stories of unexplained sounds and mysterious flashes of light. Eventually the poltergeist becomes agreed upon, but why isn't it decided that it's a rat (of which there are plenty) that makes the mysterious sounds? Or something equally mundane? Is this just reality by *consent* rather than by *proof*? Oh, for chrissakes, Steve, stop thinking and start meditating!

The temple was dark, but the barn-sized side doors allowed a large swath of setting sun to pour through the open space. The gigantic

Buddha sat in shadow on the other side of this luminous orange stream. The heat had subsided now, and a mixed music of faraway motos and evening birdsong floated in from outside. Slowly I turned toward my own breathing and focused on the inhale and exhale, trying to center myself in the present moment and leave behind my perseverations on the past and my worries about the future. Eventually there was a preternatural still-ness in the room. And shortly, the bhikkhu leading the meditation gently thumped the bell-bowl. An hour had slipped by imperceptibly. Time seemed like just an illusion, except for when I got up to return my cush-ion and discovered that my legs were fast asleep. My body came crashing back to take the front stage of my consciousness, and Indian curry topped my body's list of demands.

Peter and I ambled to the restaurant and ordered some Angkor beer. In a corner of the room, a TV played some Asian professional wrestling, but when the owner saw us he switched to BBC news coverage of the Iraq War. This was the very beginning of the Iraq War, and Peter and I watched the bombs dropping on Baghdad. For Peter, who had served in Vietnam, and for Khmer, Laotian, Burmese, and Vietnamese people, the American campaign in Iraq was dredging up many ghosts from the past. A few weeks later, things were stranger still because I was in Saigon, of all places, watching the Americans take Baghdad.

Religious conflict, particularly in developing countries, may be the greatest challenge facing the growing global village. Saying that Islam had nothing to do with the events of 9/11 is like saying that Christianity had nothing to do with the Crusades. We can protest that Jesus was the "Prince of Peace" and all coercion in his name is a corruption of the teach-ings, but this distinction hardly matters to the "heathen" who were and are getting the cross crammed down their throats (formerly by violent means and currently by economic means). Likewise we might maintain that the Prophet Muhammad was really a peace-loving leader, but again, tell it to the New York City families whose loved ones died in the act of jihad. The useful distinction that often helps us make sense of religious violence is mainstream versus fundamentalism. Thankfully, mainstreamers don't tend toward zealotry; indeed, that may be the only universally defining criterion of being a mainstream religious person. But we shouldn't just make this distinction and then absolve religion of all responsibility—fundamentalism is religion's progeny, albeit deformed, as much as mainstream moderation.

Many people insist that wars are not really "holy" or even ideological, but economically motivated—just dressed up in the clothing of theological difference. But to say that it isn't really religion that's to blame in cultural conflicts unduly privileges property and wealth by insisting that they are the only things people will kill and die for. Maybe we should start believing people when they say that their religion motivates them to raise the devil. As Peter and I sat in the restaurant after our meditation, we watched news clips of a brazen Saddam Hussein making televised addresses to the Iraqi people. (This was well before his infamous spider-hole capture.) Every other word out of his mouth was "God." Sitting in military uniform, he managed to intone God at least twenty times in a five-minute speech in which he essentially said that God was on his side against the infidel aggressor, the USA. And President George Bush, in his public statements, seemed equally tight with God, dropping His name with great zeal and regularity. In the history of warfare, all this God-talk is of course no accident. God may not be the essential reason why people fight each other, but He certainly helps people spill blood more readily.

Fundamentalism certainly lends the gravitas needed for men to give up their lives. One might counter by pointing out the carnage that godless communism reaped in Russia, China, Cambodia, and elsewhere, but a little reflection reveals an ideology there that rivals any fundamentalism in its embrace of manifest destiny, idealism, utopianism, and dogmatism. And the same might be said for zealous bullying in order to "make the world safe for democracy." The zealot tends to replace real people (who are complex and multidimensional) with abstract, absolute systems (which tend to be simple and blind). Of course, not all religion is zealous—just enough of it to make us miserable from time to time.

I'm sure crazy people would still be crazy if there were no fundamentalist religion, so we can't blame the former on the latter. But I can't help wonder whether, in the absence of absolutist religious convictions, crazy people might exhaust themselves over more harmless topics, like stamp collecting or bingo.

What about Buddhism? Some naive Westerners, raised on a diet of Hollywood representations and New Age simplifications, like to think that there is no violence or war in Buddhist countries because everyone is so peaceful. Would that it were true. Watching Buddhists fight each other in Muay Thai boxing matches will open the eyes of the overly romantic. History shows us a very long and bloody tradition of Buddhists fighting Buddhists, fighting Hindus, fighting Confucianists, and fighting Westerners. In terms of their infighting, they are no different from Christians, who have fought each other with as much gusto as they have the "heathens." For example, the Vietnamese (Mahayana), Cambodians, and Thais (Theravada) have been fighting each other for hundreds of years, and even a cursory understanding of Tibetan history (Vajrayana Buddhism) reveals a highly aggressive and warring people. But there are indeed cultural differences in the way people manage their aggression, and some of these differences are religiously based.

Peter had lived in Southeast Asia for a long time and understood many of the subterranean codes that were more obscure to neophytes like me. I knew that it was very important for Asians to not "lose face," but Peter educated me further.

He explained that on the surface Southeast Asians appear to be in much better possession of themselves than farang or barang. They seldom have outbursts of anger, for example, because getting mad means losing face—and losing control of oneself in front of others fractures the delicate social construction of public dignity and status. Thais have several terms to characterize the nuances or levels of embarrassment. *Sia na* means to lose face, while *na teak* or breaking of face is the term for a minor embarrassment. *Khai na* is to sell one's face, and *na na* is to be "thick-faced" or less bothered by others' judgments.

Thailand is frequently referred to as the Land of Smiles, but this doesn't mean Thais don't get angry. It means that they manage that anger differently than Westerners. If you cross a Thai, he will not get loud or outwardly hostile, but he won't forget it . . . ever. Some say that nobody can hold a grudge as long and as deep as a Southeast Asian, and when the payback eventually comes, it is fierce. Asian culture in general, Peter reminded me, tends to be more formal than the informal culture of America. So even anger becomes filtered and channeled through what are considered socially appropriate pathways. These pathways tend to be indirect responses, or less publicly confrontational behaviors.

The religions scholar Trevor Ling identifies three ways in which Thais, for example, manage personal animosity. First, if you've crossed a Thai, then you may find yourself the butt of an elaborate gossip campaign. Next you may experience "ritual aggression"; maybe you go to use your boat and find it missing, but then it mysteriously turns up again a week later. Lastly, the injured party may turn to "magical aggression," as in the Cambodian witchcraft case of the magic cow that we examined in chapter 2. Ling points out that all this obliqueness may be connected to the very well known Buddhist Dhammapada passage about *dosa* (hate, enmity). Hate, along with greed (*lobha*) and ignorance (*moha*), is one of the three fundamental roots (*mula*) of suffering, according to Buddhism. Most Southeast Asians are quite familiar with the scripture that reads, " 'He insulted me, he hurt me, he defeated me, he robbed me.' Those who think such thoughts will not be free from hate. 'He insulted me, he hurt me, he defeated me, he robbed me.' Those who think not such thoughts will be free from hate. For hate is not conquered by hate: hate is conquered by love. This is law eternal" (Dhammapada, 3–5). Of course, Southeast Asians have as much trouble meeting hate with love as Christians have turning the other cheek, but at least they try, as Ling puts it, to find "less dangerous ways of venting hostile feelings."

A more uniquely Buddhist personal ethic, which bubbles up to the social level, is the idea of *mai bpen rai* in Thai, or *baw pen nyang* in Lao. These phrases translate roughly as "it doesn't matter." Theravadans frequently respond to distressing events or adversity with, "It doesn't matter." Usually such a phrase is used to mean "it's nothing," as in the case of "you're welcome," but it also functions a little like our response phrase "whatever," which signals that the speaker is not going to be bothered or stressed by a potentially stressful event. This attitude of fatalistic resignation is partly a reflection of deeply entrenched assumptions of karma, but also partly an expression of Buddhist metaphysics. All things are impermanent (anicca), so whatever it is, "it doesn't matter." This attitude allows one to rise above petty infractions, and even tumultuous political fluctuations, but does it also make Buddhists too cavalier about their own survival? Will Theravadans buckle under the weight of the missionary cross and then shrug their shoulders with, "It doesn't matter"?

When my chicken curry arrived, I asked the owner to switch back to the professional wrestling. At least I could eat with fat Singaporean guys in superhero costumes belly-flopping on each other—better that than bombs over Baghdad.

"How do you think Cambodia will handle this new religious competition?" I asked Peter. "It seems like the challenge, for pluralistic societies, is how to juggle competing ideas of absolute truth. I mean, it's a no-brainer when the culture is homogenous and uniform about their cultural convictions."

"Yeah," Peter replied, swatting off a mosquito squadron, "Cambodia is still 95 percent Theravadan, but you're right. As the country modernizes it increasingly faces this challenge. And some countries that are similarly challenged, like some of the Middle East extremist clerical regimes, try to return to that cultural homogeneity through totalitarian measures."

"In the United States," I offered, "we have our share of religious tension and strife, but generally speaking, Protestants, Catholics, Jews, Muslims, Buddhists, and pagans aren't killing each other over religious differences. The reason, I think, why religions coexist so well in the melting pot is, one, the long-standing legal separation of church and state. And two, the philosophical agreement (albeit tacit) among mainstream religions that spiritual convictions are *private* and personal, while mutually beneficial *public* policies can be engineered or worked out by secular means."

"Well," he concurred, "I think it was H. L. Mencken who said, 'We must respect the other fellow's religion, but only in the sense and to the extent that we respect his theory that his wife is beautiful and his children smart.'"

We laughed hard and ordered more beer. It was a beautiful night in Phnom Penh, and the confluence of exotic surroundings, spicy flavors, booze, meditation, and good conversation with my friend made me feel very fortunate.

"I'll tell you, though," Peter said, still laughing, "living in Southeast Asia reveals a very different tradition of religious-civil interaction. And you should be careful when you overlay the American separation of church and state onto Southeast Asian culture.

"I mean, historically speaking, Thailand, Cambodia, Laos, and Burma engaged in a cosmological politics that identified the king with a god. This is called the cult of the *devaraja* [god-king]. During the dominance of Hindu ideology, Southeast Asia saw its rulers as incarnations of deities like Shiva or Vishnu—if not direct avatars, then their righteous lives actually brought on a divine status. And since the onset of Buddhism, around the twelfth century, people have identified their kings with the ancient King Asoka or other divine Buddhist kings, like the still highly revered Jayavarman VII in Cambodia—you know, you've seen his face all over the Angkor Thom temples. In Southeast Asia, the king is believed to be a *cakkavattin*, one who has attained his kingship through the meritorious virtues of his previous lives. He rules in accordance with Buddhist dhamma, with justice and compassion.

"When Buddhism was competing with Hinduism," Peter explained, "both parties engaged in the usual propaganda techniques, like scratching out or defacing the sculptures of each other's religion—again, very evident at Angkor. But things have been resolutely Buddhist here for a long, long time, and it's safe to say that Southeast Asia has been spiritually homogenous and not pluralistic—there has never been a need for a separation of church and state. Cambodian people don't really understand the idea of party politics even, let alone the idea of church-state separation.

"Traditionally speaking, Southeast Asia has not been very responsive to missionary efforts. The people's national identity is strongly tied to Buddhism because, historically speaking, they've experienced how helpful the sangha and wat have been in their daily lives."

Christian missionaries, it turns out, have been at it for a very long time in this part of the world. In the 1550s, a Portuguese missionary named Gaspar da Cruz tried to convert Cambodians but found them rather intractable. Da Cruz complained that the Khmer people were too devoted to their Buddhist monks to consider Christianity properly. He said, "It happened sometimes that while I was preaching, many round me hearing me very well, and being very satisfied with what I told them, that if there came along any of these monks and said, 'This is good, but ours is better,' they would all depart and leave me alone."

These days, however, a new wave of missionaries has swept in, trying to fill the void that communism left behind. And Pol Pot effectively erased the spiritual memory of Khmer, thereby jeopardizing the people's future allegiance to Buddhism. The Christian do-gooders are unashamedly forthright about their opportunist agenda. For example, Steven M. Ellis, an evangelical missionary working with a "church planting" group called the Cambodia Baptist Convention, tells fellow missionaries that "most Cambodians are very responsive to the gospel, resulting from years of suffering and social upheaval during the last twenty years (i.e., it has loosened the bond between nationalism and Buddhism). The Cambodian people are more open to religious change than at any other time in their past history. The shake-up and/or disintegration of their entire way of life has significantly decreased their ties to Buddhism." Ellis exhorts his Christian brethren further by pointing out that "if Christianity does not rapidly advance throughout the country of Cambodia, the Cambodian people will likely return to Buddhism for stability (as it was representative of the former peaceful and stable way of life)." But take courage, brethren, for, as Ellis points out, Christians are kicking ass in the "spiritual warfare" in Cambodia. "The mustard seed faith of this infant church is moving mountains as spiritual strongholds are being demolished, and advances are being made into enemy territory."

The pitch of this kind of proselytizing has become so high in Cambodia that the government is striking back. In March 2003, the Ministry of Cults and Religion issued a new "disciplinary order" that states, "All public proselytizing activities are prohibited. Christians are not allowed to proselytize citizens' houses by knocking on doors, or waiting for them, saying, 'The Lord is coming,' which is an interruption to daily life or may intrude on privacy in the community." The order continues, "The teaching of religions must respect other religions and avoid insulting and degrading each other, especially Buddhism, the state religion."

After the Cambodian Ministry of Cults and Religion released its antiproselytizing disciplinary order asking Christians to ease back on the "good news," there was much rejoicing by urban Cambodians. But the irony of this ministry statement was revealed to me by the French journalist Stephanie Geé. Stephanie, who wrote for the *Cambodge Soir*, was one of Peter's friends, and she had recently visited the ministry. She informed me that a swanky new conference room and various other refurbishings had been funded entirely by recent donations from Christian missionary organizations. The ministry was taking Christian money privately, but publicly reprimanding the Christians because Cambodian irritation is at an all-time high and required some official sop. This seems rather hypocritical, I guess, but it's probably also good business. As Marx (Groucho, that is) once said, "Those are my principles, and if you don't like them . . . well, I have others."

Perhaps everyone's convictions are ultimately for sale, and "integrity" just means that you'll only sell at a very high price. I suspect that the Ministry of Cults and Religion will look the other way when the Christian missionaries who gave them a fat donation want to continue their prose-

lytizing. When a Cambodian sells out his Buddhist convictions in order
to get rice on Sundays, can anyone blame him? I can't. But I *can* be an-
noyed when an evangelical Christian forces a Cambodian to make such
an obscene trade. Humanitarian aid with spiritual strings attached seems
particularly manipulative. Most people do not object if one government
offers aid to another government with reasonable stipulations that seek
to rectify human rights abuses or even open up local markets (providing
that the aid-granting country doesn't exploit the recipient), but the free
market of "ideas" doesn't seem so free when Christianity says, "We'll feed
you if and only if we can have your soul in our registry." That seems more
like coercion than free choice. For a spiritually bankrupt guy like me, this
food-for-faith calculation is a no-brainer: "Yeah, yeah, put me down for
the next baptism. Now, where's the rice line?" I don't quite understand
how an evangelical finds any inspiration in a conversion that he has essentially bought.

That night, after our dinner, I dreamed a hundred nightmares. My
unconscious burned like the overspiced curry. I ran from unseen enemies,
swam in mile-deep fathoms teeming with leviathans, failed with oatmeal
arms to fight off vicious blows, and even hazily witnessed a crucifixion of
the Buddha.

Religious competition and economic development are being intertwined
in poor countries like Cambodia, but that doesn't need to be the case.
S. C. Dube, director of the Indian Institute of Advanced Study, decried
the Western model of development, which sees "traditional" as backward
and "modern" as advanced, when he asked, "Must we disintegrate our personality for the promised economic gains?"

While I was ruminating on the missionary question, I had a completely chance meeting with Yann Martel, the Booker Prize–winning
author of the wildly popular novel *Life of Pi*. We just happened to sit
down next to each other in a café in downtown Phnom Penh; he was
passing through on his way up to tour the Angkor temples and asked me
if I could recommend a place to stay in Siem Reap. We eventually got

into a good-natured argument that spilled late into the night about which religion was superior, Hinduism or Buddhism. He took the side of the former, and I the latter, but our heated conversation ranged widely on spiritual matters. When, in the course of things, I lamented this phenomenon of "rice Christianity" in Cambodia, he said, "Well, I guess Christians are doing more good for people than Buddhism, so maybe we shouldn't regret the slow death of Buddhism." I should point out that Yann, while being an extremely smart and thoroughly likable fellow, doesn't know fuck-all about Cambodia—a fact he readily admits.

I simply cannot agree with his assessment, or any such survival-of-the-fittest interpretation of religion. It wasn't Christianity per se that was helping the starving villagers. It was a group of relatively wealthy people making poor people jump through hoops to get some temporary relief. If the rich people had been Islamic, then we'd have had "rice Muslims" in Cambodia; if they'd been rich Stonehenge devotees, then we'd have had "rice Druids." More important, Buddhism per se hasn't failed the Khmer people; thirty years of war, a couple of droughts, and continued political corruption have failed the Khmer people. If people weren't starving, then Christian bribery would never get any traction. And one of the primary reasons why people in Cambodia are so disadvantaged is because of draconian attempts to reauthor their culture by the competing forces of democracy and communism—forces that either ignored or abolished the traditional culture. Both democratic and communist utopianism have caused a great deal of misery. As Americans stormed Iraq with "shock and awe," I hoped that similarly shortsighted "utopianism" wasn't causing the same thing in Iraq.

Many Christian missionaries from developed countries like the United States think that their own successful economic prosperity is somehow tied to their spiritual convictions and that if Buddhists adopted Jesus then their wealth and health would improve. But it's more likely that Christianity is an *accidental* appendage of the richest countries in the world (unless Max Weber comes into play here), and therefore poorer countries shouldn't have to adopt it in order to join the prosperity club.

Buddhism, in fact, serves the people very well. In the 1996 Center for Advanced Study's report "Buddhism in Cambodia," my friend Peter Gyallay-Pap describes the comprehensive benefits of the Theravadan Buddhist wat (temple complex):

> Apart from serving as moral-religious and educational centers, the wats were also the foci for villagers' social and cultural activities. Wats were the symbolic centers for all community festivities and ceremonies. They were places for learning and performing such applied arts as dance, music, shadow puppetry, carving, pottery, theater, and poetry. . . . The wats provided social services by housing male orphans and children from disadvantaged families as temple boys who received basic education in literacy and numeracy. They provided for the elderly, particularly women who chose to become lay devotee nuns (*doun chee*) in their declining years while serving the wat according to their capacities. The wats served as important health and counseling centers as well as courts of justice where disputes were conciliated and mediated. Wats were regarded as sacred spaces and gardens of peace (*wataram*) for concentration and meditation.

*   *   *

Faithful believers in "competition" contend that Adam Smith's "invisible hand" will eventually arrange things into the best of all possible worlds. Why, they ask, shouldn't this competition apply to religions as well? Maybe this article of faith applies appropriately to economic globalization, but should we extend it to all the domains of life, including the spiritual? Should religions fight it out with rice briberies and "weapons" better suited to the marketplace?

It's certainly true that militant *proselytizing* is preferable to militant *violence*—and I don't want to equate contemporary Christian proselytizing with the violent jihad activities of extremist Islam. But why must we compete in the spiritual realm at all? I guess the competition is inevitable if each faith believes that it has discovered the Truth (with a capital T) and that when you find yourself in possession of the Truth you must bring other people into agreement with it—for their own sake. After all, you can't let people run around thinking that two plus two equals five— you owe it to them to rid them of their confusion. This is how the road to perdition is paved—with good intentions. Even Americans who find themselves in possession of this "Truth" can barely keep it to themselves in that private subjective way that's necessary for the church-state separation. They chafe under the separation because they perceive their faith to be about the objective world, not the subjective realm of personal taste.

As an example of this, just look at President George W. Bush's international aid policies. Bush is a self-proclaimed evangelical Christian who is born again and believes in a literal reading of the good book. With disregard for the First Amendment, Bush has sought ways to insinuate evangelical values into national and international policies. I suppose that when you feel like God is on your side, mere laws seem easily violable. In the beginning of 2004, the Bush administration passed legislation that withdrew aid money from Southeast Asian humanitarian organizations that advocated for legalization of sex work. As I learned from Phroung and others (back in chapter 1), many aid workers who live down in the trenches, so to speak, labor hard on improving women's health and economic status and see the legalization of prostitution as an important means to that end. The Bush administration, using a strings-attached approach to humanitarian help, has taken away the funding of any groups that show sympathy for the decriminalization position. This follows a similar Bush tactic, dubbed the "Mexico City policy," in which aid monies were withdrawn and denied to NGOs that worked on abortion-related issues in developing countries, leaving the director of Cambodia's National Mother and Child Health Center groveling to USAID for money to help in post-abortion health cases. "Our objective," the frustrated director said, "is to reduce the number of deaths from unsafe abortions, not to promote abortions."

In the case of aid for sex workers, Bush has pulled back funding and instead has started to route money to "faith-based" NGOs (read missionaries) in Cambodia. The message seems to be: adopt our evangelical Christian values, and then we'll help you survive. All the while, this imposition of values goes on under the aegis of the moral high ground back home, because the Bush administration spins it to look like a righteous fight against human trafficking and pedophilia. In response, the Cambodian minister of women's affairs, Mu Sochua, worries that Bush's attempts to establish "moral values as a condition to aid is not a policy that is constructive for global development."

Historically, there seem to have been three basic strategies for dealing with religious disagreement. The most problematic strategy is the aggressive elimination of competing options, whether this be in the form of Communist rejection of all religion (Pol Pot), Islamic jihad, or Christian fundamentalist attempts to blanket the world in Jesus uniformity. Their methods have varying degrees of danger (Bible-toting blabbers are relatively benign), but the mind-set is similar. This strategy is usually wedded to the fundamentalist concept of truth—absolute, universal, and scripturally literal. The Taliban idiot Mulla Mohammad Omar springs to mind here—this is the moron who destroyed the giant, two-thousand-year-old Bamiyan Buddha statues of Afghanistan in 2001. I'm sorry to say that one cannot "play nice" with fundamentalists. Rational and rhetorical arts of persuasion will not work to turn them from their aggressive mission. I recommend a blunt object of some sort.

The second strategy for dealing with religious disagreement is the one that has proved effective in the United States and may prove so in other highly pluralistic settings: a separation of church and state and a "privatizing" (psychologically speaking) of spiritual commitments. This strategy requires a secularization of the public sphere. It probably also requires that we think about our religion as a subjectively inspirational guide to ethics and values and *not* as an accurate picture of nature or cosmology (a very difficult schism of facts and values). Many Americans feel fairly comfortable about spreading this secular strategy all over the globe. Although this strategy is generally motivated by the best intentions, it fails to appreciate the very public nature of religions in other parts of the world.

The third strategy for coping with religious disagreement has a rather checkered past. Sometimes it works, sometimes it doesn't. This is the model of a benevolent religious majority that tolerates and even fosters the free expression of religious minorities. There have been times and regions where Islam, for example, treated Christians and Jews with respect and tolerance. The same can be said of the Roman Empire at certain times, as well as Christianity, at certain times, and Buddhism and Hinduism and Confucianism. Maybe this only works well when the margin between the majority and the minority positions is very large and when the majority is not threatened in any real way. (This model probably falls apart when the different religious populations have similar numbers.) But there are such places, many such places. Cambodia and the rest of Southeast Asia are examples of this strategy—overwhelmingly Buddhist with small populations of Muslims and Christians. In this context, it is naive to think that they should become or want to become like the Americans. Their modernization (read economic aid packages) should not depend upon that adoption.

Before I came to Cambodia, I was convinced that all theocracies should go the way of the dinosaur, mostly because the fundamentalist forms tend toward totalitarianism and there is no rational check on spiritual systems that claim to transcend rationality. Many theocracies degenerate into dictatorships of gnostic psychos. But now I'm revising my position: these degenerations are not the necessary outcomes of church-state conflations, I've come to see, just worst-case scenarios. Some theocracies, like the traditional Buddhist monarchy, have been relatively just and benevolent.

American policymakers observe that a particular people are dissatisfied with their current regime (whether it be Iraqis, Chinese, Cambodians, or Indonesians), and they draw the erroneous conclusion that those people must be yearning for American-style democracy. They must want to end their monarchy, or theocracy, or party structure, or whatever. But when you ask the Cambodians if they would rather end the current regime of Prime Minister Hun Sen and replace it with either American-style democracy or a return to the monarchy, they choose the royalist road. For the most part, they love the king, and they identify with a Buddhist monarchy. American policymakers would do well to understand this point. The famous Thai monk Buddhadasa Bhikkhu critiques democratic dogmatism when he says, in his tract *Help! Kalama Sutta*, that "those who insist on such views haven't considered that a democracy of selfish people could be worse than a dictatorship of unselfish people who live according to dhamma or righteousness. A democracy of selfish people means freedom to use their selfishness in a most frightening and awful manner." He goes on to call for flexibility and adaptability guided by principles of compassion. "Stop saying that democracy is absolutely good or that dictatorship is absolutely good. Instead, stick to the principle that either will be good when based on dhamma. Each society should choose which suits it best according to the particular circumstances facing it."

I'm not one of those "hands off other cultures" sorts of guys. I'm not dead-set against all interventions—they just have to be enlightened interventions that see, respect, and preserve the socioeconomic and religio-ethical structures that are working well for the locals. U.S. Republican senator Mitch McConnell, for example, started calling for "regime change" in Cambodia in 2002. I'm definitely not disagreeing with him. But he's wrong if he thinks Khmer people would be happy with U.S.-style democracy and separation of church and state. The famous classicist Leo Strauss influenced a lot of American conservatives when he said, "To make the world safe for Western democracies, one must make the whole globe democratic, each country in itself as well as the society of nations." Maybe. But we should temper that gung-ho sentiment with H. L. Mencken's "I believe in only one thing: liberty; but I do not believe in liberty enough to want to force it upon anyone."

A refreshing alternative to the myopic forms of intervention (be they political or spiritual) can be seen in the Catholic missions, particularly the Jesuits in Southeast Asia. Unlike those missionaries who give food with the ulterior motive of winning conversions, the Catholics just give food because people are starving. There is no means-end negotiation—just charity. I never thought a trip to Cambodia would bring me closer to my Catholic roots, but it did. It didn't restore my faith (that would take, at least, a Lazarus-style resurrection), but it did restore some respect.

The French priest François Ponchaud has been a strong humanitarian force in Cambodia since the 1970s, and he opened Western eyes to the tragedies that were occurring under Pol Pot with his famous book *Cambodia Year Zero*. Father Ponchaud and many Catholics worked tirelessly in the refugee camps during the 1980s and today continue to bring relief and support to poor Khmer people. But their policy about conversion is very clear, and very different from that of the rice Christian fundamentalists. The Catholics say that they only wish to "evangelize" through their humanitarian actions—not through preaching, or Bible thumping, or rice bribes. The Catholics don't want to convert the Buddhists; they just want to help them with food, clean water, housing, education, and so forth. The Catholics have a great deal of respect for Buddhism, and they work *with* those ancient spiritual-social structures, not *against* them. In fact, some overly polite Cambodians, who are already familiar with rice Christian conversions, occasionally ask Father Ponchaud if they should convert to Catholicism, now that they are receiving Catholic charity. Ponchaud responds by asking them, "First, can you tell me what you know about Buddhism?" And if the Khmer doesn't know much, Ponchaud tells them to go learn more about Buddhism first. In fact, the Catholic Church makes the rare convert go through a rigorous three-year catechism before it will baptize that person. Criticizing the rushed baptisms by the Mormon elders, Ponchaud says, "They make pressure, pressure, pressure. Christ liberated us. [Mormon conversion] is not liberation; they make more slaves."

This is a monk who lives in the cells that are carved into the sandstone mountainsides at Wat Tham Sua near Krabi in southern Thailand. In many of the shrines and cells, there are drawings of human entrails and images of corpses in various states of decay. These are meditational focal points designed to highlight the impermanence of all things. (*photo by Brian Wingert*)

My Khmer friend Kimvan and I in Udong, Cambodia. Just after this photo was taken, I was set upon by a throng of twenty-five Khmer high school students who asked if each of them could be photographed standing next to the exotic big white *barang* who had vomited all over the lawn in front of the sacred shrine. (*photo by Stephen Asma*)

The beautiful pagoda was built in 2002 at Udong, north of Phnom Penh, to house the Buddha's tooth relic. The architectural style harkens back to the high period of Khmer sculpture; this original style can be seen at Bantay Srei temple in northern Cambodia. In addition to sculptures of the Buddha, the elaborate carvings include many mythical animals from the pre-Buddhist Brahminic era, including *nagas* (cobras) and *garudas* (bird-men). There are also Chinese influences in the sitting-lion guardian figures. (*photo by Stephen Asma*)

A representative photo of the impoverished living conditions in the outlying Phnom Penh region. A student on her way home from school covers her mouth to filter out the dust. It is common for families to try to eke out a living in shantytowns on the outskirts of the city. (*photo by Stephen Asma*)

A roadside stand in the Cambodian countryside selling handcrafted spirit houses of different colors. Once these are placed in the homeowner's yard or place of business, they are filled with offerings for *neak ta* (spirits): incense in abundance, lotus and other flowers, and often whiskey or another valuable liquor. (*photo by Stephen Asma*)

A colorful shrine of fragrant garlands, incense, and carved wooden penises. This still active *lingam* shrine is in a little cave in southern Thailand near Krabi. Outside the frame of this shot is a huge pile of hundreds of penises previously offered to Shiva (who takes the form of the phallic lingam). (*photo by Brian Wingert*)

The River of a Thousand Lingas at Kbal Spear in northern Cambodia. Scholars believe that sometime in the ninth century C.E., one thousand penis-shaped stones were carved into the riverbed. The belief was that the water would pass over these fertility phalluses (Shiva incarnations) and acquire generative powers to feed the crops below. This photo shows the linga heads residing inside and outside a square-shaped carving. This invaginated square represents *yoni*, the female phallic symbol of fertility power. (*photo by Stephen Asma*)

A giant monument to honor a Buddha footprint at Wat Tham Sua (Temple of the Tiger Cave), near Krabi in southern Thailand. This view is only possible after a 1,227-step vertical hike. A wild dog followed me up every step to the top and then collapsed into deep sleep. The golden flags are Thai Buddhist flags bearing a wheel-of-dhamma design; the white, red, and blue flag is Thailand's national flag. (*photo by Brian Wingert*)

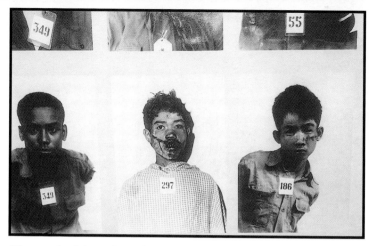

Thousands of these photos line the walls of the S-21 prison museum today. The Khmer Rouge chronicled their twisted interrogations and documented all incoming prisoners. Many of the innocent victims were just children who had no idea why they were being tortured. (*photo by Stephen Asma*)

A torture bed inside the notorious S-21 prison in Phnom Penh. The prison was used by Khmer Rouge to torture over 17,000 victims, all of whom were taken to nearby Choeung Ek and killed. When the compound was finally stormed in 1979, only seven survivors were liberated. The stains on the floor are dried pools of blood. (*photo by Stephen Asma*)

My Khmer students and I on the steps of the Buddhist
Institute in Phnom Penh. I'm quite sure they taught me
more than I taught them. (*photo by Peter Gyallay-Pap*)

A typical bustling side street in Ho Chi Minh City, Vietnam.
This backpacker region near Pham Ngu Lao Street in District 1
was my base of operations in Saigon. (*photo by Stephen Asma*)

Considered one of the wonders of the world, Angkor Wat was built as a funerary temple for Khmer King Suryarvarman II. The temple's architecture is highly symbolic—the central spire represents the mythical Mount Meru, a geographic symbol of the cosmic first principle of creation. The temple is formally dedicated to the Hindu god Vishnu. (*photo by Brian Wingert*)

My tenacious young guide Bo at the Preah Khan temple, Cambodia. Bo, who gets a daily shakedown from bullies and cops, recites an elaborate tour from memory and pockets his net profits to pay for school. Here he shows me the *lingam/yoni* fertility altar. (*photo by Stephen Asma*)

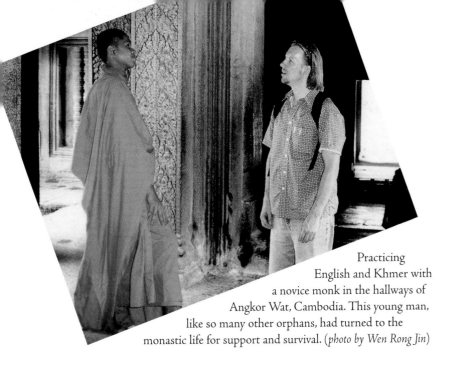

Practicing
English and Khmer with
a novice monk in the hallways of
Angkor Wat, Cambodia. This young man,
like so many other orphans, had turned to the
monastic life for support and survival. (*photo by Wen Rong Jin*)

Nature overtakes the
ancient ruins at
Ta Phrom temple. Of all
the Angkor-era temples
in northern Cambodia,
Ta Phrom is the most
haunting and poetic. The
jungle is absorbing the
architecture before your
eyes, largely owing to the
fact that Franco-Khmer
restoration teams
decided to leave it in the
decaying state in which
they first found it.
(*photo by Stephen Asma*)

Father Enrique Figaredo Alvagonzalez, prefect of Battambang Cambodia, argues that the gospel is not for preaching but for *doing*. Catholics bring humanitarian help through charitable actions rather than through words, slogans, or oaths. The Church, at least nowadays, has little interest in remaking the globe in its own theological image. Maybe the fundamentalist missionary thinks that he should help other people because he wants to save their souls; Catholic missionaries want to help other people because this is how they save their own souls.

The funny thing here is that, according to the Buddha, there is no human soul. He points out, in the Potthapada Sutta, that a man who busies himself with souls is like a man who is madly in love with a woman whom he has never seen or otherwise experienced and about whom he knows absolutely nothing. In other words, playing with souls is a mind-game. But worse, it is a dangerous game, because it continues to create two worlds—this mundane, imperfect, and impermanent world and the perfect and permanent next world. The Buddha seeks to heal the radical divide of two worlds, a divide that leads people to devalue flesh and blood in favor of immaculate figments. When there is no next world, then *this* world becomes holy. Perhaps when people are less convinced that martyrdom brings posthumous paradise, they will be less motivated to strap bombs on themselves. And maybe missionaries will be less motivated to force religious conversions as well.

In Buddhism there are levels of reality. The top level is pretty much the world we see around us. Our day-to-day experiential world is made up of individual beings who seem separate or individuated from each other. There's a guy named Steve Asma, and there's a guy named Eric Clapton, and a woman named Rosa Parks, and so forth. And these people are relatively the same with themselves (over time) but different from each other. However, if you go down beneath this conventional layer of reality, you find a deeper layer in which each person is only a momentary confluence of five streams or aggregates (khandas), namely, body, perception, feeling, will or disposition, and consciousness.

The idea of compositional levels here is not that different from what we already accept from the physical sciences; it's just not as materialistically reductionionist. We are accustomed, for example, to seeing that biological organisms are composed of smaller and less visible chemical interactions, while those chemical interactions are themselves composed of atomic and subatomic interactions. In Buddhism one goes deeper (as seen in the Abhidhamma scriptures) to discover that beneath the stratum of the five aggregates there are more fundamental elements of mind and body—almost like atoms of consciousness (and below this, emptiness). This idea of levels is important for understanding all the aspects of Buddhism. And when you apply it to the domain of values, you begin to grasp the meaning of mai bpen rai—"it doesn't matter."

At the top layer of reality, for example, human beings tend to see things as "good" or "bad"—we are attracted to some things and repelled by others. But when we see things from a deeper perspective, we find that we have imposed these properties of "good" or "pleasurable" or "bad" on things but the things themselves are neither good nor bad. Values are subjectively placed on an otherwise value-neutral reality. An illustration of this is helpful. The Vietnamese monk Thich Nhat Hanh points out that even love and hate are human misunderstandings of a deeper unified reality. Humans, he says, are naturally attracted to flowers but repulsed by garbage. And yet, from the level of deeper reality, the flower is on its way to becoming garbage and the garbage is on its way to becoming a flower. So the attitude of the wise is one of acceptance—mai bpen rai.

If I successfully deceive someone, for example, Buddhism says, yes, on this level of reality I have wronged someone and I seem to have gotten away with it, but on a deeper level I am still bound by karma and I will pay. On a deeper level still, there is no such thing as good or bad, as justice or injustice, because these dichotomies are merely human constructions. The constructions keep creating layers of alienation between oneself and all other beings, but in reality there are no important distinctions. Some Westerners see this view as nihilistic, or at the very least profoundly relativistic, but they fail to see the final arc in this downward analysis. The final arc swings upward to the top again, forming a circle of wisdom. After we have reached the bottom layer and grasped the emptiness of all things, then we return to daily life with new eyes. We no longer see the layers of metaphysical, political, and ethnic nonsense that have accumulated like barnacles on the man in front of us. We don't worry about his soul, or his party, or his skin color. We just see that he suffers and needs help. We respond with compassion.

Will this radically embracing and antidoctrinaire aspect of Buddhism cause it to be swallowed slowly by aggressive competing religions? Is it too accepting and acquiescent? An interesting answer comes in the form of a parable told by the highly revered Khmer monk Maha Ghosananda. I had the amazing privilege of meeting Maha Ghosananda, the man whom most Khmer people believe to be the holiest person in all of Cambodia. Not only was I fortunate enough to have a private audience with Venerable Maha, but I managed to have him visit my classroom and meet my awestruck students—more on this later.

Almost no one in America knows of Maha Ghosananda, but it would be difficult to overestimate the role this elderly monk has played in recent Cambodian identity. He's been nominated for the Nobel Peace Prize three times, and the Dalai Lama actually prostrates himself on the ground in a sign of deep respect and worship when he visits Venerable Maha. When it was almost certain suicide, Maha defied the Khmer Rouge directly and opened makeshift Buddhist temples in the late 1970s. This was after the Khmer Rouge had demonstrated their hatred of Buddhism by killing over thirty thousand monks. Maha Ghosananda traveled through the refugee camps, where Cambodians were physically starving and spiritually demoralized, and he constructed makeshift wats and chanted the Buddha's dhamma. He continues, right up to the present, to lead peace marches through the rural provinces of Cambodia, and he is deeply respected by the villagers who make up the silent majority of Khmer people.

He tells a story about the need to balance compassion with wisdom. One must strive for tolerance, openness, and compassionate acceptance, but one shouldn't be stupid about it. In Maha's parable, a violent dragon meets a bodhisattva on the road one day. (Interestingly enough, the bodhisattva is much more celebrated in the Mahayana tradition, and the presence of this figure in this Theravadan monk's parable illustrates the inclusive nature of Buddhism.) The bodhisattva tells the dragon that he should not kill anymore and should instead adopt the Five Precepts and care for all life. The bodhisattva inspires the dragon, and afterwards the dragon becomes completely nonviolent. But now the children who tend to the animal flocks nearby, seeing that the dragon has become gentle, lose all fear of him. And they begin to torment him, stuffing stones and dirt into his mouth, pulling on his tail, and jumping on his head. Soon the dragon stops eating and becomes very sick.

When the dragon encounters the bodhisattva again, he complains, "You told me that if I kept the precepts and was compassionate, I would be happy. But now I suffer, and I am not happy at all." To this the bodhisattva replies, "My son, if you have compassion, morality, and virtue, you must also have wisdom and intelligence. This is the way to protect yourself. The next time the children make you suffer, show them your fire. After that, they will trouble you no more."

This little story applies not only to the personal quest for a middle way between tolerance and self-defense but also to the Buddhist cultural response to missionary zealots. The lesson is simple: don't let people push you around, even if you're a Buddhist.

The fact that Khmer Theravada rallied back after Pol Pot from the brink of annihilation bodes well for its survival abilities. But my own fears about the survival of Buddhism weren't truly quelled until I stood on the corner of Cach Mang Thang Tam and Nguyen Dinh Chieu in Saigon, Vietnam.

At this nondescript intersection three blocks south of the War Crimes Museum, bicycles, cyclos, and motor scooters dashed in all directions. Women in traditional *Ao Dais*, with perfectly erect postures, pedaled past me, most of them wearing opera-length gloves, brimmed hats, and handkerchiefs wrapped around their faces to protect them from the sun. (Asian women are desperate to have the palest skin possible.) A guy on foot passed me on the corner and nodded politely. His arm was outstretched, carefully carrying a netting sack that contained dozens of live scorpions away from his body—he was undoubtedly on his way to the market to grind them up for various medicinal purposes. An ugly three-story office building made of concrete served as backdrop to a small memorial tower near the street side. Just an ordinary intersection. But this is the spot where, on June 11, 1963, the Buddhist monk Thich Quang Duc emerged with a gas can from the car that he had driven down from Hue. He sat down in the lotus position, dowsed himself with gasoline, found the still-point of mindfulness within himself, lit a match, and burned himself to death.

David Halberstam, then reporting for the *New York Times*, witnessed the event and described it in this way:

> I was to see that sight again, but once was enough. Flames were coming from a human being; his body was slowly withering and shriveling up, his head blackening and charring. In the air was the smell of burning flesh; human beings burn surprisingly quickly. Behind me I could hear the sobbing of the Vietnamese who were now gathering. I was too shocked to cry, too confused to take notes or ask questions, too bewildered to even think. . . . As he burned he never moved a muscle, never uttered a sound, his outward composure in sharp contrast to the wailing people around him.

Many of the people who have seen the famous photograph of the burning monk (the photo was front-page news in America) mistakenly think that Thich Quang Duc was protesting the Eisenhower-Kennedy interference in Vietnam. In fact, Thich Quang Duc immolated himself in protest against South Vietnamese president Ngo Dinh Diem's anti-Buddhist policies. President Diem was a fanatical Catholic, and he sought every opportunity to persecute the Buddhist sangha and lay communities. Diem, believing in the superiority of Catholicism and not trusting the Buddhist official stance of neutrality between North and South, attempted to demonize Buddhists as Communist sympathizers. Totally out of touch with the vast Buddhist majority in Vietnam (something like 80 percent), Diem instituted strict rules to prevent the free practice of Buddhism. On May 8, 1963, Buddhists tried to celebrate the Buddha's birthday by flying flags in Hue, but Diem had them torn down and then forbade a Buddhist radio program from airing in the evening. A frustrated crowd formed at the radio station, and Diem had troops fire on the crowd, killing seven children and one woman. Two days later, ten thousand Buddhists protested in Hue, demanding that their traditional Buddhism be granted equal respect with the Catholic Church. Diem responded by arresting many of the monks and activists and increasing his persecution efforts.

One month later, after writing an open letter asking believers and supporters to strive to preserve Buddhism, Thich Quang Duc drove from Hue to Saigon and immolated himself as an act of religious self-defense. The social unrest that followed led Diem to attack pagodas all over South Vietnam, killing and arresting Buddhist monks and other insurgents. But Thich Quang Duc's dramatic gesture had a powerful and decisive effect on the political future of Diem and his anti-Buddhist regime. In four months' time, Diem was overthrown and executed, and the pro-Buddhist coup leader, General Duong Van Minh, freed seventy-five thousand political prisoners, including many monks.

Burning himself alive was not a cowardly act of suicide by Thich Quang Duc, but a courageous act of self-sacrifice in order to protect his people and their beliefs. Standing on that grim street corner, I looked at the famous photo carefully. I asked myself whether I'd be able to do something like that; I felt distinctly weak, flimsy, and pusillanimous by comparison. This guy is sitting perfectly still while a ten-foot conflagration eats him alive. I guess I don't ever have to worry about Buddhist acquiescence in the face of enemies. They will hold their own against missionaries and crusaders. No problem.

*   *   *

The history of Buddhism is not populated by many missionary movements, but they are not entirely absent either. After all, how else could it spread so widely? Perhaps the most famous campaign to spread the dhamma was that of Emperor Asoka, the Indian king who sent envoys throughout Asia. But notice the enlightened attitude of Asoka compared with other missionaries. In one of his edicts, which he carved into rock (it's still readable today), he says,

> One should not honor only one's own religion and condemn the religion of others, but one should honor other's religions for this or that reason. So doing, one helps one's own religion to grow and renders service to the religions of others too. In acting otherwise one digs the grave of one's own religion and also does harm to other religions. Whosoever honors his own religion and condemns other religions, does so indeed through devotion to his own religion, thinking, "I will glorify my own religion." But on the contrary, in so doing he injures his own religion more gravely. So concord is good: Let all listen, and be willing to listen to the doctrines professed by others.

Four

"BRITNEY SPEARS? NEVER HEARD OF HER"

The Virtues of Being Uncool

"Teacher, can you tell us if there was ever a caste system in Cambodia?"

I looked right at Boramy and I heard him ask the question, but I couldn't formulate a response. Only a moment passed between his question and my halting grinding response, but it seemed like an hour. He and all the other students appeared to be sitting on the other side of some frosted pane, but it was only the oppressive humidity. This day was hot even for them, and they'd grown up in the tropics. I had completely slipped my moorings and felt my lecture floating gradually to ever more shallow depths until we were all beached on dull platitudes.

Our Buddhist philosophy class met on the stifling second floor of the Buddhist Institute in one of the only air-conditioned rooms of the building, but the air conditioner was broken. I felt guilty for feeling any misfortune about the breakdown, when air conditioners themselves were such rare luxuries. But I couldn't really see straight anymore. Some of the students looked at me with pity; others just had the same blurry expression that I had. We'd been together now for a few months, chewing on a steady diet of abstract philosophical concepts, but everything tasted off today.

These students were unlike any I had previously encountered, and they will always hold a special place in my heart. There were twelve of them altogether, and they were very fortunate to be in this new Buddhist studies master's program—so they were extremely motivated. The program was their lifeline out of wretched destitution. Only 35 percent of Khmer can read and write, and the female part of that percentage is dismally low.

It was a rather competitive testing process that had brought these students into the program, and the sad fact, hanging like a sword of Damocles, was that some of them wouldn't be able to master the mountain of information and skills to graduate with a master's degree. They were expected to become research-proficient in Buddhist philosophy (my job), Khmer history, political science, Khmer literature and linguistics, French, English, Pali (the ancient language of the Buddhist palm-leaf scriptures), Khmer archaeology, and social science methodology. And probably some other stuff that I can't even remember.

The students were split evenly between men and women, and they were between twenty-two and twenty-six years old. They all dressed in a self-imposed formal fashion, as a sign of respect—white cotton shirts or blouses, dark pants for the men, long skirts for the women. They spent every day, all day, six days a week, in this classroom studying. Such an intense life of study is a widespread Asian practice that is unknown in the West. Formal education, especially higher education, is rarer and more competitive in the East. It is considered a great privilege rather than a right, and it is seldom squandered. I can't say the same about my American students.

Every day, on my way from my tiny office to the classroom, I could see my students dallying in a rare moment of relaxation between classes. But when they saw me approaching, they would race to take their seats and compose themselves in a quiet manner. All this was funny and touching to me, since I was accustomed to my American students answering their cell phones in the middle of my lectures.

Many of the students would greet me in the traditional Khmer style, by folding their hands in prayer and bowing slightly. They could never quite understand my full name, or they were bashful about mispronouncing it, and even though I invited them repeatedly to call me "Steve," many years of more formal protocol simply forbade them from doing so. They called me "Teacher." They began their questions with it, like: "Teacher, can you tell us if there was ever a caste system in Cambodia?"

When I entered the classroom, one of them would always bring me a fresh glass of filtered drinking water from the cooler, and they seemed to compete a little for this privilege. When I started to erase the chalkboard at the end of class, one or two would leap up to relieve me of this subprofessorial duty. I felt like a rock star or a royal. My American blue-collar background always gave me the faint dread that they'd somehow mistaken me for someone else, someone worthy of all this respect. When class was over, no one moved until I left the room, a tradition that was not explained to me ahead of time. At the end of our first few classes, I inadvertently tortured them (particularly the ones who had to go to the bathroom) by standing around casually chatting and slowly packing my books. I dismissed them, but they would continue to sit there until after my departure.

Three of the male students were orphans and had no homes, so they slept in monks' cells at nearby Buddhist wats. They'd study feverishly by day and sleep in a monastery at night. Education was no joke to these kids—it had been and will be their only way out. According to UNICEF's most recent figures, over twenty thousand children live on the streets of Phnom Penh. My students were trying to break the cycle, but they were doing it in a unique way. Those few of their peers who had also clawed their way up to higher education were choosing to study commerce in the quickly reproducing business schools of Phnom Penh, not Buddhism.

Toweling the sweat off my face, I gathered enough competence to direct the class to the Buddha's Aggana Sutta. I asked Boramy to read the passages where Buddha explicitly criticizes the Indian caste system. Indian society has been carved into rigid social classes since the ancient Vedic scriptures articulated a cosmic system of hierarchical order. The divisions of society were considered isomorphic, with the anatomical parts of a primordial cosmic being (*purusa*); the priestly Brahmin class came from the head of the purusa, while the *ksatriya* (warrior) caste came from the arms of the cosmic being.

Buddha offers several arguments against the caste system—which at that time had already existed for over one thousand years—but perhaps his most persuasive is to point out that one encounters good and bad ethical behavior across *all* the caste divisions. Brahmins aren't any more moral than other castes, so the only true way to say that a person is higher or lower than another is to use ethical behavior as the measure. Righteousness comes only from righteous action, not class membership. I explained to Boramy that Buddha's official position is clear in this scripture, but of course that did not preclude the possibility of a caste system in Cambodia prior to the arrival of Buddhism. Perhaps it was imported with other Brahministic teachings. I didn't know the answer. I often didn't know an answer, and part of maturing as a teacher has been learning to comfortably say "I don't know." But I knew someone who did know: I suggested that we consult the anthropology professor later. This afforded me a convenient pretext for wrapping up the lecture.

I ended the class a little early and stumbled blinking back to the office, where I found Kimvan and Peter hunched over the one and only sacred computer. Both of them were soaked with sweat, and Peter had his glasses off and was massaging his temples.

"Come and look at this!" Kimvan said to me, half smiling. The guts of the hard drive were hanging out of the housing carriage, and parts were strewn around the desk.

"Here is where mouse got inside," he explained. "And here zis mice shit ereywhere. Now there is no working. No more."

"Oh no," I groaned, and it was not false empathy. All the administrative records for our program were on that computer.

"Thank God," offered Peter, "at least we have backups saved for most things." He looked blankly at the wreck on the desk. "Welcome to Cambodia," he said to no one in particular.

A knock on the door interrupted our quiet heatstroke. A novice monk stood in the doorway with a slate of wood and a hammer. Kimvan became excited.

"Now we stop all mice from coming inside!" he said, with military conviction. Kimvan set about his "foolproof" defense plan: nailing a piece of board over the gap at the bottom of the office door.

Aldous Huxley's insight came back to me over and over again in Southeast Asia. "One is all for religion," he wrote, "until one visits a really religious country. Then one is all for drains, machinery, and the minimum wage." My own experience in Southeast Asia resonated with Huxley's insight about the ways in which different cultures romanticize each other. Many people in the West feel alienated and see the East as a cure for the woes of industrialization and development. Most of this attitude is pure romanticism that one overcomes quickly by actually living in the undeveloped East. Nonetheless, I did come to see a different sort of alienation in the West. I was already pretty dark on American pop culture before I came east, but I had to admit that the view from Southeast Asia made it seem even emptier and more trivial than I had thought possible.

It's no accident that American pop culture and a glamorous elite became so engaging in the second half of the twentieth century—after the War to End All Wars. For over half a century now, Americans have not really suffered very much. We have the biggest leisure class of any country in the world. Of course, individual Americans have suffered, and September 11 should never be overlooked, but en masse, as a people, we've had it relatively easy. I had found myself slipping into a Nietzschean hostility toward all things middle-class and comfortable. Did our cushy American lives, our prosperity and privilege, lead us to produce a culture of banal trivia? Obviously I'm not the first to muse this way, but it was my extended respite from pop culture that made me feel positively embarrassed about the "products" of all that Western wealth. Viewing America from deep in the sea of Southeast Asian spiritualism made my nation seem like the homeland of bimbos.

American pop culture, in the form of television programming, music CDs, Hollywood-produced films, fast-food chains, clothing styles, and so forth, seemed, from the perspective of Southeast Asia, to be even more consuming, numbing, distracting, and worthless than I'd already concluded—and Americans seemed blind to its trifling character. This wasn't a tired and typical railing on youth culture—you know, a thirty-something guy bitching about the MTV Generation. (Actually, come to think of it, the thirty-somethings and I *are* the MTV Generation.) No, I came to see the white noise of American cultural detritus extending from today's children straight back to the baby boomers.

I did not feel self-righteous or seek a blameless soapbox. Frankly, living in Cambodia made me loathe myself because, when I took stock of my own head, I found that I knew something about the ups and downs of Cher's personal life; something about Anna Nicole Smith's inane adventures; something about Justin Timberlake and Britney Spears's trials and tribulations; something about that Joe Millionaire guy and the other reality dating shows; not to mention something about Michael Jackson's prosthetic nose, Pamela Anderson's breasts, and Jennifer Lopez's latest engagement. I'd probably be enlightened by now if I could just get this stupid shit out of my head.

The vast majority of Cambodians have never heard of the Rolling Stones or Elvis. They haven't grown up with the same background radiation of the Western psyche. They don't know about the Brady Bunch, Julia Roberts, Michael Jordan, Steven Spielberg, or Nike. They've never heard of *Star Wars* or *Apocalypse Now* (even though its denouement happens in Cambodia). Eminem? Never heard of him. Hip-hop? Hip who? And huge crowds of Cambodians gathered in absolute disbelief recently at the opening of the first escalator in Phnom Penh! Most impressively perhaps, Cambodians have never patronized or even seen a McDonald's or Starbucks.

In my cynical moments, I imagined the next MTV *Real World* episode set in Phnom Penh, Cambodia. Americans love the manicured pseudo-drama of reality TV. With the right editing and sound-track music, you can make the pathetic nonproblems of prosperous people seem gripping and tense. "My God, did you see the way that Puck looked at Latoya when she didn't do the dishes on her night? And isn't it just sad the way that Skippy is so controlling toward his boyfriend Allen?" How about this instead? Puck gets voted off the show because he has his legs blown off by a land mine and has to spend too much time begging down by the riverfront. Latoya can't do the dishes on her night cuz she's contracted AIDS working in the sex industry in order to send money home to her starving family in the provinces.

Again, I wouldn't say that the frivolousness belongs exclusively to teens and twenty-somethings. Most baby boomers also seem to be living in a fog of mediated dramas and narratives, created by pop-culture industries. Some Americans seem unable to relate to each other, or themselves, without the mediation of *People* magazine and *Entertainment Tonight* (which CNN resembles more and more). We also demonstrate cultlike devotion to our sitcoms, soaps, and law firm–cop–emergency room dramas, the supposed high art of American culture. It is also not uncommon to find that the "news" is actually just summaries of other shows (like award shows) that celebrate . . . um, *other* shows. Even the "hard" news frequently boils down to reporters quoting other reporters (masked as "sources say . . ."). The simulacrum of mass media and entertainment is not even trying to mirror reality anymore—it's a simulacrum of itself, as Baudrillard would say. We Americans seem perfectly happy to focus on people, like Paris Hilton, who are famous simply *because* they are famous and not for anything they've actually done. Who cares about their talent or their character? We love them, even if they're ciphers, because the lens is focused on them. Never mind that the level of egotistical narcissism in our celebrities is enough to make the ancient Roman emperors look temperate and selfless.

As disturbing as it may be to contemplate the effect of this petty chaff on the consumer's psyche, it's even more troubling to examine the producer's relentless agenda. Industry seems to be weaving together more and more of the pop-culture threads so that we can more efficiently consume the related products. Magazines, for example, are struggling to stay afloat in the web-savvy new millennium, so they are starting to integrate product advertising into the actual news content of their articles, violating every journalistic ethical code imaginable and irresponsibly betraying the public trust (caveat emptor, I guess). Additionally, the purely fictional products are woven together such that blockbuster Hollywood movies are literally re-created comic books nowadays. And along with your Spiderman, Daredevil, X-Men, Hulk, and Batman movies (and collectible DVDs), all your favorite pop singers have contributed to the sound track. But not the *real* sound track—that's a list of your *other* favorite pop artists. You've got to have that one too. No, these are the jams that were "inspired" by the characters of the movie but never actually made it into the sound track.

While you're listening to the kick-ass Hulk-inspired jams of Limp Bagel and Aerosmug, you can stop and throw the CD into your PC, where it will take you to the Hulk website. After you "interact" a little with a questionnaire (designed to get more demographic specs from you), you can order the Hulk shirt, hat, and mug and enter the contest to get tickets to meet the Hulk at Disney's Hulkfest. The whole family can consume together. And the family that consumes together, stays together. Wait a minute. Log off for a sec, cuz there's a half-hour "news" show on TV about the making of the Hulk, and J-Lo is rockin' the mic on her new "Hulk, On and On and On" single, y'all. Commercial break for the Gap: new green Hulk sweaters. "The Gap: It's What's On You . . . and Everyone Else."

All this is symptomatic of a new cultural category, and when I say "new" I mean it's been growing since the 1950s. It's the culture of the *cool*. The people on TV, in movies, on CDs—they all have it, and we want it.

"Cool" is what's left to sell to people when they already have everything else. Thankfully, nobody in Cambodia is "cool"—they can't afford it.

I don't think I ever slipped into some knee-jerk anti-Americanism or anti-Westernism. I love America, and I loved it more and more as my wisdom teeth grew more impacted and I knew that I was going home soon and wouldn't have to resort to the Khmer guy down the street with the big pliers. I'm also officially in print, both in the previous chapter and in other books, as saying that Western science is superior to other ways of trying to understand nature (a singularly unvogue stance nowadays). Nonetheless, experiencing a radically alternative (non-consumer-based) culture on a daily basis made me seriously question certain Western values. Looking around at the starving orphans on the streets of Phnom Penh, I was nauseated that America worships Sean "Puff Daddy" "P-Diddy" Coombs, a guy who doesn't hesitate to spend one million dollars on his own birthday party. It's one thing to *imagine* the thousands of lives that such money could save or improve, but it's more crushing to actually *see* these lives every day struggling to survive. I hated the cool people of American pop culture, and I hated the sheep that worshiped them. I didn't want my students to become those sheep.

Buddhists in Southeast Asia have a different kind of "cool" than Americans—one that's a little closer to the meaning of the word. They have a quiet, detached, low-temperature way about them. As I already pointed out, they're laid-back in the same way that all people living in the tropics are laid-back. It's too goddamn hot to be bubbly and perky. But if they are trained Buddhists, then this quietude is accompanied by a specific mental culture called *sati* (mindfulness).

One of the things that distinguishes Buddhism from other forms of spirituality is this doctrine of mindfulness. Types of yogic meditation existed long before the Buddha, and in his quest for enlightenment he mastered various techniques. There are four jhanas, or meditative trance-states, and if we include the ascetic "formless" jhanas (abstract contemplations of infinity and nothingness) there are eight jhanas altogether. They start simple enough, with quiet sitting and the attempt to close out the external world of sensory stimulation. The trance-state elevates further and eventually stops the incessant babble of internal thought, and then rises upward and onward to increasing levels of rarefied consciousness. One moves through the trance-states until finally reaching the realm of "neither existence nor nonexistence."

Even though the Buddha mastered these abstract forms of *samadhi* (concentration), he also found them incomplete for attaining freedom. They are merely temporary glimpses of nibbana and last only as long as your trance—they do not lead to *vipassana* (true insight). He saw mindfulness as superior to yogic trance because mindfulness is a way of meditating *while* you go about your daily business—you don't have to separate yourself and contemplate your navel in a cave somewhere.

Mindfulness is being aware of your actions (no matter how mundane) as they happen in the present moment, without letting your mind wander into the past or future. Anyone who has ever tried this knows how difficult it is. For example, try to focus carefully on your first fifty bites of dinner tonight, without letting your mind float into thoughts about either the past (*Work was a drag today. Why didn't I ever learn to dance the salsa? What was that kid's name in high school? Is the steak cooked properly?*) or the future (*I wonder who's on Letterman tonight. Am I going to get that paperwork done tomorrow? I'm going to eat less red meat from here on out. I hope I get laid this weekend.*). Focus on nothing but the chewing. Or make it even simpler. Try to be mindful of the next fifty breaths, and nothing else. Good luck. Your monkey-mind can't sit still.

In the Mahasatipatthana Sutta, the Buddha explains that we should be mindful about four things in particular: the body, the feelings, the mind's mental processes (psychology), and the theories and ideas of the mind (mind objects and ideologies). And you can be mindful in two ways: you can be mindful with regard to your reflective thinking, but also with regard to your actions.

Mindfulness of action is somewhat easy to understand. For example, you can be so focused and immersed in an activity (planting a tree, making tea, playing your guitar, folding your laundry) that "you" temporarily disappear. You lose yourself in the moment and just become the laundry. I could've picked the sexual orgasm as my example here, but *le petit mort* is just too obvious. Losing yourself in the laundry—now that takes discipline. Notice that mindfulness in activity should actually be called mindlessness, because you lose self-awareness in the activity.

Mindfulness in reflection is harder to explain and harder to attain. In addition to becoming mindful of your own body by "dissolving" it in some absorbing activity, you should also think and theorize about the body properly. As I pointed out earlier, Theravada has a rather macabre emphasis on decaying flesh and bloated, bursting corpses. When I was at a monastery in southern Thailand, I chanced upon some reproductions of "dhamma paintings" from the mid-nineteenth century. These pictures were from a Chaiya manuscript discovered nearby, and they depicted, in detail, the "Ten Reflections on Foulness" (*asubha kammatthana*). The paintings illustrate the various uses of corpses as objects for contemplating impermanence. Following the great Theravadan philosopher Buddhaghosa's Visuddhimagga text ("Path of Purification"), the artist rendered decaying corpses in rather comprehensive stages of dismemberment and putrefaction. I was interested to discover that staring at a bloated corpse will be particularly useful to me if I'm feeling overly attached and arrogant about the shape and morphology of my body, but if I'm feeling snobby or bigoted about my skin's color or complexion, then I should focus on the livid corpse that ranges from green to blue-black in color. If I mistakenly feel that my body is my own, I am to rectify this error by meditating on a worm-infested corpse (*puluvaka*), for as Buddhaghosa explains, "The body is shared by many and creatures live in dependence on [all parts and organs] and feed [on them]. And there they are born, grow old, and die, evacuate and pass water; and the body is their maternity home, their hospital, their charnel ground, their privy and their urinal."

Having sati about the body is being aware of its transience, its brevity, its fugacity. The physical body is slowly macerating, and to try to hold on to it or recompose it is a pipe dream. Compare this view with the body obsessions of the West, where, in America, for example, the plastic surgery statistics went from 681,000 procedures in 1989 to 8.5 million in 2001. And after the amazing success of surgery makeover reality shows and Botox parties, one suspects that future figures will be much higher.

What about your feelings? The Buddha says you can become mindful of your feelings in a way that de-centers them. Perhaps you're feeling a little depressed. If you focus mindfully, you start to think about that feeling not as *your* feeling but just as *a* feeling that is moving through—like a cloud arising and passing away in the sky. You step back and detach from the feeling (de-center it) and consider it, almost as an objective scientist would observe an impermanent cumulus formation. You observe the causes of the depression, the full strength of it, and its passing away. Venerable Walpola Rahula explains that "when you observe your mind, and see its true nature clearly, you become dispassionate with regard to its emotions, sentiments, and states. Thus you become detached and free, so that you may see things as they are."

Being mindful of your own specific psychological and theoretical tendencies can help you overcome some stupid patterns. For example, you call your friend and leave a message. A couple of days go by with no response, and you start to wonder. After a couple of more days, you're inventing theories, almost all of which cause you anxiety. You nervously contemplate your friend dead, face down in a gutter somewhere. Or maybe your friend thinks she's too good for you and doesn't feel the need to get back to you—the outrage sets in. No, no, she was never *really* your friend, and she's been secretly laughing at you all along! Your mind reels on this stuff, filling your head with worry, self-doubt, indignation, and then the phone rings, and your friend invites you for a pint at the pub, and you feel like a moron for ever entertaining such negativity. All of this nonsense can be trained out of your thinking if you start by being mindful of the proclivity.

What is the purpose of such mindfulness training? First, it brings you freedom from unhealthy attachments to anxieties—or, simply put, peace of mind. But also, in mindfulness you begin to realize that the ego (the self) is a habitual fiction and that it doesn't really exist. So you can stop acting in a self-ish manner. Contrary to your everyday consciousness, you are not a stable being that exists through the past, present, and future moments. You are just a temporary aspect of the flow of becoming. Belief in a self (an essential soul), for Buddhists, is what causes us to strive to profit ourselves and injure others—to treat others as mere *means* rather than as *ends* in themselves.

The Buddha, in the Samyutta Nikaya (35.206), offers the simile of the Six Animals. Imagine, he says, that your six senses (remember that the mind is also considered a sense in Buddhism) are like six different animals: a snake, a crocodile, a bird, a dog, a hyena, and a monkey. Imagine now that each animal is bound on its own rope-leash but that all of the ropes are tied together in a central knot. Since each animal has its own habitat, each will pull, crawl, or fly toward that habitat home. The crocodile will struggle to get to the water, the bird to the air, the monkey to the forest, and so on. But when the animals become exhausted and can no longer struggle, they will submit and surrender to whichever animal happens to be strongest on that day. This, according to the Buddha, is what it's like to live without mindfulness. Our senses are drawn toward their particular pleasures, and we haphazardly pursue whatever is momentarily strongest. We are locked in an internal struggle. When I read this, I thought about myself on a weekend bender in Las Vegas—not exactly a spiritual high point for me, at least the bits I can recall. Then I thought about Vegas itself, and eventually America itself. It seemed like everyone I knew, including myself, was a roped-up, six-animal tug-of-war.

The solution, according to the Buddha, is to live in the present without attachment and slavery to sensual and intellectual cravings. He says that you should take your six animals and tether them to a strong stake or pole. In this way, they will still struggle for their respective pleasures, but they will grow tired and then stand, sit, or lie down right there next to the stake. The discipline and restraint of mindfulness brings this peacefulness, this equanimity.

*   *   *

I've traveled in America, Europe, the Far East, and Southeast Asia. Nowhere have I met people more adept at doing *nothing* than the Cambodians. I'm not exaggerating when I say that a Cambodian can spend three or four hours straight sitting in a chair (alone or together with others) just staring off into the distance without any respite of magazine, book, TV, or even conversation. They "chill out" for excruciating stretches of time without seeming to grow restless. In the West (where we have "no loitering" laws and where people are raised on the Protestant work ethic), this hyper-lounging seems suspicious, maybe criminal, and certainly wasteful. But in a culture where mindful meditation is a crucial spiritual foundation, some of this daily trance behavior makes sense. Khmer people have many hours each day to be reflective, to be contemplative. I think it's harder to find this time in America because wealth gives us more material distractions, the procuring of that wealth eats up most of our time, and finally TV takes the rest (the average American watches four hours a day).

I'm not naive. Much of this Cambodian meditation is the result of having nothing better to do, but for now I'm more interested in the effect of this mindful quietude than its cause. After living in Southeast Asia for a few months, I began to see that the culture itself had more sati than my own culture. Khmer people in particular, but also Thais and Laotians, seemed more present in the here and now than Westerners. Always on guard against my own temptation to romanticize these exotic peoples, I tried hard to universalize their sense of ease, but I struggled to find an American correlate to their modest tranquillity.

Of course, not everyone who's slacking in Asia is doing so because of Buddhism. But the monkey-mind ambition of Western individualism, always seeking to maximize pleasures and increase profits, is less powerful here because from the time you're a baby you always see yourself as part of a clan or a collective family or village. Your selfish drives are probably being trained, sacrificed, and subjugated more regularly. And the irony is that these people who have less affluence, less choice, and less individual freedom actually seem to have more happiness.

*   *   *

The wife of my friend Peter Gyallay-Pap is Cambodian, and when I was in Siem Reap to explore more of the Angkor Wat ruins, Naht invited me for a traditional Khmer dinner. When the fabulous meal was over, I realized that I'd never eaten food so fresh; nor have most people living in urban America. The chicken I ate had been running around their backyard just hours before; the pig had been killed at market that morning (and it makes a big difference in the flavor). The fish was caught that afternoon by her brother-in-law in the nearby river, the vegetables were from their garden, the jackfruit dessert was from the tree in front of the house, and the coconut juice was from the tree out back. In America I get my plastic-wrapped boneless, skinless chicken breasts from the supermarket and some vegetables out of the freezer section and am forced to take it on faith that this stuff ever walked on legs or grew in the ground.

The whole extended family was there—three generations under one roof. And the meal—indeed *every* meal—must have taken hours to collectively prepare. Naht and her son live half the year with her American husband in Colorado, and during the rest of the year they are all in Cambodia while Peter works down in Phnom Penh at the Buddhist Institute. They'd been doing this back-and-forth for seven or eight years. Naht has had the choice between Western convenience and culture, on the one hand, and traditional Khmer ways, on the other. She's had McDonald's and Kentucky Fried Chicken. She's read *People* magazine.

Naht thinks the food issue is tied to much larger cultural differences. She thinks the only reason why we Americans think that getting our food very fast is a luxury is because we have already committed to a culture of radical busyness (not mindfulness). She thinks we spend so much time in the rat race that we neglect our own families, our own happiness, and our own health. She would rather spend two hours with her sisters, son, husband, and parents cooking a meal than spend no time together and then race to get some McNuggets or some other fast food at the end of a harried day.

Asia, however, is starting to feel the lure of Western fast food. In

Bangkok and in tourist parts of Thailand, I could get most of the predictable big-chain burgers and fries. In other developed and developing parts of Asia, the story is beginning to break. Faster and fattier foods are more prevalent now, so an unprecedented wave of obesity is sweeping Asia. Couple this new diet with the fact that populations are becoming more urban and more sedentary, and you see why cardiovascular diseases are now Asia's leading killers. Children all over Asia are fatter than they've ever been, and the World Health Organization reports that six out of every ten deaths in developed Asia are obesity-related.

After dinner I was looking past Naht, out to the backyard. I could see her son and six of his cousins running around playing soccer with a tattered sandal. Dimly trying to salvage some value of my own pop culture, I rebutted her folksy philosophy with a pro-modernization query.

"But wouldn't your son prefer," I asked, "to play with a Gameboy or a Playstation than play with his shoe?"

"Oh," she replied, "it's not the *shoe* that you should be noticing. What's important is that he is playing with six of his cousins. And with a Gameboy he'd be playing by himself."

Having grown up in Cambodia but having also spent several years living in America, Naht has a privileged position. There's no romanticizing of the other culture here; she's past all that. So I listened carefully to her assessments. Totally unprompted, she told me the same thing my ex-wife always says to me: "Americans have too many choices to be happy."

My ex-wife Wen is mainland Chinese and grew up in Shanghai and Nanjing, eventually moving to the States when she was twenty years old. By the time we met, she had already been living in the States for almost ten years. She, like Naht, knew the two worlds very intimately and did not take an overly maudlin view of their differences. They both concurred that too many choices lead to increased anxiety and misery and that a more Asian lifestyle, wherein family constraints dominate your possibilities, actually lets you focus better and live more deeply in your activities. In America people spend a lot of time and energy trying to maximize the most satisfactory choice. They gather data about their choices and stress out about their imminent decisions. They regret many of their decisions, because the possibilities are so endless, and then this regret is compounded by their worry that they wouldn't be able to avoid regret after making their decisions. Frequently, all these choices leave people paralyzed and unable to commit. When they do commit, they obsess and fret over the missed opportunities that their actual choice forced upon them. This is why shopping has become a science for many Americans, and perhaps it is also why romance itself now seems more like shopping. But our overabundance of choices often leaves us living in the past and future rather than the present.

Most of us assume that more choice always means more happiness. But a recent study by the psychologist Barry Schwartz suggests that Naht and Wen are correct. According to recent figures published in the *Journal of the American Medical Association*, Americans are more depressed than ever. And Dr. Schwartz claims that it is because Americans, despite their relative wealth and myriad life choices, are fundamentally lonely. The most important factor in happiness is close social relations, something Americans lack. Being connected to others, he argues, is the ingredient that Americans have lost in their pursuit of individual success. Things like demanding family obligations, serious long-lasting friendships, religious fellowship, and community closeness may bind us, but paradoxically they also create happier people.

Americans complain of a lack of intimacy in their lives. Dr. Schwartz points out that "we spend less time visiting with neighbors. We spend less time visiting with our parents, and much less time visiting with other relatives. Partly this is because we *have* less time, since we are busy trying to determine what choices to make in other areas of life. But partly this is because close social relations have themselves become matters of choice." In other words, we used to live in a world—more like contemporary Cambodia—where the social bonds were simply given, but now we must actively cultivate fundamentals like family and friends. For example, Cambodians always live in very close proximity to their families; usually multiple generations reside under the same roof. But in the States the family can be spread out over the whole country, forcing people to work hard (and fail) at endeavors that used to be no-brainer natural conditions. Friendships too grow flimsy at continental distances. Schwartz concludes that "our social fabric is no longer a birthright but has become a series of deliberate and demanding choices."

Freud debates this briefly in his *Civilization and Its Discontents* when he first points out the benefits of a modern technological culture that, for example, could bring to him the sound of his faraway son's voice on the telephone or provide him with a cable that notified him of his friend's safe arrival in a distant country. But taking up the opposite side, he points out that "if there had been no railway to conquer distances, my child would never have left his native town and I should need no telephone to hear his voice; if traveling across the ocean by ship had not been introduced, my friend would not have embarked on his sea-voyage and I should not need a cable to relieve my anxiety about him." These examples sound quaint to us now, of course, but recent technological jumps have only strengthened this debate, not put it to rest. This same question of deep conflicting values is bubbling under the surface of every interface between developed and developing countries, whether they be in Southeast Asia or the Middle East or North America.

I felt all this keenly at dinner with my friend Naht and her family. Everything that was important to her was right there, all around her. And all of the people that mattered most to me were thousands of miles away on the other side of the planet. I felt a twinge of estrangement from the things that mattered most, but then I realized that it was largely because of my affluent, choice-riddled status as an American that I was able to be sitting, eating, and making friends on the other side of the planet. It may be a luxury for me to travel to Cambodia, but it is also a privilege.

If you brought Gameboy, Playstation, *People* magazine, and Kentucky Fried Chicken to Cambodia, would they go for it? Of course they would. (For God's sake, the kids don't have toys so they play street soccer with their own sandals.) Would they be better off with those luxuries? Well, the answer here is less clear. I certainly don't want to be paternalistic about the issue. I do not want to suggest that developing nations should stay primal just so I and other like-minded Western tourists can have a Thoreau-style vacation every now and then. Obviously, Cambodians themselves have to decide if they are better off with Western luxuries. But I wondered if it was getting harder and harder to find places in the world where the solvent of pop culture hadn't corroded the local culture. I'm all for development if it means decent medical facilities and education, but the biggest export that America has to offer these days is pop culture. Open your markets to us and we will bring you Britney and Keanu and Red Lobster. Let the Progress begin.

My students were living on the razor's edge of an East-West culture clash. Every day brought a new temptation to sell out their heritage and join the increasing ranks of their grifter peers. The contrast between young people in Phnom Penh and Ho Chi Minh City, for example, or Bangkok, is shocking. In the more rural parts of Vietnam and Thailand, there remain very honest, unjaded, and innocent young people, but in the big cities you find a different species altogether. Jaded, cynical opportunists abound in urban areas, and some nefarious folks seek to exploit both locals and travelers. One comes to regard many supposedly friendly encounters with suspicion in Ho Chi Minh City and Bangkok. Of course, this is also true in Chicago, New York, Paris, and so forth, but it bears mentioning because Khmer people are, by and large, so refreshingly different.

Frankly, it's hard to believe their sincerity, their optimism, and their disinterested goodwill until after months and months of it you begin to accept its reality. I suspect this beautiful naïveté in young people may be the result of thirty-some years of Cambodian isolation. It's paradoxical that Khmer people have experienced so much violence and yet their goodwill remains so genuine. Still, some of this is already slipping away in Cambodia because the younger generation is having to find ways to survive in a modernizing culture overseen by a corrupt government that cares little about their well-being. Without real support for education and gainful employment opportunities, urban young people become locked into dead-end sweatshop labor, or they gravitate toward more disreputable means of support. My own students were relatively uncorrupted and still hopeful, but without increased opportunities for budding intellectuals, they too would end up selling jackfruit on the street or much worse.

Compared to my American students, Khmer students, who had fine senses of humor, were relatively devoid of irony and sarcasm. So many of my "cool" American students, in contrast, are desperate to show their contempt for sincerity. And they learned long ago, in school, that to take a posture of superiority toward "nerdy" things like knowledge and study can both save them the irritation of learning and puff up their egos nicely. The result is a frightening combination of ignorance and arrogance. Not so in Cambodia. As Socrates famously pointed out, ignorance is a precondition for learning, and he readily admitted his own, but humility is also a precondition for learning, and this virtue is much harder to find in America than in Cambodia.

Around the time when the annual rains started, all of the Buddhist Institute folks and some educators from the Royal University of Phnom Penh gathered one evening for a retirement party on a Tonle Sap riverboat. All twelve of my students found it hard to contain their excitement at the prospect of this party, and we struggled to focus that day in class. When evening rolled around, I made my way down to the river and managed to get on the boat just before it groaned out of the dock. The party vessel was filled with some "big fish" of Khmer studies—academics from various disciplines. Sri Lankans were heavily represented; they always know more Buddhist philosophy than the average Asian, partly because they historically represent the Theravada motherland, but partly because their religious ideas have been clarified and tempered by years of struggle with Tamil Hindus. The Tamil (largely Hindu) minority of Sri Lanka has been warring with the Sinhalese (largely Buddhist) majority in an attempt to break away as an independent Tamil state. Bloodshed was significant between 1983 and a ceasefire in 2001. Invariably, I could meet a Sri Lankan bartender or grocer, anywhere in Southeast Asia, and he could weigh in on the most abstruse aspects of philosophical dharma. One seems to refine and better articulate one's beliefs and values when they are either under attack or forced to vie in a pluralistic society of alternative options.

With this many academics around, I headed straight for the bar. After securing the necessary sustenance, I socialized a bit and wandered below deck to where the rest of the party had spilled. My eye caught a stunning beauty across the room, wearing an iridescent silk traditional Khmer dress. Lacking mindfulness, I could feel one of my six animals dragging me in that direction.

"Wait a minute ... wait one minute," I heard myself say out loud. "That's Samphors! That's my student." And there was Bunnary and Thyda and the others sitting nearby—all dressed to kill. I had not recognized them with their finest clothes on and their hair piled up and carefully coiffured. And, my God, were they wearing makeup?

The students were all excited to see me and asked me to pull up a chair. Here, outside the classroom, I saw them as young men and women, not kids. But they were still painfully sweet and guileless in their demeanor. Several of the male students gathered in so we could talk over the din of clinking glasses and traditional Khmer folk music. All the young women quickly retreated to the far side of the table, laughing and locking arms. I looked up in surprise.

"The girls go over here now," Sreang explained, seeing my confusion, "because that is proper Khmer way." Sreang was Sino-Khmer and, because he scored higher on the English proficiency test than the other students, he acted as a kind of class captain. The male students shook their heads in agreement, and as with many previous lessons, they took great pleasure in educating their teacher.

"Girls and boys should be separate at socializing. Not too much mixing is to be happening," he explained gravely, then added, "but when boys and girls get older, we can have the more together mixing." Of course I found this incredibly charming, since these "boys and girls," already in their early twenties, still felt too young for full-on mingling.

Later Samphors leaned into our discussion for a moment, creating a fragrant interlude as she passed on her way to the upper deck.

"Teacher," she smiled, "you must be careful not to have the wetness on you this night." Pause. I mulled this over for a moment while the other students nodded in agreement. Finally I gave my usual look of grave bewilderment.

"Khmer people," she explained, "believe that the first rain of season is causing of bad health. So people cannot want to be getting wet tonight."

I smiled comprehension, and she was quickly off again, lest Khmer propriety be compromised.

The young men descended on me that evening with all manner of questions and issues, as if the informal party surroundings and the all-male company had freed them to finally ask me about matters too delicate or embarrassing for the classroom. The biggest surprise was that my quietest student, Hokmeng, seemed like a different person at the party. Barely able to make eye contact in the classroom, here he regaled me with one query after another. Hokmeng was a slightly chubby fellow, with boyish features and a little archaic Buddha smile. He was one of the students who had come from the provinces and, having no family in Phnom Penh, lived in a Buddhist wat. After studying all day long, he retired every evening to very spartan digs where he slept on a monk's cot.

Hokmeng had taken a degree in biology at the Royal University of Phnom Penh before being accepted into our Buddhist studies program. Since my own doctoral work was in the philosophy of biology, I took an immediate interest in him. But despite my regular interrogations of Hokmeng, I could never find any common subjects over which we might bond. One day in class I had made some reference to Charles Darwin's evolution theory, and the students collectively drew a blank. I looked to Hokmeng to help me explain Darwin to the other students, and he told me he had never heard of Darwin. And on this night of the riverboat party, Hokmeng, with the nodding support of two other students, mysteriously rambled at length about the phenomenon of spontaneous generation— looking to me to corroborate and amplify his understanding of sponta- neous maggot creation. As a teacher, I was expected to know about all sorts of subjects, so this wasn't the first time I had been quizzed on ob- scure matters.

I explained to him that belief in spontaneous generation was very old and widespread, but in fact Louis Pasteur, whom Hokmeng had also never heard of, had finally resolved the issue in the 1850s. I sketched Pas- teur's experiments and explained that there was no such thing as life arising from nonliving matter. Cases that seem to be spontaneous, like worms appearing in putrefying meat, actually involve microscopically small eggs. Hokmeng would have no part of it. Out of respect for his teacher, he was of course outwardly deferential, but I could see that he was unmoved by my short history of nineteenth-century European "flummery." He made some vague appeal based on his own witnessing of spontaneous generation, and I just let the matter go because I could see that his supporters, now presented with new information, were starting to question his authority. As was true of all my students, I liked Hok- meng too much to make him lose face over such a trivial thing.

He took a moment later in the night to approach me, this time with- out backers or audience, and ask whether I believed in the existence of ghosts. I told him that I was skeptical. He explained that he thought he had seen ghosts in a graveyard near his village home, and his family be- lieved in them too.

I always try to walk carefully around this sort of thing, which also arises regularly in the questions of my American students. I could bark a barrage of arguments and counterhypotheses at the credulous, but some- thing deeper is usually being asked in such queries. Often the student is intellectually poised on a pivot between the new wisdom of his urban formal education and the old wisdom of his family and rural culture. Students are faced with the awkward possibility that their parents and other long-standing founts of wisdom are only one option among others. And added to this anxiety for Hokmeng was the tugging competition of Khmer ideas and Western ideas. This is a deeply personal tension, and early in my teaching career, before I understood it properly, I'm sure I handled such questions badly. Here, with Hokmeng, I tried to handle it better.

"Well, I have never seen a ghost, Hokmeng," I offered. "Of course, that doesn't mean they don't exist—maybe they do. But I don't think the Buddha cared much about ghosts. The idea of them fills us with fears and anxieties and cravings, and so we should probably conduct our lives as if they do not exist. Otherwise, we will not attain peace and equanimity." I told him about my art students back home who dumped their traditional monotheisms to become Goth-glamour Wiccans, worshiping unseen spirits and casting manipulative spells. They all felt empowered by their break from traditional authority and their new ownership of personalized ritualism and the vaguely naughty totemism. But in the end such look-at-me "liberation" is still just bondage by another name, because it sees this world as dependent on a spirit world. The irony lies in the fact that many lapsed monotheists in the West feel so radical and spiritually rebellious when they adopt New Age and/or Wiccan practices, but those new theologies are just more populated versions of the old metaphysics. They switch the names of the spirits, but they cling tight to an invisible co-present dimension. By comparison, the Buddha focuses on *this* world—there is no true distinction between the hidden and the manifest. What you see is what you get, but of course you can always learn to see it better through mindfulness.

Keeping in mind the stakes of Hokmeng's question, I tried to demonstrate some respect for the supernatural tendencies of his family, and those of most Khmer people, and those of most people period for that matter. I told him that my own parents had buried a Saint Joseph statue upside down in our backyard as an old Catholic trick to help them sell their home. It seemed to be an emotionally satisfying thing for them to do. Of course, dhamma (truth) is not measured by an emotional barometer, and pointing out kooky practices and beliefs in other places doesn't lend credence to any of them. But it does show some cultural solidarity, or maybe it's emotional solidarity with different cultural veneers.

Several of the other male students had approached us while Hokmeng and I discussed ghosts, and now they hovered impatiently.

"Teacher," Boramy interjected, "can you . . ." He broke off nervously, looking around for support. The other young men prodded him forward. "Can you tell us more about the climax of the orgasm sex?"

Okay, enough about spontaneous generation and ghosts, I thought. Here, I surmised, as the young men leaned close and smiled tentatively, was a topic they were eager to flesh out. In class I had casually mentioned the age-old example of coitus as a case of temporary ego annihilation. It had been weeks since I offered this intuitive example of "living in the moment" and "losing the self," but they had not forgotten it. It was the sort of thing I could say and did say to my American students, who usually had the requisite experience to make the illustration work. But I had only obscured things for my Khmer students by offering an even more mysterious phenomenon (sex) as an analogy for the less mysterious phenomenon of mindfulness. My students were unembarrassed to explain that only one of them, the mischievously grinning Heng, had tasted of these carnal mysteries—a trip to the brothel had made him an overnight authority figure to the other curious male students.

I did my best to explain the unexplainable, and thankfully they seemed satisfied just to hear me say words like "sex" and "orgasm." And they could scarcely contain themselves when I explained that some forms of Tantric Buddhism actually celebrate sexual union as a form of transcendental selflessness.

I wondered if this excitement about sex was the main reason why the new "imperialism" of American pop culture was so unavoidable in developing countries (and why reactionary regimes will always fail to stop it). Arguably, the American sexual revolution brought the subterranean erotic expressions up into the light of everyday commercial culture—marrying them together, as it were, whereas these two cultures remained somewhat bifurcated in Southeast Asia. Perhaps the one good thing about American pop culture—the thing that will always make it naturally attractive to other youth cultures—is that it liberates and celebrates our sexual dimensions in all their irrational, dark, and hedonistic glory. In this sense, I suppose that pop culture's shallowness is its virtue, because it doesn't prance delicately around feigned morality or politically correct decorum. It just screams out James Brown's "Sex Machine," or Madonna's "Like a Virgin," or Sir Mixalot's "Baby Got Back." This stuff will always appeal to the youth of socially conservative cultures like those one finds in much of the developing world. Unfortunately, in the United States we are already way past the initial shock and liberation phase and have simply taken that sexual dynamite and packaged it slickly to serve the agenda of consumerism. The sexual energy of popular culture may retain some of its intrinsic punch, but it's also been successfully shackled into service by the marketplace. I wondered how all this might play out in places like Cambodia (or Iraq) in the years to come. Thailand, for example, is already well on its way to a more sexualized commercial culture.

After the riverboat docked and the party broke up, some of the students and I ended up at a run-down karaoke club over the Chruoy Changvar Bridge. Prime Minister Hun Sen officially banned karaoke bars in 2001, claiming that they were lascivious sites of misconduct and corrupted the youth. But everyone just ignored the ban. Hun Sen, in another attempt to stem the tide of encroaching Western sexual fashion, also banned Khmer women from wearing short skirts on Cambodian television.

Here at the karaoke bar, however, there were plenty of short skirts, and while the sexual climate at many karaoke bars is as steamy as the tropical air, we had come there for the music and drink. Still, I couldn't help but marvel, from my comparative vantage point, at the complexities and paradoxes of sexual cultures. In America I could watch a parade of tits and asses on primetime television, and I could access ridiculous amounts of porn, but the real mainstream culture (not the *commercial images* of our culture) is relatively conservative, monogamous, and sexually conventional (one might even say "uptight"). In Phnom Penh I can search in vain for any public *images* of sexuality, but I can get a blow job on almost any street corner.

I've always hated karaoke. For the longest time I thought it was just a kitschy joke, sort of like going with your college buddies to the local VFW hall polka party just because it was such an absurd and quirky thing to do. In Asia, however, singing on stage to canned song tracks is serious business—there's nothing kitschy about it. That doesn't mean I grew to like it when I lived there. On the performance end, it certainly didn't help me sing any better to know that people were really listening, and on the audience end, there are just as many tone-deaf wannabe singers in Southeast Asian bars as anywhere else. So the actual enjoyment part of karaoke remained stubbornly truant for me. Nonetheless, the opportunity for socializing with locals and expats was wonderful.

As we sat drinking Angkor beers, I had to endure a young woman's nauseating version of the treacly "Tie a Yellow Ribbon Round the Old Oak Tree" and a barrage of Lionel Ritchie tunes that made me want to shoot myself. In fact, all over Southeast Asia there is an eerie obsession with Lionel Ritchie tunes. In Saigon one day, for example, I counted four painful hearings of Ritchie's "Hello" piped into various business establishments. Something of the melodramatic sadness of these American tunes really echoes the lachrymose folk songs of the Thais, Khmer, and Vietnamese. But the most important thing I learned from my many hours listening to amateur vocalists was that some of my fears about an American pop culture takeover were ill founded.

Many enemies of "globalization," including myself on certain days of the week, have argued that globalization is really just Americanization by another name. And while it is true that AOL Time Warner, Disney, and Viacom are all insinuating themselves into worldwide markets like a rhizomic disease, there is a more complicated and perhaps optimistic story in Southeast Asia.

Throughout most of human history, people have lived in rather provincial local cultures; things like deserts and mountains were enough to keep communities entirely ignorant of each other. Mass media, high-speed travel, and the Internet have quickly transformed all this, and cultural identity is struggling to keep up with the technological quantum leap. Apart from the serious economic-ecological ramifications of living on a much "smaller" planet (for example, American SUVs changing greenhouse-gas emissions for people all over the globe), there is the creepy prospect that everyone everywhere will eventually drink Coke and listen to Britney Spears. Having traveled all over Asia and lived in the developing world for an extended period, I can finally say that this is not going to happen.

While I had to grit my teeth through some dodgy renditions of American pop songs at the karaoke bar, the overwhelming majority of songs were Khmer, and in Thailand they're Thai, in Vietnam they're Vietnamese, and so on. This is true everywhere. Asians may adopt the poses of hip-hop, the fashions of bubble-gum blondes, and even the instruments and arrangements of American music, but they are resolutely interested in hearing their own stories in their own language. There is greater cultural "fusion" than ever before, but that is not the same as cultural conquest. Local cultures are extremely resilient. After all, how else could Buddhism survive the Khmer Rouge? Local cultures are also extremely adaptive, and I was optimistic to see Southeast Asians enjoying Western culture in addition to, rather than instead of, their own culture.

Even that paragon of inane American frivolity, MTV, has been forced to "go native," because Asian viewers were not interested in American pop stars. Once the programming began to offer local artists, the popularity exploded. MTV Asia started broadcasting in 1991 and now operates eight twenty-four-hour programming services—MTV China, MTV India, MTV Indonesia, MTV Korea, MTV Mandarin, MTV Philippines, MTV Southeast Asia, and MTV Thailand. Including programming blocks in various parts of Asia, MTV has a combined distribution of more than 150 million homes. Each of these incarnations has its own independent roster of indigenous pop stars.

On the one hand, there's something unsettling about the ubiquitous reach of Viacom (and the extension of "cool" marketing), but on the other hand, one has to recognize that the local cultures were hardly devoured by a homogenizing American culture, and in fact the desire of local people to see themselves reflected back in the cathode mirror actually recreated the programming. So indigenous cultural expressions are only fusing and mixing and evolving—something they've always done—and are not in danger of vanishing.

In some deeper recesses of my cynicism, however, I'm reminded to follow the money, and then things look less optimistic. I wonder if these diverse masks of local culture (MTV India, MTV Thailand, and so forth) are simply hiding the bigger homogenous cultural import: consumerism. If it is true that the ultimate teleology of American pop culture and mass media has become consumption, then Southeast Asia needs to heed the advice of the Latin American economist Hernando De Soto. De Soto argues that budding capitalism will work in the Third World only if it is accompanied by the creation of significant "property rights"— an issue currently under discussion in Cambodia. After the Khmer Rouge and the occupation period, many people settled on property by squatting; even age-old family farms have no legal protections. Without property laws, farmers and workers cannot obtain loans or credit, and without these basic tools of capitalist development, developing countries will bog down in a no-growth condition. What does this have to do with MTV?

De Soto's point is relevant for the pop-culture question. If you're going to show poor kids in the Third World televised "windows" into wealthy lifestyles, then you'd better give them some access to real capitalist growth (property rights), or you're going to have a lot of very angry people on your hands. Angry people who find themselves shut out of the prosperous life will simply pursue alternative noncapitalist ideologies of power.

As my students and I parted company that night, I wondered whether their Buddhism would protect them from Nike and the Gap and pornography and fast food and ultimately narcissism. I wondered if my own Buddhism had protected me from any of these things. Did anybody really need protection from this sort of stuff? I walked down Norodom Boulevard toward the purple lights of the Independence Monument. I thought about the Buddhist emphasis on impermanence and the focus on non-attachment to desire, and these philosophical positions seemed like good defenses against crass materialism. I felt better after this realization. If the background culture of the dhamma could be restored in Cambodia, then people would have a foundation of deep values that could immunize them against the culture of me, myself, and I. But as soon as I had consoled myself with this thought, I remembered that the original American spiritual tradition of Christianity (even with its emphasis on the impermanence of this mundane world and its rejection of selfish desire) had offered little resistance historically to the relentless juggernaut of materialism. Instead, it revised and accommodated so that fat men could regularly fit through the eyes of needles. And even as Buddhism increasingly finds its way into America, for example, it gets twisted and turned so that affluent, Benz-driving practitioners can still wear it comfortably as a badge of honor. Buddhism will certainly change and adapt just like other parts of Khmer culture, but I hope the fusion with modern consumer culture will not enfeeble its curative properties.

The thick clouded sky above churned like my beer-soaked brain. Maybe I should have taken that ride home on the back of my student's moto. The sensuality of the tropical night—the night of the first rain, pregnant with the monsoon season—was deep and murky. It seemed as though I could feel the ancient cycle turning slowly, like samsara itself— the wheel of becoming. This part of the world had swayed rhythmically to the same seasonal forces for thousands of years. Even Theravada Buddhism itself, with its monsoon retreats and *kathina* (robes) ceremonies, ebbed and flowed with the rains.

The streets were completely empty. The first drops hit heavy on my face, and then the sky really opened up and the torrent pounded me all the way home.

Five

KARMA AND
THE KILLING FIELDS

Even though I lived within walking distance, it took months before I mustered enough courage to visit the infamous S-21. Pierrot, the Swiss owner of my guesthouse, told me that he still refused, after ten years in Phnom Penh, to visit the horrible building. After working for fifteen years in the Red Cross in places like Afghanistan and Rwanda, Pierrot explained, he'd seen enough suffering to last him a lifetime.

"You will not get me in that place, mon ami," he said. "It is the maker of bad dreams, and I wish to sleep well. Now, here is the cloves that I tell you about, no?" The Khmer cook, a young girl of substantial culinary talents, appeared from the kitchen with a handful of clove spices. Pierrot insisted that I clench the cloves between my aching gums. My impacted wisdom teeth had decided to make a painfully inconvenient commotion in the very dentistry-challenged Cambodia. My moto-dup friend Li assured me that his uncle had some dental tools, and he would be happy to work "cheap, cheap," but I wasn't even tempted by this frightening possibility. I bit down hard on the spiky little cloves and resolved to jump the border to Bangkok if the pain got unbearable.

Like Pierrot, I didn't want to go to Security Prison 21 either. I felt obligated to go, like one feels obligated to visit a Nazi concentration camp. I wasn't exactly sure what the moral duty here was, and I shrugged at my inability, even as a philosophy professor, to articulate my own ethical sentiments. Partly, I think I wanted to go as an act of honoring or acknowledging the thousands of victims who suffered so unimaginably. Memory takes on grave importance for those of us who don't have the consolation of faith in a higher justice. I wished that some being with an infinitely comprehensive mind could store and safeguard every nuance of every life that had unfolded, but in lieu of that omniscience, I guess I felt that I should do my own little part. Like the antimetaphysical Chinese Confucians, for example, I always felt a moral duty to preserve the memory of lost loved ones, because that is the only real immortality they can have.

But I think I also felt obligated to go because part of me believed in the view of human nature that one finds in *The Lord of the Flies*. Golding's famous Freudian tale of boys who sink into aggressive depravity without the ameliorating effect of civilization seemed like the only coherent way to explain most of the twentieth century. Contrary to more popular demonizing scapegoat theories, the *Flies* story shows us that bad things really are inside us all. The ethical challenge then is to prevent our own darker potential from becoming actualized. The way to do this is by taking our heads out of the sands of denial and facing the cautionary tales of history with unblinking resolve. Well, *some* blinking seems reasonable, I suppose.

Over and over again, however, one hears the same story of torturers, whether it's Nazis, Pinochet lackeys, American soldiers at Abu Ghraib, or Khmer Rouge teenagers at S-21—they were just "following orders." As lame as this seems, and before we dismiss these people as barbarians who bear no resemblance to us, we should remember Stanley Milgram's famous psychology test that resulted in the average American Joe Six-pack shocking victims with "lethal" doses of electricity simply because a guy in a white lab coat insisted that he do it. Milgram, you may recall, only thought up this test because he wanted to understand how so many average Germans could have been complicit in the Nazi horrors.

I suppose I obsess a little over what I would do if I were a test-subject in Milgram's famous study, or how I would act if I were told that these people under my guard are enemies of freedom and we must "pressure" them to give up information about their imminent terrorist plan. Or worse yet, what would I do if someone held a gun to my head and told me to cut someone else's throat? That's what happened at S-21, over and over again. I guess I felt that going to see it was part of my own ethical training. Perhaps, if I did the difficult work of imagining myself in the shoes of the tortured and the torturers, then I would be better prepared to do the right thing if and when, God forbid, such a challenge fell to me.

I walked the dirt back roads to the uneventful-looking compound S-21. It looked uneventful because before 1975 it was simply known as the Tuol Svay Prey High School. It was converted into Security Prison 21 by Pol Pot's security forces, and it became the central detention center for suspected enemies of Angkar, the mysterious and authoritative higher "organization" or "party" of the Khmer Rouge. Angkar, in the indoctrination propaganda of the time, became a looming, abstract Big Brother to the young boys who were essentially abducted into Khmer Rouge service. Khmer people grew to fear Angkar, to love Angkar, and to kill for Angkar. The Cambodian scholar John Marston points out that when "Angkar" was intoned in the many horrible commands and demands that the Khmer Rouge made on the general public and on themselves, sometimes it was used to imply a personified authority—like brother number one, Pol Pot—and sometimes it represented the patently false "will of the people." In either case, it usually allowed the perpetrator of torture or murder to escape responsibility for his actions and to assign it to some nebulous higher authority.

Brother number one, Pol Pot, argued that there had been five social classes in prerevolutionary Cambodia. These were feudalists, capitalists, bourgeoisie, workers, and peasants. Trying to eliminate what he saw as "social parasites," Pol Pot, and the Khmer Rouge, articulated a "Constitution of Democratic Kampuchea" in 1976 and in it reduced all classes to workers and peasants. King Sihanouk remembers that in 1975 he and the revolutionaries Khieu Samphan and Khieu Thirith visited Chinese premier Zhou En-lai, who warned Cambodians to develop their social revolution slowly. Cambodia should not make China's mistakes and "leap forward" without intermediate phases. But as Sihanouk remembers, the revolutionaries were smug and superior and suggested after the meeting that they would be the first nation to build a communist society without wasting time and energy on intermediate stages. The results of that arrogance were disastrous.

Standing outside the entrance, the yellow- and cream-colored walls seemed innocent enough, and the barbed wire didn't really hint at the building's ominous history because, after all, every other building in Phnom Penh had barbed wire on it. Apart from a handful of people, the place seemed relatively deserted. Some creepy-looking Khmer thug accosted me near the entrance and asked if I wanted to go get "some young pussy." Jesus Christ, I thought, I'm trying to brace myself to face the historical monstrosities of this former torture prison, and now I need to contend with other monsters hovering at the front gate. The look of disgust on my face sent the guy packing, and I made my way inside.

The Khmer Rouge converted this high school into a torture and interrogation compound shortly after taking control of Phnom Penh in 1975. By 1976, approximately 2,500 prisoners had passed through the bloody corridors of S-21, and each year that followed saw increasing numbers of tortured prisoners, until they totaled around 17,000 by 1979, when the Vietnamese army liberated Phnom Penh. When Vietnamese soldiers stormed S-21, they were horrified by the carnage they discovered. Only seven prisoners were found alive in the compound. No one else who entered S-21—*no one* out of 17,000 people—made it out alive.

There was a small receiving station just inside the main entry, and I stopped there to talk to a man smoking absently at the counter. After a casual exchange, I negotiated a guide to walk me through the prison. The man barked at a kid playing behind the station, and after a half-hour interim the kid returned with a woman who introduced herself as Ladin.

Ladin was a small woman in her thirties with a broad and somewhat sad face. She smiled and gestured for me to walk with her across a small field of dust and burnt grass. We were the only people moving through the compound. All the classrooms of this former high school had been converted into prison cells and torture chambers. Iron bars were installed over the windows and doors, and barbed wire snaked everywhere. On the ground floor, little brick cells had been fabricated to hold one prisoner each, with not even enough space to lie down. Larger rooms held hundreds of prisoners chained together, unable to move—starving, dehydrated, injured from interrogation torture, dying.

Ladin led me to one of the torture chambers. The floor had checkered tile, and the walls were mottled and dirty. A battered bed frame sat in the center of the room, and the shackles and chains sat on the bed. Underneath the bed was a huge dried stain of blood that had pooled there from countless victims. The room was left just as it had been found when S-21 finally fell in 1979. The last victim, tortured to death as the Vietnamese were entering Phnom Penh, was discovered here and photographed. The gruesome photo now hangs over the bed. It shows a mangled man lying in this bed before me, his head caved in, his throat slit, blood everywhere, a rooster standing on the body picking at the corpse. Feeling like I was going to throw up, I left the room quickly.

The phenomenon of this torture prison is a testament to human depravity, because the vast majority of the men, women, and children who were brought here had done absolutely nothing wrong and were as mystified by their imprisonment as you or I would be if someone dragged us out of bed tonight and charged us with bogus crimes. Hearsay, suspicion, and paranoia led the Khmer Rouge's Security Office, Central Committee, and minister of defense to descend violently upon innocent farmers, teachers, engineers, students, workers, and whole families, accusing them of being enemies of the revolution. The damaging agricultural policies of the early Khmer Rouge, inspired by Mao's Great Leap Forward, were disastrous, and they left tens of thousands of people starving, ill, and exhausted. People were being forced through Herculean manual labor efforts to re-create the countryside with new dams and expansive field plots, but it was too much too soon for a labor force that was already weak and famished. Pol Pot and Angkar interpreted this failure as a corruption and betrayal from within and set out on a paranoid witch hunt that resulted partly in the S-21 catastrophe. The frightening twisted logic of the institution began with forced confessions, which were usually just invented by the suffering torture victim, and then a list of other "counter-revolutionary" names were gathered from the tormented victim. These poor souls, accused of affiliation with the CIA, the KGB, or the Vietnamese, were then captured and put through the same frightening process. Torture included severe beating, electrocution, hanging suspensions, and rape.

As the prison filled up, the young soldiers—many of them just twelve-year-old boys under the direction of S-21 chief comrade Duch (a former mathematics teacher)—took the prisoners to an orchard outside Phnom Penh known as Choeung Ek, aka the Killing Fields. There they killed the prisoners by smashing their skulls with hoes or cutting their throats. They dumped thousands of bodies into mass graves, and I eventually went there to see the memorial glass monument containing thousands of human skulls. Imagine aggressive pubescent boys who've been ripped out of their homes at an early age ("cleansed" of their cultural and family principles), fed a steady diet of party-line suspicions, and then given weapons and impunity, and you have a pretty accurate sense of the Khmer Rouge's most violent branch.

Perhaps the most disturbing thing about walking through S-21 is the photo documentation of the victims. The Khmer Rouge kept meticulous records of those who passed through the facility. Filling the walls now are thousands and thousands of small black-and-white photos of prisoner "mug shots" taken by the Khmer Rouge when the frightened victim had just entered the prison camp. You can see terrible fear in many of their eyes. In some you can read resignation, in others confusion. Ladin, my guide, explained to me that none of these people survived S-21. I was looking at the last pictures taken of people just before they were tortured and killed. Many of them were women and children. Some photos were taken before torture and some afterward. One young boy's eyes pleaded with me, his face smashed, swollen, and bloody. My throat tightened. I felt the burning sensation in my nose and behind my eyes, and I gripped my forehead and couldn't stop my own tears.

I tried to compose myself, but then I realized that Ladin had quietly started to cry as well. I felt doubly awful that my lack of control had probably triggered her own memories, memories that usually stayed well below the surface. She explained to me that she was ten years old when the Khmer Rouge came to her home, forcibly removed her father and brother, and sent her to work in the fields from sunrise to sunset until she almost starved to death. She never saw her father and brother again and still has no knowledge of their fate. I wondered how on earth she could come to this wretched place day after day and offer "tours" of places and events that had shredded her own life. Perhaps, in walking these terrible hallways, there was some paradoxical therapeutic effect for her. I didn't understand it. Standing in the macabre gallery of near-death portraits, I didn't understand any of it.

I tried to distract us both a little bit by asking her about Buo Meng. While I was in Phnom Penh, an amazing revelation hit the front pages of the newspapers. Buo Meng, one of the seven survivors of S-21, reappeared in Phnom Penh after almost two decades. His appearance shocked most Cambodians because he was assumed to have died sometime in the late 1990s. He, like one of the other survivors, Vann Nath, was spared because he was an artist: the Khmer Rouge kept him alive to paint flattering propaganda images of Pol Pot. The infamous S-21 chief Duch told Buo Meng that if he did not make the portraits look like the photos of Pol Pot, he would be killed. Buo Meng, whose wife and children died at S-21, had now returned to the capital from Svay Rieng because he was irritated to read of his own "death" in an article and wanted to set the record straight and possibly participate in a future Khmer Rouge trial. Meng said, "If there is a trial, I want to be there as a witness. I want to tell the world about Pol Pot's crimes and the torture they inflicted on me. [The Khmer Rouge] must pay compensation. I still wonder why they killed our countrymen." He had not been able to come back to Phnom Penh earlier because he was too poor to make the trip from Svay Rieng, where he scratched out a living by painting Buddha pictures at a pagoda. Ladin told me that only three of the original seven survivors are still alive now, and she expressed hope that a UN-sponsored war crimes trial would finally bring justice before everyone was too old. Thirty years after the fact, Duch, the head of S-21, sits in jail awaiting trial for his crimes against humanity.

Most Cambodians today are doubtful that a war crimes trial will really bring justice unless it is conducted in a thoroughly independent fashion. The current government, Hun Sen's Cambodian People's Party, acts as if it saved the people from the Khmer Rouge, but a lot of Cambodians believe that an independent investigation would reveal that many former Khmer Rouge criminals are inside the higher ranks of the CPP. In addition, the lower-level former Khmer Rouge locals, men who acted viciously as Angkar soldiers, respond to their confrontational neighbors with claims that they too were victims, since they were forced into a kill-or-be-killed situation. Ladin and I discussed these issues through the remainder of the tour, and it helped, strangely, to give us (or at least me) a little abstract distance from the terrible images in front of us. As I was leaving, she told me that no matter what happens, karma will catch the Khmer Rouge offenders even if a tribunal does not.

Karma (Sanskrit), or kamma (Pali), is an increasingly popular idea in the West. It literally means "action," but it has come to mean all things to all people. Ten years ago only a handful of my American students had heard the term, but now almost all my students use the word freely to apply to every manner of kismet. Everything from finding a dollar on the street to cheating death in a car crash is chalked up to the rule of karma in their lives. In the West people use the word in a loose and informal way, but in Southeast Asia kamma is serious business, and it leads to radically different ways of thinking about success, luck, and misfortune.

Venerable monk Tep Vong, the current supreme patriarch of Mahanikay Buddhism, became rather controversial recently because of his obstinate opposition to monk voting, despite the fact that the Cambodian constitution grants monks the right to vote. In a lesser-known, albeit equally controversial, statement, he actually suggested in an interview with the Documentation Center of Cambodia that the Cambodian people may have deserved Pol Pot and the Khmer Rouge atrocities as karmic payback for previous sins. In this shocking statement, Tep Vong is only giving voice to a widely held belief in Southeast Asia. Kamma holds that your good actions create merit and are rewarded, whereas your evil actions come back to haunt you—even if they have to chase you through many lifetimes to catch you.

Tep Vong explains the far-reaching power of kamma when he tells an apocryphal story about one of the former lives of the Buddha. In the Theravada tradition, earlier incarnations of the Buddha are often referred to as a bodhisattva. (These adventures are chronicled in the Jataka Tales, located in the Khuddaka Nikaya.) Many generations before the Buddha was born as Gotama and became enlightened, he lived in a province where a demon terrorized the people. To help the people, the bodhisattva killed the demon. But before he slew the beast, the beast warned the bodhisattva that one day he would return to exact karmic revenge. Sure enough, thousands of years later, when the bodhisattva was finally born as Gotama the Buddha, the karma of killing caught up with him. Remember the parinibbana story of the Buddha's death, how he ate some tainted pork and died of food poisoning? Guess who it was that had been reborn as the diseased pig? The demon returned as the pig to exact his karmic payback. Of course, from a philosophical point of view, this story not only is bizarre but also violates fundamental Buddhist dhamma, like anatta (no-self) and the Enlightened One's freedom from kamma. In the Buddha's Sabbasava Sutta, for example, he clearly argues that you should transcend mental "cares and troubles" by avoiding questions like Did I exist in the past? What was I in the past? Shall I exist in the future? He says that these concerns will give rise to the "false view" that you have a permanent self, or even the skeptical obsession with the idea that you don't have a self. Either way, Buddha calls it a jungle of binding, imprisoning views. But Tep Vong's story still conveys the gist of popular or folk Theravada.

Tep Vong admitted that isolating the precise kamma causal chains is never an exact science, even for the supreme patriarch. When the interviewer, San Kalyann of the Documentation Center, asked Tep Vong if the millions of people who died during the Khmer Rouge genocide had bad karma from their previous lives, the patriarch replied, "I am not sure about this. If it was not Pol Pot's evil deeds, it was our sin of bad deeds we had done from our previous lives. You and I had sin," Tep Vong told the interviewer, "but ours were minor. That's why we survived."

I really recoiled from this notion when I first read it. It seemed like a pernicious case of "blaming the victim." I couldn't imagine a prominent Jewish rabbi, for example, telling his people that the victims of the Holocaust had somehow *deserved* their fate.

Tep Vong had combined two philosophically distinct ideas in the same way that most Southeast Asians combine them. The doctrine of kamma is logically distinct from samsara (the cycle of rebirth or transmigration), even though they are often linked in people's heads. Before the Buddha articulated his unique idea of kamma, there were similar ideas floating around India. In mainstream Hinduism, karma usually meant "action in accordance with law (dharma)," and it was more like legalistic adherence to the Brahmin rules of ritual sacrifice and social caste. The Buddha rejected not only this notion but also the more dramatic version of karma offered by the Jains. Jainism interpreted karma very literally as "all action"; they came to believe that the holiest life is one in which a person manages to do almost nothing. Since action of any kind only creates more karma chains, they argued, it would be best to practice extreme asceticism, and like the patron saint of Jains, Mahavira, one should strive to pass out of existence without causing any ripples of future causality. Rejecting this idea, the Buddha gives us a typical Middle Way redefinition of karma, arguing that its binding causal power applies only to those actions that stem from our conscious intentions. In this way, the Buddha rescues the idea of karma from the overly legalistic and external notion of Brahministic duty and also steers us away from the extreme Jain alternative of karma binding *every* activity. Strictly speaking, only actions based on our *choices* can give rise to karma, not accidental actions or those flowing from physical laws. In the language of Buddhist metaphysics, karma flows only from the sankhara, or volitional, part of our five khandas (the aggregates of our personhood).

Samsara, which literally translates as "wandering on" over lifetimes, is a logically distinct idea, but it usually gets mixed up with karma because people wish to extend karma over many lifetimes. This is Tep Vong's move, for example, when he tries to link Killing Fields suffering to some unobservable past transgression.

Most people have come to think of reincarnation in pretty much the same way: my essence or my soul or personality has lived through many lifetimes, and I have a shadowy sense of some of these incarnations (usually famous historical personalities like Cleopatra or Mozart). This parody–like model is more Hindu than Buddhist, but Eastern folk religions (and Western New Agers) have painted it all with the same brush. And I suppose that the atman of Hinduism makes intuitive sense when thinking about reincarnation, because this permanent soul can do the actual time-travel through history. Atman, or soul, conveniently provides the continuity when everything else (matter, time, place) has changed.

In the Hindu Katha Upanishad scripture, a famous simile illustrates the relationship between the soul and its earthly vessel. It is not the simple Western mind-body split that one finds after Descartes. Rather, it asks us to imagine a horse-drawn chariot. The chariot represents our physical body, and the chariot driver is symbolic of our intellect, which has hold of the reins. The reins, representing our mind, are connected to the horses, which stand for the senses. Finally, the rider and owner of the chariot, sitting relaxed behind the charioteer, is the symbol of atman— the soul within us. Samsara happens when the soul gets out of one broken-down chariot and finds a new one. Atman is the god within you, according to Hinduism. But since atman, the chariot owner, is supposed to be pure and permanent, like an unscratchable diamond in a dung heap, it's hard to see how karma would ever arise from it or stick to it. Atman is the ultimate Teflon. For that matter, it's hard to see how any personal history would be remembered by your atman in the next life, because the mind, the senses, the intellect, and the body are all discarded at death. The Buddha couldn't make sense of it either, which is why he dumped the whole idea (more on that later).

Not only do I find it hard to believe in this cartoon kind of reincarnation, but I find it hard to believe that other people believe in it. Of course, it wouldn't be the first time I failed to fathom my fellow human beings. Still, the simplest empirical test of samsara always strikes me as appropriate, and yet no one ever tries it. If I thought I was a soul moving through many lifetimes, I'd do two things. First, I'd mark a giant tree or some other long-lasting monument with something like "Steve was here in 1810." Then I could go back to it in a later lifetime and at least know for sure that reincarnation is true. Second, I'd leave some serious notes to myself, maybe some sort of life-manual of lessons learned, or at the very least some gold. I could bury it as a time capsule to myself. Come to think of it, I don't know why everybody hasn't done this simple act of Self-help. Okay, I'm being facetious here (or I'm demonstrating how far away from enlightenment I really am), but the point is that these types of simple evidentiary tests are uninteresting to the true believers. People who believe in reincarnation tend to brush away issues of proof and verification. Some spiritualists brush off scientific skepticism because they think that doubt or the need for experiment will itself ruin the spirit effect—like the ghost won't appear if he sees that you've set up measurement equipment, or Jesus won't heal you if you test the holy water. So perhaps if I marked a tree with "Steve was here," I'd actually ensure failure because atman won't play that kind of game with arrogant punks like me. This seems like such an adolescent sort of spiritualism, wherein the "hidden world" will choose to stay hidden unless you grovel first, that I find it difficult to get on board.

Others reject my empirical attitude toward metaphysical issues like samsara as a matter of principle, saying that empirical testing is methodologically oriented toward the measurable material world and spiritual issues are by definition incapable of sensory detection. This is a markedly Western way of thinking and only arose with force after the Scientific Revolution. At least this position sounds more sophisticated. But on closer examination, these people don't really stick to their pretended distinction between the phenomenal and the noumenal worlds, and they end up saying something like: spiritual reality *can* be *experienced* at certain times (in the answered prayer, in the cured cancer, in the oceanic feeling), but just *not* when you want to *test* it. Stated in that way, it doesn't sound any more sophisticated than the previous position.

The more important reason, I suppose, why believers aren't running simple empirical proofs for metaphysical claims like samsara is that they don't think it's important. People who believe that they've been here before and will be here again and that their actions matter to the ultimate meaning of things tend to see the whole universe in anthropomorphic terms. They use the human heart as the template for understanding the cosmos itself, whereas the science-minded skeptic sees the human heart as just one more object at work in a neutral universe. Skeptics tend to live in a staggeringly immense universe in which their very existence (indeed life itself) was a lucky accident, but the believer lives in a much more intimate (almost pre-Copernican) universe. If you already see life in terms of a cosmic drama wherein good and evil struggle for ascendancy, or justice ultimately prevails, or souls "train" over many lifetimes, then subjecting any of that stuff to objective testing seems utterly beside the point. Adopting an objective scientific outlook is already expunging the subjective drama out of the center of reality and treating humans as other objects in a value-neutral cosmos; the believer has no interest in adopting this viewpoint.

Some Buddhists want it both ways with regard to samsara. For example, many Tibetan Buddhists put great stock in Lama litmus tests. A group of incarnation candidates are lined up and asked to pick out begging bowls (or other objects) from their previous incarnations. In this way, a young kid proves that he was indeed the Lama in a previous life. The current Dalai Lama, for example, was "recognized" by elder monks when he was only two years old as a reincarnation of the Thirteenth Lama because he successfully picked out the correct walking stick and drum. I suppose this kind of testing is like my little tree-marking experiment. As such, the testing of spiritual claims brings the metaphysical reality under the umbrella of experiential and negotiable physical reality. For folk religions this is where it has always resided anyway, because, as a prescientific way of thinking, folk religion is not *opposed* to science but rather is a primordial version of it.

The believer in reincarnation is sure to make a big deal of these kids who pick out prayer wheels and begging bowls as evidence of preexistence. And seeing as how I'm open to the tree-marking test, I should be more impressed by this "evidence" of samsara. In truth, I'm so doggedly incredulous that I'd probably see my own tree message to myself from the distant past and chalk it up to a trick or misinterpretation. I guess, for me, samsara seems like an extraordinary phenomenon that, like other extraordinary phenomena, requires extra-ordinary evidence. A kid picking out a begging bowl just doesn't do it for me. I guess I'm wary of things that become "unknowably mysterious" when you inspect them further. But having said all that, what was I to make of the metaphysics of karma generally and the idea, espoused by Tep Vong, that the Khmer people may have somehow *deserved* the Khmer Rouge atrocities?

My student Samphors was working on a master's thesis about the way in which Khmer Buddhists apply karma concepts to the escalating health crises caused by AIDS in Southeast Asia. She interviewed monks, NGO workers, infected men and women, and general laypeople in order to understand the way Theravadans apply karma to this devastating disease. She discovered that karma is used in a variety of ways. Most Buddhists see HIV infection as a consequence or bad fruit of violating one of the Five Precepts—in this case, sexual misconduct. Many Buddhists do not conceptualize "getting infected" as a case of bad luck with an efficient, self-replicating virus. They see it as karmic justice first, and a biological phenomenon second.

As usual, the archconservative patriarch Tep Vong has offered the dogmatic position by dissuading the sangha from working to prevent HIV infections or care for people with AIDS. He said, "If we help sick people, then we will only encourage them not to be afraid of catching the virus. . . . It is the mistake of the people who get AIDS. . . . They do not have good morals. Everyone should unite and punish the people who have lost their good morals." Tep Vong here seems very far indeed from the goal of Buddhist compassion. Karma is invoked by Tep Vong, but also by more kindhearted Buddhists, as a cautionary tale to promote abstinence and monogamy among those who are not infected. By linking HIV to "immoral behaviors" through the Buddhist law of cause and effect, people are able to take responsibility for their future decisions and the inevitable outcomes without giving over to rigid fatalism. But for those who are already infected, karma functions in a different manner.

For infected people, karma offers a way to resign oneself to a reality that cannot be undone. I suppose there's some Spinoza–like comfort in recognizing your own particular human bondage once you're sufficiently bound by it. Perhaps the saddest victims of the growing AIDS crisis are the faithful wives who contract it from their idiot husbands who visit brothels without using condoms. Samphors discovered that these husbands and wives understand their karma in different ways. The men clearly identify their own actions at the brothel as the karma that produced bad fruits, HIV in this case. The women, who rightly blame their husbands to varying degrees, nonetheless apply the law of karma to themselves and, failing to find misdeeds in *this* life, assume that they must have sinned greatly in a past life in order to justify this great punishment.

The idea of karma has distinct psychological uses and shouldn't be scoffed at. But its dangerous side must be acknowledged as well. Since many Southeast Asians perceive their diseases and ailments as the fruits of karma (in this life or a previous one), they sometimes adopt a fatalistic attitude and do not trust or pursue medical treatments for themselves. Most people are more balanced and take a pluralistic approach, making merit for atonement but also getting conventional medical treatment. The true believer in karma, similar to the Western theist, sees things like biological viruses as the tools or instruments or means by which justice gets worked out in the cosmos, whereas someone like me thinks that all this may be only a fallacy of *post hoc ergo propter hoc* (*after* this, therefore *because* of this). In other words, true believers in karma usually find a way to interpret *coincidences* as *causes*.

A couple of years ago, for example, while walking down the street on my way to work, a small but heavy piece of brick fell off the building I was passing by and narrowly missed my head. When I arrived at work and laughingly told of my near-miss, my true-believer friend said that it was certainly "karma," and he wasn't being metaphorical. When I quizzed him, he couldn't really say whether it was good karma (because I had been spared) or bad karma (since I had been frightened); he finally settled on something like "it was a sign." He, like other true believers, saw causes where I saw coincidences. The only "sign" I could read in this event was that I should walk on the opposite side of the street from the dilapidated building. Taking his suggestion seriously, though, I tried to imagine what *cause* (besides bad masonry) could be responsible for this "karmic" effect. I felt that if it had happened to my true-believing friend, he would quickly and positively identify some karmic culprit of his own previous actions, but I feared then and fear now that this sort of causal chain identification is a purely subjective overinterpretation of one's experience—sort of like seeing a "dog" or a "quiche" or "Jesus" in a cloud passing overhead. Let's say it was a good fruit of karma, for example, because I had been spared the nasty hit. When I thought back over the preceding few days, I, like most people, could name several good deeds but also an equal number of bad ones. How could I narrow down the options? And since karma can be either instant or delayed, how can I narrow the search down from the totality of my life or even many lifetimes? Could I have given a crust of bread to a beggar in 1640 and ended up being spared a brick to my head in 2003?

This sort of analysis may seem tedious, but the point can only be made by showing the infinite possibilities of karma interpretation. If someone tells me that an event in my life is the result of karma and the result of a specific previous moral action, but that the specific action is one of millions of possible contenders and it is impossible to know which one matters, then that person hasn't really offered any kind of meaningful explanation.

But here's where the rational mind has to relax its interest in "proving" predictions and explanations. Karma is intentionally general rather than specific because it's an attempt to get people to *behave* well. And it has the same effect or even a stronger effect if you *can't* predict or specifically identify which causal chain connects events, because then you have to err on the side of caution. Since you never know when or where the payback is coming, you better make every current action as pure as you can in order to ensure future safety.

A few days after my disturbing visit to S-21, I was relaxing on the terrace of my guesthouse, preparing my lectures and noodling occasionally on an old guitar, when one of the doors was flung open and a new intense face appeared.

"Hey, man, that's fucking Elmore James!" he shouted at me. "Fucking brilliant, man, I couldn't believe it. I'm layin' here in my bed, tryin' to sweat out the siesta, and suddenly I hear Elmore James riffs outside my window. Goddammit, Phnom Penh is such a trip, man. I'm Chaminda, what's your name?"

Chaminda and I made fast friends that afternoon, swapping the guitar back and forth and chatting about Chicago, Texas, and Delta blues music. Slowly, I began to get some picture of him. He worked as an ecological economist for a conservation NGO based in Bangkok, and before that he was teaching something in South Africa. He was a dark Sri Lankan mystery of a man who seemed to have lived everywhere for a short time—which was all the more surprising since he seemed, like me, to be only in his midthirties. In fact, the more time we spent together, the more enigmatic and unfamiliar Chaminda became to me. He seemed to understand his own unique complexity and subsequently only parceled himself out in small doses to strangers like me. The consequence of this guarded presentation was that every time I thought I knew where he was coming from, he would drop some story on me that forced me to revise everything.

"So, what's a white boy like you doing in Phnom Penh, Cambodia?" he asked me on that first afternoon. "Looking at you, I'd first guess Christian missionary, but then I hear you playin' the devil's music on guitar," he laughed, "and now I don't know what to make of you." I realized over time that I was as puzzling to him as he was to me. I told him I came to Cambodia to teach and study Buddhism.

"Oh no! C'mon, get the fuck outta here. Wait, wait, let me guess." He mocked, "You're, like, really into the Dalai Lama, right? And like, you started reading his deep and moving books after you saw the Beastie Boys talkin' about him at a hip-hop show? And you have a 'Free Tibet' bumper sticker, right? And let's see, you definitely have your own prayer beads, right?"

"Wrong on every count, my friend," I coolly answered his blast of sarcasm.

"Really?" He looked incredulous but newly intrigued to find someone who did not fit the stereotype. "God, that's a relief, man. I meet so many of these cookie-cutter Buddhist wannabes from the States and Europe and Australia, and they're all so fuckin' clueless, man. I should have known you were different, brother—you don't have that deer-in-the-headlights ashram stare." This seemed as close to a compliment as I was going to get, so I took it accordingly.

I too, in my Asian travels, had encountered many of the hapless wannabe creatures that Chaminda described, but he was forthright in his loathing. As a Buddhist "insider," he was not as uncritically gullible about his own cultural heritage as we "outsider" Western neophytes tend to be. He reminded me of my Japanese college buddy Jun, who took me to a Pure Land Buddhist temple in Chicago once when I was a wide-eyed greenhorn. After the ceremony, we met the head monk at a tea social hour. I was very keen to connect with the whole scene, but for Jun none of this was exotic; he indulged my excitement, but was hoping to get back in time for a softball game. Mostly, Jun went to temple because his mom kept after him to find a nice Japanese girl to marry. I asked the head monk at one point how I should understand the Pure Land pursuit of heavenly paradise and *Amitabha* (the deification of Buddha) when the original teachings of the Buddha seemed so different. He grew quiet and reflective. Then he offered, in a soft voice, "Well, my friend, how does the butterfly understand its movement from one flower to the next?" This was followed by a long silence, and I nodded my head slowly, taking in the morsel of enigmatic deep wisdom. Then my friend Jun rolled his eyes and demanded of the monk, "What the *hell* does that mean?" And for me this was one of those Zen moments of clarity. The monk became flustered and attempted more evasion but ultimately found some pretext to move on. I could see that while Jun had made things a little awkward, he was fundamentally right to ask for explanation. Asking for more explanation and clarity is one of the things that Westerners are afraid to do regarding Eastern thought, and it frequently leads them to fawn over the emperor's new clothes. But in my experience, Asians themselves are not afraid because they know their traditions are rich and profound and insightfully responsive to tough questions. That's how Chaminda saw things too.

As a highly educated Sri Lankan man who had also lived and studied in the West, Chaminda had a unique perspective on East-West spiritual yearning. Moreover, he turned out to be astoundingly well trained in Buddhist philosophy—one of those dimensions of himself that he guardedly revealed little by little.

"That shit isn't Buddhism," he said with impatience.

"You mean," I asked, "the Richard Gere–type neophytes are just bandwagoners on the latest fad, right? Like the Madonna-inspired Kabbalah craze?"

"Oh yeah, that goes without sayin', man. I mean, Gucci is now selling a yoga mat for $350—it boggles the fuckin' mind. No, I mean that Tibetan shit isn't Buddhism.

"Everybody in the West thinks of that Lama nonsense when they think of Buddhism, and it's totally ridiculous for those of us who actually grew up as Buddhists. I mean, imagine if you came to Asia and everybody thought that Christianity was just Mormonism! Vajrayana [Tibetan Buddhism] is every bit as small and as idiosyncratic and as marginal as Mormonism in the West—or maybe the fuckin' Amish!

"And did you know that dozens of these Tibetan rinpoches are touring the developed world and offering little magical ceremonies for meditation groups? Bourgeois Buddhists in the States are eating this stuff up. Wealthy wives of stiff-necked company men are holding modern-day séances and lavishing donations on monks who claim to offer "empowerment blessings" that give special powers to devotees. These Tibetan monks advertise that their blessings will remove sickness, increase prosperity, and overcome all obstacles. Can you imagine? And these snake-oil salesmen have the gall to call themselves Buddhists!"

Chaminda grew more animated and passionate as he articulated these long-standing injuries. He explained that Vajrayana Buddhism and Tantrayana Buddhism were much later developments within the Mahayana school (about a thousand years after Gotama's death), and they represented magic-based corruptions of the real teachings. Tibetan beliefs make up only 6 percent of the worldwide dharma pie, yet Westerners mistakenly see this small slice as paradigmatic. I already knew this stuff, but I let him get it all off his chest.

"The thing that really burns my ass," Chaminda continued, "is when some California twit prats on to me about *The Tibetan Book of the Dead*— a book that is so far away from the Buddha's teachings that you might as well call the Torah a Buddhist tract. I mean, here's a Tibetan system of beliefs that focuses on the *bardo* planes of existence, where your soul travels after your death and before your reincarnation, and it's precisely this sort of speculative garbage that the Buddha warned against when he called off those unanswerable investigations [avyakata]!"

I had to admit that hearing Chaminda say this with such conviction (which is sort of how he said everything) was a little reassuring to me. I didn't entirely share his views on Vajrayana, but I felt better about what I had told my student Hokmeng concerning ghosts. I felt a little vindicated to hear Chaminda also go on to denounce speculative metaphysics as anathema to Buddha's teachings. And his rant spilled over into a compelling diatribe about "those mantra-chanting Soka Gakkai twits" who keep giving Buddhism "a bad name" by linking it to "childish chanting for gain." The Soka Gakkai sect, which was started in Japan but flourishes in the States, recommends chanting *Nam-myoho-renge-kyo* ("reverence to the wonderful law of the Lotus") as a magical panacea for everything. Chaminda said that if he didn't know anything about Buddhism and he met a Soka Gakkai or a Vajrayana devotee, he'd definitely write Buddhism off as a quack religion. I could see that he was genuinely hurt by the confusion, because for him Buddhism was, and is, his motherland. Sri Lanka is like the "Rome" of Theravada Buddhism. It was the landing place of Asoka's third-century B.C.E. southern envoy, and it has remained the citadel of Theravada orthodoxy ever since.

"Look," he said, winding down a little from his tirade, "the problem with these silly sects that masquerade as Buddhism is that they're not just confused—that would only make them humorous and harmless. No, they're actually contrary to the dhamma—they are actually the same craving errors that the teachings are trying to overcome. That's what makes them fucking dangerous. The Tripitika is very clear, man. Magic is for the weak and the manipulative and should be avoided, yet here are these bullshit sects offering magical spells, totems, and demigods. Specu-lations about the afterlife are dead-end mind-games, and here are these sects offering 'authoritative' accounts about it. And speaking of authority, the Buddha gives us an egalitarian philosophy that rejects oppressive priests, and here are these pop sects making everybody grovel to sancti-monious gurus. The Dalai Lama, who the Americans think is a benign little man, requires the Tibetan people to treat him like God on earth. Tibet under the Lamas was a master-slave society, man, but the West has re-created it in their minds as a spiritual paradise. Shangri-La, my ass!"

When I thought he was all through, he suddenly burst the empty moment with one last flourish.

"Worst of all, these faux Buddhisms have all gone back to the atman idea that Buddha tried so desperately to get rid of." Here I felt solidarity with him, despite his purple style. "They're always talking about reincar-nation and the soul and paradise, and all that crap that anatta is designed to overcome."

I tried to tell him about my credibility problem regarding samsara reincarnation. I thought, here is a highly metaphysical and speculative belief right at the core of mainstream Theravada—where it would not be so easy for Chaminda to dismiss the devotees as faux Buddhists. But before I could broach the topic, my toothache soared suddenly to excru-ciating heights. The chronic dull throb crescendoed without warning, and I pathetically crammed cloves into place.

"Jesus, man, you look awful," Chaminda observed. After a minute, he added, "I have just the thing for you, my boy! What are you doing tonight for dinner?"

"No plans," I said, gingerly massaging my jaw and wondering if I'd be able to eat anything at all. He gave me an address along the riverfront and asked me to meet him there at 7:00 P.M. With that, he was off, and I was left holding my head and wondering about the Dalai Lama.

That night I walked casually along Sothearos Boulevard past the Royal Palace, then turned east along Phlauv 178 and ended up at Happy Herb's pizza restaurant. This was prime expat territory, where grizzled, long-time émigrés mixed with young backpackers to get a little taste of the familiar. Chaminda had not yet arrived, so I pulled up a curbside table and watched the busy street action. Moto drivers swarmed at the mouths of all the restaurants in this area, and they vied with each other for passengers. Once you've lived here long enough, you learn how to bait them into a bidding war and drive down the price of your ride. This part of town was the big money. A moto-dup could earn as much in one night working this area (between four and seven dollars) as his counterpart could in a week of more rural taxi work.

I ordered a coffee and watched a group of moto drivers jockey for strategic position. A little boy came up to me and set a carved flute on my table, then he played a short atonal melody for me and suggested that I buy a flute. This pitch happened every five minutes when I was up north near the Angkor ruins. Eventually one grows desensitized to the constant assault for cash and looks for standout stories or personalities to reward. I told the boy that I already bought three of these flutes the week before, which was true, but that didn't seem like a sufficient excuse to him. He was so young, maybe only five years old. After a good-humored exchange, he finally said to me, "You buy from other peoples. Okay, okay, but you not buy from *me* yet, mistah! And look, look, you have the long hair, and I have the long hairs too, so . . . must buy from me now!" Well, I admitted to him that his logic was truly unassailable, and I forked over a dollar.

These grifter kids were some of the shrewdest people I ever met, and their appeals were always made with humor and panache. A few weeks before I had a hilarious negotiation in Saigon, for example, with a six-year-old hard-sell merchant girl. She followed me around in front of the Continental Hotel, where Graham Greene and Somerset Maugham stayed. I was listening to a string quartet across the street playing a fantastic version of the *Mission Impossible* theme song. Adding to this surrealism, the little girl kept trying to sell me a bootlegged copy of Greene's novel *The Quiet American*, but I told her that I'd already read it. She said, in surprisingly perfect English, "Oh really? Well, if you've read it, then you can tell me what happens, right?" So I offered a half-baked plot summary, but she remained unimpressed. I was standing with her, scratching my head and trying to remember the story line, amused that her sales pitch to me was a quiz. Finally, exasperated, she asked me, "Okay, what was the female character's name?" And I surprised myself when I shot back "Phuong." Ha, the little girl was defeated! But of course her charm had worked on me and I bought some gum from her anyway.

Chaminda arrived regally in the chair of a dilapidated cyclo, with an old driver puffing behind him in a wide-brimmed straw hat. He explained to me that Happy Herb's Pizza was an institution in Phnom Penh. It served specialty pizzas with marijuana as the not-so-secret ingredient. Against my better judgment, Chaminda convinced me that my toothache condition warranted an "extra happy" pizza, and he ordered accordingly. We sat in the open air, enjoying the street theater and talking about music and books mostly. He told me about an interesting novel he'd just read about a Hindu boy who gets trapped in a lifeboat with a Bengali tiger. I laughed at the strange synchronicity and told him that I'd chanced to have dinner recently, down the street, with the author of this very book, Yann Martel. I confessed sheepishly that I'd had a little too much to drink and that I'd told Yann that his religious ideas were "infantile." But, thankfully, he'd taken my critique in the best possible way. Or at least that's how I remembered it.

Our "extra happy" pizza arrived, and I chewed very carefully to avoid my tender gums. I decided to raise some Buddhist issues before we were too blitzed to discuss them properly. I told Chaminda about Venerable Tep Vong's claim that the Khmer people had brought Pol Pot's atrocities upon themselves as the fruits of bad karma from previous lives. Here was an example of mainstream Theravada metaphysics, and I wondered if Chaminda was orthodox about this highly speculative theory or not. He turned out to be as critically analytical about his own Buddhist tradition as he was about Mahayana.

"No," he said, in between bites, "that sounds like rubbish to me, man. I don't care if it was Tep Vong who said it or Peter Pan. Did you know that the Khmer Rouge used to make mothers watch as they tortured their children? And someone is gonna say that the mother and the child somehow deserved *that*?! I don't see how that fatalistic explanation helps. Isn't it bad enough that you have to witness the torture of your loved ones? Now you have to feel personally responsible and guilty for it too? I'm not havin' it, man."

"What Cambodians need," he went on, "is a good strong dose of Buddhadasa Bhikkhu. And they can tell Tep Vong to take a hike."

Chaminda went on to tell me about the most famous reformer in modern Theravada Buddhism, a Thai monk named Buddhadasa Bhikkhu (1906–93). Buddhadasa was, and is, hugely influential in Southeast Asian Buddhism, but he remains virtually unknown in the West. Forging a Middle Way between the hyper-scholastic Buddhism of the Theravada patriarch Buddhaghosa (fifth century C.E.) and the micromanaged monastic life of ritualistic practice, Buddhadasa sought to reclaim the lost heartwood of the dhamma. To do this, he relocated the scholarly philosophical activity of Buddhism to the Thai forests, so that the flights of intellectualism would always be revitalized and rectified by close contact with nature. And at a time when Buddhist education was becoming nationalized and standardized in Thailand (elaborate sequencing of Pali exams, and so on), Buddhadasa reemphasized the importance of vipassana (insight) meditation.

In 1932 Buddhadasa founded an innovative new center of dhamma learning and practice called Suan Mokkh ("Garden of Liberation") in southern Thailand. Here he studied the Pali Tripitika, wrote tracts, offered lectures, began publishing a Buddhist journal, meditated intensely, and eventually found himself surrounded by other reform-minded monks, lay practitioners, social activists, and scholars. He created a powerful sangha (community) that still exists, outside Surat Thani, Thailand. Chaminda had done several intensive meditation retreats at Suan Mokkh and knew the reform movement from the inside. The retreats, offered at the beginning of each month, are so difficult and demanding that half of those who begin the ten-day stint never make it to the end. Chaminda said that the New Agers are always gone after two days of severe contemplation. And some of the hippie neophytes pester the monks during the evening dhamma talks with questions like, "So, dude, like when do we start to get the special powers, and when do we start to levitate?"

Feeling that contemporary Theravada Buddhism had strayed from its roots, Buddhadasa set about to show the relevance of dhamma to the unique challenges of modern life. In the middle of the twentieth century, modernization in Southeast Asia was suddenly racing forward and changing the cultural landscape. Political, economic, educational, and social frameworks were evolving rapidly, and Buddhadasa believed that the essential teachings of the Buddha could heal the growing selfishness and materialism that he perceived to be on the rise.

Three major forces had led people away from the restorative powers of Theravada Buddhism. One was the age-old superstitious tendencies of pre-Buddhist animism. (Mischievous spirits run rampant in the Thai psyche.) A second was the effete scholasticism of academic monks who had deemphasized the emancipatory power of the dhamma in favor of the intellectual games of cosmology and metaphysics. And the third force was the confusion of authentic Buddhist ideas with pre-Buddhist Hindu ideas. What was needed, according to Buddhadasa, was a return to the Four Noble Truths and a return to the three fundamentals of the dhamma: anatta (no-self), anicca (impermanence), and paticca samuppada (dependent arising or causality). Everything else could be purged from Buddhism, and this more focused dhamma, trained on rooting out tanha (craving), could more effectively bring peace at the personal and social levels.

One of the most important things to purge from Buddhism, according to Buddhadasa, was the belief in samsara. This bold reform seems heretical at first, because almost all Buddhists you meet in Southeast Asia are extremely concerned with their past and future lives. But while this concern is very widespread, it is not, according to Buddhadasa, a helpful preoccupation. In his book *Me and Mine*, Buddhadasa says, "As for reincarnation, it does not exist in Buddhist teachings, or rather it is not a

truly Buddhist doctrine, because it is coupled with the doctrine of
kamma which predated the period of the Upanishads." He reiterates the
widespread belief that an eternal soul cruises through the cycle of birth
and death and then points out bluntly,

> It is absurd to say that this is a Buddhist doctrine. The Buddha's en-
> lightenment was the discovery that, in truth, there is no such thing as a
> person or self; that there is simply the arising in the mind of ignorance
> and attachment which leads to the false assumption that there is a self;
> and that birth and death pertain to this "self" alone. This assumption
> creates enormous problems and leads only to suffering. To spread the
> Buddha's teachings, then, is to spread the truth that there is no such
> thing as "me" or "mine." When this truth is entered into, the problems of
> birth, age, illness, death, and samsara will immediately end.

Many Southeast Asians see the idea of enlightenment or full liberation as something that only happens after many lifetimes. While it
remains the ultimate goal, laypeople see themselves as rather far away
from nibbana, so they focus on merit-making bribes in order to ensure a
good rebirth. This, according to Buddhadasa, is just bad Buddhism.

Under Buddhadasa's fearless scrutiny, the time-honored idea of
karma also takes it on the chin, so to speak. Again, he points out, the idea
of "do good receive good, do evil receive evil" is a much older idea than
Buddhism and should be thought of more as cultural baggage in the
Buddha's discourses than as essential doctrine. There are references to
karma in the Sutta Pitaka, but, according to Buddhadasa, the Buddha
mentions it only to show how one can use the dhamma to overcome
karma—to rise above praise, blame, good, and evil. Eliminating ego-
consciousness (through mindful detachment) eradicates the self-interest
that one has in both "righteous" and noncompassionate actions. In this
way, all fruits of karma, whether good or bad, are transcended. Buddhadasa says, "This, then, is the true Buddhist doctrine concerning
kamma, because the aim of Buddhism is to help free human beings from
bondage to kamma."

Chaminda explained that Buddhadasa's main emphasis was to stop the obsessions with past and future lives and the constant fixation on merit-making behaviors and instead to get back to the crucial problem of human life, namely dukkha (suffering). The Western scholar Donald Swearer, a student of Buddhadasa's, amplifies this point when he says,

> Buddhadasa sees the preoccupation of popular Buddhist practice with merit-making (Thai: *tham pun*) to gain material benefits as a refutation of the central Buddhist teaching of non-attachment. He contends that the figure of the Buddha has become, in effect, a wish-fulfilling deity, instead of the teacher whose dhamma provides a "raft" to gain "the further shore" (nibbana). He challenges both monks and laity to a more serious study and practice of the Buddha's path to enlightenment rather than reducing it into a magical means of self-aggrandizement.

"The way I see it," Chaminda offered, "is that you don't have to believe in reincarnation, or even karma, to be a true Buddhist. I know that's shocking for some people, man, but look at the core ideas that Buddhadasa is talking about. If the basic point of Buddhism is to overcome suffering and the way to that is through non-attachment, then how do ideas like karma and samsara help? Those ideas are just leftovers from earlier attempts to make people act morally toward each other. They're not much different from Western heaven and hell!"

Maybe the happy pizza was starting to kick in, but it occurred to me that you could keep some notion of karma and samsara in Buddhism (expunging it seemed like a Sisyphean task), but reinterpret it symbolically rather than literally. Moving from literal to symbolic understanding of a scripture is an old story in the West. Even Pope John Paul II articulated this point when he said in his famous pro-evolution encyclical that the Bible is not about how the heavens were made, but about how to get to heaven. Unlike fundamentalist Christians, Catholics read Genesis as a symbolic work. Similarly, a Buddhist could reinterpret the idea that one's previous selves create the realities of one's consequent selves in a naturalistic way. The Asian scholar Herbert Fingarette has gone so far as to suggest that this way of thinking of reincarnation and karma is not very different from the psychoanalytic tradition of seeing one's previous experiences as "parenting" one's later psyche. With this model, you can think of the multiple "selves" and multiple "lives" as unfolding entirely within the span of this lifetime. Good karma, then, means acting well so as to ensure a healthy psyche in the years to come (the fruits of karma).

Chaminda and I worked on this new philosophical angle while we devoured copious amounts of doped pizza. I pressed him on this symbolic interpretive move, applying it in a scattershot way to other dhamma issues, and he served as a thresher to separate out my sense from my nonsense. Just as in the West, where intellectual believers have symbolically reinterpreted Bible doctrines to avoid absurdities, so too Buddhism could synthesize its own conflicted dhamma by focusing on the core (the Four Noble Truths, and so on) and treating other issues, like samsara, as purely figurative. Just as a creation "day" doesn't really mean a twenty-four-hour period in the Book of Genesis, so too a Buddhist "previous life" doesn't really mean "before you were physically born." And just as the body of Jesus isn't literally *in* the communion cracker, so too my bad luck isn't really the result of the sins of my previous incarnation. Once I got Chaminda to concede this point, it seemed possible to temper some of his earlier critiques of Vajrayana and Mahayana Buddhism.

It is true that Tibetan Buddhism is heavily populated with deities, spirits, and wish-granting bodhisattvas, but if we make this turn toward symbolic interpretation, then we do not run counter to the Buddha's antimetaphysical dhamma. Sure enough, some Tantric Buddhists use the vital imagery of bodhisattvas not as *wish-granting beings* for prayer, but as *meditational devices* designed to bring the practitioner to greater ego annihilation. The practitioner doesn't think of the Buddha image as a deity but as a tool for focusing meditation, and the point of the meditation, residing squarely inside the heartwood of dhamma, is to overcome the self.

Since I felt like I was on a roll, I pushed on and suggested that in shifting from a literal to a symbolic interpretation, we could bring that whole *Tibetan Book of the Dead* and bardo stuff into the dhamma too. Chaminda rolled his eyes, but I pressed ahead. Perhaps if we rethink these metaphysical bardo planes (where the "soul" is transmigrating) as figurative stages of self-development, then we can say that this death and rebirth and transitional stage is really about how we evolve to overcome our own selfish tendencies *in this lifetime*. It's a psychological, not a metaphysical, doctrine. I was breaking a sweat now, and it seemed clear to me that I had brilliantly healed the divide between Hinayana and Mahayana Buddhism.

"Man, you're fucking *high*, Steve!" Chaminda responded. And sure enough, he was right. "First of all, you're talking about an interpretive move that's so sophisticated that very few of your Western Christians, outside of a handful of intellectuals, have been able to pull it off. Try telling the average Christian that Jesus wasn't really the Son of God, but just a *symbol* of the selfless ethical lifestyle—maybe Ivy League divinity PhDs will get on board with this, but not 99 percent of other Christians. Yeah, I'd love to see you introduce that idea at a Sunday service. Why do you think the Gospel of Thomas was quashed, historically, in favor of John?" I shook my head up and down but had no idea what he was referring to. This happened a lot.

"Don't get me wrong," Chaminda continued. "I'm sympathetic to your attempt here. I've tried to have my cake and eat it too. I've grown up in Sri Lanka under Buddhist nationalism after all, and I've tried to find a rubric for affirming both the *culture* and the *philosophy* of Buddhism. But in the end, I had to make peace with the fact that these two things do not truly cohere. You're making excuses to keep this spooky crap in Buddhism, when you know damn well that average people, the laypeople in the villages, aren't gonna make this symbolic turn. They're gonna keep believing in and praying to Avaloketesvara, or Guan Yin, or Amitabha, in order to get favors, not to refine their meditational awareness. What you've been calling a 'symbolic' interpretation of Buddhist ideas already exists among some of the scholar-monks. And they call it the 'esoteric' interpretation of Buddhist images and practices. Maybe it helps these highly educated people to play around in these virtual worlds, where dramatic stories and images help you to visualize the dhamma, but for average people this virtual reality just becomes *real* reality. Besides, you can get people to understand the dhamma very simply—it's not rocket science and doesn't need all this symbolic junk. I'd just take all those wistful dreamer Buddhists and tell them to focus on the Eightfold Path instead of bardo planes and bodhisattvas and mantras and samsara. It's hard enough to keep reminding ourselves that we are as impermanent as the fleeting pleasures we chase after. I think it's better if we just say that samsara made sense a long time ago but it's dumb and distracting *now*. Get over it. I think we'd be better Buddhists if we did that."

"Well, I hear what you're saying, Chaminda," I concurred, studying the increasingly beautiful waitress. "I have enough trouble with the day-to-day cravings. I mean, if I don't get the touch of a woman soon, I'm gonna shoot myself."

"Amen to that, brother," he shot back. "Now you're onto a worthy topic. I'll tell you one thing about Asian women, though, something you've probably never experienced but something I know *all* about. They're racist as hell. Well, I don't mean 'racist' exactly. I mean they're obsessed with light skin color. Ever since I moved to Bangkok, I can't get any play from these Thai women because they think I'm too dark! Fucking ridiculous. Asians associate dark skin with low class or peasantry—only someone poor who works outside in the fields gets really dark, or some stupid shit like that. Whatever it is, I'm getting really sick of it. I never had these problems with American women when I was in the States."

While I was listening to him, taking a momentary break from our narco-pizza, I suddenly felt a light "smack" on my neck and then instantly the twitch of legs. Chaminda's eyes grew large. *This can't be good,* I thought, sitting bolt upright and swiping at my neck. Into my dinner plate dropped a huge lime-green praying mantis, easily as big as my hand. It was sort of creepy and beautiful at the same time. I'd never had a praying mantis crawling on me before, but once was definitely enough. As quickly as it arrived it was gone again, and we carried on eating pizza.

"But here's my problem," I said to Chaminda. "Buddhism makes sense to me when we're talking about overcoming the cravings for sex or whatever. I mean, the suffering or dukkha that's involved there can be transcended by mental and physical discipline, and in that sense I can see that the *cause* of dukkha is, as Gotama said, craving. But there seem to be other kinds of suffering that don't fit the model."

"Go on, professor." Chaminda smiled.

"Well, this Khmer Rouge security prison, Tuol Sleng Prey, or S-21, has been giving me nightmares lately. I look at the suffering of those innocent prisoners, and I have a hard time applying the Four Noble Truths. Can we really say those people suffered *because they were attached*? Do you, as a Buddhist, believe that some act of renunciation or self-discipline could have alleviated their suffering?"

"I don't want to trivialize your point," Chaminda responded, "but there are yogis and arahants who are able, through meditation, to disassociate completely from their own physical pain."

"Like Thich Quang Duc," I offered. "The Vietnamese monk who burned himself alive in protest?"

"Yeah, that kind of thing is amazing," he replied, lost for a moment in a foggy reverie. "But it's not something the average guy can tap into when the Khmer Rouge puts him on the rack."

"I suppose," I went on, "the ultimate cause of any suffering is our psychobiological organism that registers incoming pain, and if you could turn it off, you'd transcend that pain. But I can't even 'turn off' my petty little wisdom-tooth ache, let alone torture. So maybe the *ultimate* cause of the S-21 victim's pain is his perceptual faculties, but that's cold comfort when the *proximate* cause is some fucker's boot on his neck! And rather than putting the locus of dukkha on the torture victim, I think that we can say that it's the torturer's selfish attachment to ego that brings more noncompassionate behavior into the world.

"Now, if you telescope out again to the highest level of ultimate reality, you find that there really isn't any difference between the torturer and the tortured, between the subject and the object, because there really are no independent *selves* that exist—only the decentralized flow of matter and consciousness (the five aggregates), linked causally, producing new experiences (increased suffering or increased compassion) like some streaming élan vital. All fine and good, but tell *that* to torture victims who are being electrocuted or bled to death—tell them they don't *really* exist, or they don't exist in any permanent or lasting way. They're gonna say, 'Okay, okay, thank you very much. Now could you please stop the electricity that's coursing through my impermanent body?' I mean, how is Buddhism really supposed to . . . um, how is Buddhism really supposed to . . . wait, what was I talking about? No, no, I got it. How is Buddhism really supposed to help in this extreme situation?"

"Whoa, whoa." Chaminda raised his hands. "I get your point. I think we have to acknowledge that Buddhist renunciation is not some ultimate superhero power that protects you from every sort of enemy. The dhamma is like a shield that can protect you from arrows and swords, but if someone aims a tank howitzer at you, you're basically fucked. All you can do is use the dhamma to help construct a compassionate society that won't fire missiles at you.

"Now," said Chaminda, gesturing dramatically toward the back of the restaurant, "let's do something useful and productive. Let's play pool." He stood up quickly and almost fell over from dizziness. That's when I noticed that the walls were breathing. *Oh, this ought to be an interesting game*, I thought.

Two hours later, we were still playing the first game of eight ball. My full debriefing of the happy pizza incident is as follows. First six hours: fantastic. Surrealism at its finest. I grasped profound interconnectedness of all things around midnight during a Sri Lankan board game called Carrom. Following twenty hours: still very, *very* "happy." Totally annoying. Caught at some point in rainstorm in Cambodian food market—discussed politics at length with merchants. I believe we spoke in Russian (which I don't know), or perhaps it was an artificial language like Esperanto. Very hazy. Woke up at some point on my bathroom floor. Late next day greeted by many queries such as, "Are you okay?" and, "Jesus, what happened to you?" Concluding advice regarding the happy pizza: order the small.

Six

SEEING A MAN
GET SHOT TO DEATH

Mai, the caretaker, mercifully asked us to get off the floor, where Peter and I were bowing and showing respect, and to take our seats. This struck me as eminently reasonable since my legs were fast asleep now, but Peter, out of devotion or smug yogic flexibility, ignored Mai's request. I was completely out of my depth here and had to follow his lead. I shot a glare at him, but he was blissfully oblivious. My friend Peter Gyallay-Pap had arranged for me to have a private audience with the holiest man in Cambodia, Venerable Maha Ghosananda.

Bodily flexibility was never my forte, but then neither was humility, and I wondered if I was especially uncomfortable because I was subserviently positioned. Like most other Americans, I had all the classic misgivings about authority and hierarchy that a native ideology of individualism and democracy can provide. And for me there were additional reasons to be suspicious about social and spiritual hierarchies. One of the principal virtues of philosophical thinking is its ability to expose illegitimate authority, to use logic and evidence to unmask posers and charismatic bullshit merchants. It's what Socrates did best, after all, and it's what got him killed in the end. Power and authority are not inherently dreadful, according to philosophy, but they must justify themselves by passing through the gauntlet of rationality—the authority within each of us. On top of my contrarian training, I had also experienced the classic fall from grace that marks the ubiquitous lapsed Catholic. Having been raised with profound devotion to a mysterious, ineluctable hierarchy, my fall into skepticism had left an atmosphere of vague betrayal around every subsequent case of authority. All this was at work inside me while I floundered on my knees to bow three times in prostration before this small old man in monk's robes. But even my brief experiences with Maha Ghosananda revealed a man who was worlds above the factionalism of politics and the pettiness of power, and he restored my feelings of humility and reverence—two feelings I had lost long ago with regard to religious teachers.

Maha Ghosananda, the supreme patriarch of Cambodia, was being cared for by a petite Vietnamese woman named Mai and her American husband, Tim, who worked for the American embassy. They were living temporarily in a very stylish home in Phnom Penh but planned to return to the States after the coming *dhammayietra*, or "peace walk." When we arrived at the outer gate of the compound, which was wreathed by barbed wire, we were greeted by security guards, who had clearly been briefed about our visit and gave us quick entry to the house. The place was heavily fortified with guards because the recent political skirmishes (anti-Thai riots, voter intimidation, and so on) were making everyone understandably nervous about Maha's safety. A powerful independent force like Maha could easily become a target. In fact, just three days earlier, you'll recall, my friend Li and I had stood outside Wat Lanka (only blocks from Maha's home) where monk Sam Bunthoeun had been gunned down, supposedly because he advocated monk participation in Cambodian politics.

Maha Ghosananda was no stranger to danger. Peter, who had worked with him in the refugee camps on the Thai border, had filled me in on the patriarch's backstory. This formidable Theravadan monk is referred to as

the "Gandhi of Cambodia," partly because he studied with Gandhi's dis-
ciples in Bihar India in the early fifties and partly because he is the most
powerful and effective peacemaker in the past twenty-five years of Cambodian history. As I related earlier, he defied the Khmer Rouge directly
and opened temporary Buddhist wats in the late 1970s. In 1978 a sea of
famished and broken survivors of the killing fields were making their
way to the Thai border when they were suddenly shocked to see a small
saffron-robed monk appear over the horizon. The traditional robes of
Cambodian monks had been forbidden for years, and the sight of Maha
Ghosananda, defiant in his robes, overwhelmed them. Waves of survivors
fell to their knees, and some combination of memories that should not be
remembered together with the profound comfort of Buddhist healing led
them to wail uncontrollably. The refugees were completely inspired by
this little monk's courage. He opened a floodgate in them, and they began
to fight, albeit nonviolently, to redeem their Buddhist heritage. Maha led
a peace march all the way from the Thai border to Phnom Penh.

The political climate of the 2003 elections was highly reminiscent of the
UN-sponsored elections of 1993. During that troubled year, Maha led a
sixteen-day dhammayietra through the embattled Khmer Rouge territory from Angkor Wat to Phnom Penh (over 125 miles). In Siem Reap
the marchers were caught in the crossfire of a Khmer Rouge attack.
Three of the peace demonstrators were injured, and a hand grenade was
thrown into the room where Maha Ghosananda had gathered two hundred of the march participants. Luckily, the grenade did not explode, but
throughout the remaining trek the marchers were beset with violence.
When some questioned whether the dhammayietra should continue,
Maha rallied the group to walk "where the troubles are." And he called for
the slowly recuperating sangha to take a strong leadership role in the pursuit of peace. "We, as monks, must serve our people. We depend on them.
Indeed, they are our rice bowl; they sustain us. If the people are suffering,
we too suffer. We cannot sit and meditate in our temples. We must walk
where the suffering is the greatest, to share the sorrows of our people, to

dry their tears. With each step, we will build a bridge, a bridge from war and suffering to peace and tranquillity. We are not peacekeepers like the UN, but peacemakers, so we must walk where there is no peace yet to keep."

On ditch roads, in between land-mined fields, through monsoon rains, and in 100-degree heat, the marchers walked on to Phnom Penh, gathering momentum and numbers as they passed through villages. The dhammayietra had begun as a few hundred people in Siem Reap but grew to three thousand by the time they reached the capital. Maha's famous annual walks for peace were performed primarily by villagers. And Maha Ghosananda continues to have an almost divine status among villagers and rural Khmer. The current government perceives this reverence and devotion as a potential threat because they see that the people are heavily influenced by an independent moral force—one that criticizes political corruption. For this reason, extra care is taken to keep Maha safe during this latest pre-election tension.

Such was the anxious political climate during my meeting with the patriarch. Once inside the home, we took off our shoes, as is the custom, and the elegant marble floors felt cool on my bare feet. Mai, who spoke in hushed tones, was the quintessential host, leading us up a giant sweeping staircase and settling us in a beautiful receiving room. There we made chitchat while an extremely formal servant brought us tea. Mai explained to us that the supreme patriarch was still napping because he hadn't been feeling well. She said she would go wake him up so I could meet him, but I nervously raised my eyebrows, thinking that we should just rain-check the whole thing. If I'd been him, I think I'd have resented being awakened in order to meet some know-nothing American twit. Then again, this guy was so enlightened that he probably hadn't felt "resentment" in many years.

While we were making small talk and sipping tea, Maha, who is in his seventies, emerged quietly from the next room. It was hard to miss him since he was wearing a blindingly orange robe and had a thick knit saffron stocking-cap perched precariously on top of his head. The conspicuous crown looked like a cable-knit cap that my mother might have constructed in the 1970s—something tasteful to match my homemade Budweiser sweater. Maha shuffled in slowly, not entirely awake yet. Everyone immediately dropped to their knees and offered Maha Ghosananda a display of respect that is usually reserved for the central Buddha statue in a pagoda—three quick prostrations.

What followed was not really a conversation per se. Following Mai's lead, we made carefully phrased comments to each other and *toward* the patriarch, and he would quietly smile and nod his head. Peter introduced me as the teacher of Buddhist philosophy at the Buddhist Institute. I got a very weird feeling from this introduction, like I had just learned the C major scale and somebody introduced me to Mozart as a "music teacher." After half an hour I began to understand Peter's claim that Maha Ghosananda is a spiritual presence rather than a rhetorically charismatic figure. This may be part of the reason why he is not well known in the West despite the fact that he, together with the Dalai Lama and Thich Nhat Hanh, is one of the spiritual leaders behind the International Network of Engaged Buddhists. But the effect of being with Maha for even a short time was very powerful. To be in the presence of somebody who has suffered so much (his whole family was killed by the Khmer Rouge) but who still inspires all Cambodians to return to the central Buddhist virtue of compassion, well, it's pretty goddamn sublime. This man doesn't just teach peace, he *is* peace.

Eventually, with a lot of nudging from Peter, I got up the nerve to ask Maha Ghosananda if he might stop by my class one day and meet my philosophy students. It seemed a presumptuous request perhaps, but then again, my students were a unique group of kids—pursuing Buddhist studies when no other Khmer their age were similarly inclined. To my utter amazement, Maha agreed to come for a visit. The next day, when I told the students that the Nobel Peace Prize nominee Maha Ghosananda might be coming to meet them, they practically fell out of their seats. It was like telling a Christian that Saint Francis might be stopping by next week.

Our meeting that night ended as quietly as it had begun. As I was leaving, Maha handed me a little flyer announcing the next Walk for Peace and Reconciliation. I closed my hands over my head to show gratitude. Here, in 2003, Maha was about to embark on another annual dhammayietra. This time, just as in 1993, the walk was to quell hostilities and anxieties about the coming elections. Villagers and monks, according to the flyer, would be walking for six weeks from Siem Reap to Phnom Penh, starting in April. Most of the flyer was printed in Khmer script, but at the bottom it said in English, "Hatred never ceases by hatred in this world, but by love alone is it healed. This is the ancient and eternal law."

About one week later, my students gathered in a fidgety and nervous group at the entryway of the Buddhist Institute. Maha Ghosananda was arriving up the drive in the backseat of a van. For safety reasons, only my students and the Buddhist Institute director had been informed of his visit, but as soon as he emerged from the van he began to be recognized by other monks, nuns, teachers, and laypeople. My students dropped to their knees in a group, as did the rest of the crowd that was now gathering in the driveway of the institute. Some of the older Khmer, those who had lived through the horrible years of violence, began to weep quietly, and some sought to touch his robes or help him mount the stairs. When we entered through the institute library, about two dozen students were studying quietly at tables. They had no idea that Maha Ghosananda was coming to visit, but as soon as he shuffled into the room they all stood up en masse and then dropped to their knees. I was completely overwhelmed. I had never experienced authentic reverence and respect in so palpable a form. Never had I seen such a spontaneous, unstaged outpouring of admiration and gratitude. In no time at all the entire population of the Buddhist Institute was quietly following behind Maha Ghosananda as the director gave him a tour of the new facilities. Finally, he ascended the stairs to my little classroom and took a seat at the front near the blackboard. Only my twelve students, a handful of novice monks, and the head administrators could fit inside the room, so the others waited patiently outside the door watching through the large glass pane.

To facilitate a good interaction between my nervous students and the patriarch, I asked the class captain, Sreang, to explain to Maha about our recent work in Buddhist philosophy. The other students looked relieved that so large a responsibility should fall to someone else, and Sreang gallantly, albeit tensely, shouldered the burden. Sreang stood up beside his desk and explained that we had been discussing the Eightfold Path. We had been examining Buddha's call for a Middle Way in the domains of sila (moral action), samadhi (concentration), and panna (wisdom). Maha Ghosananda nodded his head slowly and then began to quiz Sreang and the other students about the Eightfold Path. Following a pedagogical paradigm that is dominant in Asia, he called on them to recite lists and sublists of dhamma principles. The students came to each other's aid while Maha put them through their paces for almost an hour, weaving back and forth between Khmer, English, Pali, and French. I struggled to keep up and felt thankful that I wasn't called to recite dhamma.

The students asked Maha about the jhanas, or trance-states of meditation. They wanted to know about the different levels of concentration, and he noted that there are further levels of awareness even *within* the established eight jhanas. He explained that there are four levels even within the first level of meditational awareness. After about an hour, Mai gently interrupted and informed us that Maha was tired and needed to eat. But he continued talking to the students for another half-hour and practically had to be dragged away by his caretaker. Monks cannot eat whenever they like because, according to the rule, they must fast after noon, so Mai was rightly concerned. Surrounded by the same outpouring of affection, Maha Ghosananda made his way back down the stairs and out to the waiting van. The students and I, inspired and exhausted, bowed as he was driven away.

As I mentioned before, I was not and am not a "respecter of persons" in the sense that I take someone's word on faith because he is a guru or a purported holy man. It's not my style to bow to spiritual authorities, but here I was, bent over and authentically humbled before a very great man. I'm still skeptical of self-proclaimed gurus, maharishis, and sages, but I learned a valuable lesson by spending time with Cambodia's supreme patriarch. Some people, by their courage and compassion, deserve real reverence, even though—and especially when—they're not interested in receiving it. Maha Ghosananda is not a holy man because he is closer to God, or has a divine status, or channels the spirit realm, or any of that other two-world twaddle. He's a holy man because his heart is a huge, indomitable force that didn't break or wither in the face of staggering loss and devastating brutality. He is a saint because he wasn't crushed by forces that should have, by most standards, crushed him. I felt real humility in his presence.

Humility, something most Americans have in short supply, is close to the heart of Buddhist dhamma. It is an experience of self-effacement, an act of ego transcendence. It is a shrinking of self-importance, and as such it expresses a *felt sense* of the anatta (no-self) philosophy. I felt small in Maha's presence, and I felt that my problems were relatively trivial by comparison with what he had seen. I felt compelled to let go of the grudging slights and minor ego injuries that fed and grew in the nursery of my bloated self-regard. But self-loathing was not the final result of this experience of humility; that would just be more self-regard. Rather, a sense of true inspiration followed from my experience with Maha Ghosananda. If people are ever throwing hand grenades at *me*—as happened to Maha—or, worse, killing members of my family, I doubt that I would ever be able to rise above it. I'm not sure I would even want to. But after spending time with Maha, I *do* think I can rise above the less dramatic forms of suffering in my life.

In the Dhammapada scripture, the Buddha says, "Unlike those who don't realize that we're on the verge of perishing, those who do: their quarrels are stilled" (3, 6). Never did that stanza ring more true than after I witnessed a political assassination in Cambodia. I had seen dead bodies before, and I had even drawn many cadavers in my anatomy class at university, but I'd never seen anybody killed before.

The little guesthouse where I lived was located in Kapko Market, a very old and rather shabby little street of shops. I was way off the beaten path, and hardly any other barang lived in my neighborhood. The Swiss expat proprietor, Peirrot, was a generous-hearted man who reminded me of a much older version of Evelyn Waugh's Sebastian Flyte. Every day he slept off the previous night's festivities until his Khmer girlfriend rousted him around 10:00 A.M. with a tall glass of chocolate milk. Then the music in the open-air bar would get switched over from traditional melancholy Khmer love ballads to awful 1970s classic rock—Frampton, Fleetwood Mac, and so on—and Peirrot would slowly transform into the charming and adept proprietor.

Every day I went next door to eat lunch and sometimes dinner at a Khmer outdoor street-side market. The food stand was a wide-mouthed shack that reached back off the street to house dozens of customers under a sheet-metal rooftop. A picnic table in front had several large pots of fresh stews and staple rice dishes. The amenities were extremely spartan, but the dump was renowned for tasty fare. The average plate of steamed rice, spiced eggs, and pork with chilies cost me only about one dollar—two dollars if I ordered an Angkor beer. I would sit there under the awning, chowing down, between twelve and one o'clock almost every day. But on February 18 I diverged from my usual routine.

On that morning I had arranged to meet some monks. They were bhikkhus who had studied Buddhist philosophy extensively, and we had agreed to meet at my place around noon for some dhamma discussion. I ran next door to the restaurant earlier than usual and grabbed some curry to bring back with me. I decided to eat on the balcony overlooking the restaurant, where I could keep an eye out for my bhikkhu friends.

At that hour, the narrow street was swarming with people. I sat in a rattan chair under the shade of an Asian palm tree, looking down on the bustle of bicycles, cyclos, motos, and the rare car, which had to slowly fight its way through the throng. Young women in their sun hats wheeled carts of food, drink, and sundries to the curb, while the man on the opposing balcony draped his usual red shade-sheet across the terrace. A large, dark SUV edged up the street carefully, then parked on the curb in front of the restaurant. A group of well-dressed Khmer men emerged casually from the vehicle. They didn't look like the usual patrons. These guys were well-heeled business or bureaucrat types, wearing pressed cotton shirts and top-end sunglasses. They didn't seem to have that film of sweat, dust, and grime that the rest of us had by this hour of the day. They strolled in a leisurely way to the food stand and looked over the day's offerings. My attention wandered to the old woman shouting her trademark seller's chant, the same reveille that woke me every morning. Not far from her, two naked kids were sword fighting with sticks. Altogether, it was the usual street theater of my neighborhood.

Suddenly I heard a very loud shot. I was not accustomed to gunfire, nor was I expecting to hear any, but I knew instantly what it was. The bang was much louder, more clipped, and angrier than any moto backfire. One of the bureaucrat types collapsed down below me, and the other men swarmed in toward him, blocking my vision. The street crowd instinctively dashed in opposite directions away from the obscure epicenter of action. I leapt up to see better over the terrace railing. One of the men dashed back to the SUV, while others began to pick the victim off the ground. I couldn't tell what was happening. It was impossible to read the causal chains. People were running now to and from the restaurant awning directly underneath me. I heard a motorcycle's engine revving and then Doppler-shifting away.

There was pandemonious movement in the street, but no one screamed or shouted. In fact, for a few short moments the sounds of the usually blaring street were preternaturally still. Then, from under the exact same tables and chairs where I usually sit, three men hoisted the poor victim. They carefully guided him toward the backseat of the SUV, while bystanders began crowding around to see the victim. The wounded man must have been going into shock, and as they carried him directly beneath me I could clearly see him shaking uncontrollably. I could also see blood on his leg. Everything happened quickly, but it felt like slow motion. When he was safely in the car, another well-dressed man, with blood on his hands, patiently cleared onlookers away from the front of the vehicle. His calmness made it look like he'd been in this sort of situation before. The SUV drove off slowly.

I ran down to the street, where everyone was discussing the event and trying to interpret what had happened. The details were vague, but the consensus in the street was instantly clear: this was a political hit. The wounded man and his colleagues were certainly officials, the bystanders argued. Just look at how they were dressed, I was repeatedly reminded. One of the guesthouse staff girls told me that she had run up to the jeep to have a look: the victim seemed to have sustained only a minor leg injury. Even though they did not know who was shot, everyone in the neighborhood agreed that the broad daylight shooting was just standard Cambodian politics—straight, no chaser. According to witnesses who were closer than I, the hit was performed by a two-man team. One young man leapt off the back of a motorcycle, shot the victim, and then leapt back on while the other navigated the bike through the crowd. When I pressed a restaurant worker for some theory about the perpetrators, he spoke for the whole crowd when he said despairingly, "We *know*, but it is not safe to talk more."

A single police car lazily arrived about twenty minutes later, and officers questioned restaurant workers and diners in a perfunctory manner. Within thirty minutes of the shooting, the bustling street had resumed its frenetic pace and seemed entirely oblivious to the still fresh horror. I could not gather my thoughts and felt deeply disoriented. While I stood dumbly on the street curb, a smiling, saffron-robed monk pulled up on the back of a moto. It was my friend, Venerable Sovanrattana, arriving to discuss Buddhist ideas of impermanence.

The next morning, I discovered that the street wisdom was dead-on. Mr. Om Radsady, a senior adviser to FUNCINPEC president Prince Norodom Ranariddh, was the man I saw get shot. FUNCINPEC, you'll recall, is the royalist party that shares in the ongoing three-way political struggle with the Sam Rainsey Party and the dominant Cambodian People's Party. Radsady died a few hours later at Calmette Hospital. Apparently the leg wound that seemed so minor to the staff girl had actually been the exit wound from a very damaging entry blast that traveled down from his back, lacerating the internal organs irreparably. I kept replaying the image of him shaking uncontrollably. I kept picturing him dying, the life seeping out of him. I thought about how unpredictable and contingent it all seemed. One minute he's going down to the restaurant for some Amok chicken, and the next he's laid out dead on a cooling board in Calmette Hospital. I suppose anyone who enters Cambodian politics has a clear understanding that it's a dangerous vocation, but the sheer spontaneity of the event and the banality of the surroundings must have caught Om Radsady off guard. It seemed additionally unfair that he hadn't somehow been given a little time to prepare for his own death. But maybe he was prepared. Who can say?

Om Radsady was a well-known and well-liked public servant who preferred to work behind the scenes rather than enter the flamboyant front-stage of Cambodian politics. Nonetheless, he was very well connected, first as the chairman of the National Assembly Commission of Foreign Affairs and Information, and more recently as Prince Ranariddh's right-hand man. Being the prince's adviser meant that Radsady was a royalist and therefore out of step with the "strong man" government of Prime Minister Hun Sen's CPP. At the time of his killing, Radsady was helping to smooth over a highly publicized fight between Princess Vacheara and Hun Sen. The princess was accusing the prime minister of complicity in the recent Thai embassy riots, and the prime minister was retaliating with a threat to sue the princess for defamation. Many of the people I spoke with believed that Hun Sen was sending a clear message to the princess, through Om Radsady's assassination. Meanwhile, the royalists from the prince's FUNCINPEC party claimed that the assassination was an intimidation tactic sent from Hun Sen's CPP ruling party—a message to warn all opposition politicians to back off as the July elections approached. There were a few other speculations about the exact meaning of the message, but there was no ambivalence at all about *who* the messenger was. For weeks no suspects were taken into custody.

Sometime later one of the assailants, Mom Sophann, was arrested by police, and he confessed to killing Om Radsady because he wanted Radsady's cell phone. I don't think anyone in all of Cambodia believed that pat explanation, and the prince himself said, "We cannot accept that this crime was committed simply to steal one mobile phone. . . . This killing has disgraced the honor of Cambodia." It only added fuel to the reasonable conspiracy theories when it came to light that Sophann and the other assailant had been members of a governmental paramilitary cadre. It also seemed highly suspicious that Sophann was able to escape from the Correction Center One prison for a short time just before his trial date. A year later, the whole business remained shrouded in typical Cambodian mystery.

For days after seeing Radsady killed, I was an emotional tangle. First of all, I had never before been in such close proximity to this sort of political violence, and it pulled the optimistic rug out from under me. I also felt very strange about the fact that sheer coincidence had spared me from my usual seat at that lunch table on that day and put me a few yards away on the balcony. And last, though perhaps most disturbingly, I was shocked by how remarkably accustomed all the witnesses were to such a brutal atrocity. My friends from the guesthouse who witnessed it and my students and colleagues, to whom I described it, all seemed positively numb about the event. My friend Li's comment to me earlier kept echoing in my head: "Life is cheap in this part of the world." I'm sure that I too would be desensitized if I had grown up in a world of violence, but I felt really alone after the killing.

I kept wandering back to the shooting in my class lectures and describing it to co-workers, vaguely frustrated that they were just getting the "outside" or the "shell" of the story, missing the interior of the thing. But of course most of the people I spoke with, especially the Khmer, knew all about the "interior" of death and loss and impermanence. It wasn't callousness that made them numb—it was intimacy with death. They knew it from the inside all right, and they hadn't just seen strangers executed, as I did. Many of them had seen their own families killed. Witnessing that kind of stuff must make you radically different. Psychologists could spend centuries trying to understand the impact of genocide on survivors, and even then their findings would capture merely the exterior. I felt shaken up by Om Radsady's murder, but I had the buffer of not actually knowing him. Most people in Cambodia, however, have really seen man's heart of darkness, in a way that Americans—save perhaps our returning veterans—have not. No matter how similar I sometimes felt to my friends Li and Kimvan or to my students, I had to acknowledge, after my encounter with violence, that there was this huge divide between us. They had each swallowed a sea of violence, and they would be working for the rest of their lives to keep the toxicity level down, while I, and most of my homeland compatriots, had been mercifully spared this crucible.

The Buddha's observation seemed especially appropriate: "Unlike those who don't realize that we're on the verge of perishing, those who do: their quarrels are stilled." I knew intellectually about my own impermanence, but I didn't really understand it in my belly, so to speak, until after the assassination. I slowly began to grasp how the most obscure doctrine in Buddhism, the teaching of anatta, is really just a rarefied expression of the human emotion of compassion.

Compassion is that defining human emotion that leads us to identify with the suffering of others; it is the emotional engine that drives our desire to help. Watching a man get shot to death really dredges up this usually buried emotion, drawing it up to ascend above its usual monarch, the ego. Albert Einstein's description of the delusion of individuality hints at the way in which compassion and anatta (no-self) are two sides of the same coin:

> A human being is part of the whole, called by us "Universe," a part limited in time and space. He experiences himself, his thoughts and

feelings, as something separated from the rest, a kind of optical delusion of his consciousness. This delusion is a kind of prison for us, restricting us to our personal desires and affection for a few persons nearest to us. Our task must be to free ourselves from this prison by widening our circles of compassion to embrace all living creatures and the whole of nature in its beauty.

Einstein is echoing an old Buddhist truth: the "self" is a virtual fiction. It is practically useful to see ourselves as essentially differentiated from other selves; after all, we've all had different life histories, and each of us has different goals and motivations. My "self" acts as a metaphysical place-holder that serves as a repository of all my memories, personality traits, and core values. It's the essential me. But in reality this self is only a mental construction, a convention that erroneously groups diverse experiences into a virtual unity.

Nothing in Buddhism is more confusing to people than this doctrine of anatta (*anatman* in Sanskrit). It is as confusing for the lay Buddhists of Thailand, Cambodia, and Burma as it is for Westerners. Part of the bewilderment comes from the fact that it runs counter to our common-sense folk thinking, and part results from failing to see the Buddha's arguments in their historical context.

To understand what the Buddha was critiquing with his anatta doctrine, we can look at the famous Hindu scripture, the Bhagavad Gita. The Gita, known to Westerners as the favorite of Hari Krishna airport proselytizers, was actually written later than Gotama, but it nicely crystallizes and summarizes pre-Buddhist Hindu philosophy. It effectively summarizes all the things that Buddha fought against.

The Gita tells of a military leader named Arjuna, from the ksatriya (warrior caste), who, for complicated reasons, ends up leading an army against an opposing legion of his kinsmen. On the battlefield, just before combat, Arjuna has an existential crisis and confides to his chariot driver (Krishna in disguise) that he is morally conflicted about the impending battle. Why should he kill his cousins? Indeed, why should he kill at all? These deep apprehensions plague Arjuna's mind in the beginning of the text, and the remainder of the scripture is a series of arguments and revelations that Krishna offers to inspire Arjuna into battle. Scattered throughout the rather beautiful, albeit disturbing, story are three arguments for why Arjuna should go into battle and kill his kinsmen. First, Arjuna should kill his enemies because God says so—simple, straightforward, divine authority stuff. Arjuna, like the filicidal Abraham in the West, is commanded to do something that demonstrates his devotion to the sacred powers. This expresses the fact that *devotion* is one of the main pathways of the spiritual life. The second argument that Krishna offers presupposes the realities of the Hindu caste system. Arjuna was born into the ksatriya class, which means that it is his sacred *duty* to fulfill the actions of a warrior. Social caste was understood in cosmic terms, and the harmony of the universe itself was tied to the social harmony that resulted when each caste fulfilled its function or destiny. When we do not execute our sacred duties, the world itself slouches toward chaos. And third, Krishna attempts to assuage Arjuna's guilt over murdering his kinsmen by pointing out that it is only the physical body that gets destroyed. The soul, or atman, of his kinsman is divine and eternal and will not perish on Arjuna's sword; in fact, the atman will be liberated by the killing of the body. The Gita explains,

> This physical body is perishable. But the embodied soul is described as indestructible, eternal, and immeasurable. Therefore, do fight. Neither the one who thinks it kills nor the one who thinks it is killed knows the truth. The soul neither kills nor gets killed. The soul is never born, nor does it die at any time. It has neither past nor future. It is unborn, ever existing, permanent, and ancient. . . . Just as a man discards worn-out clothes and puts on new clothes, the soul discards worn-out bodies and wears new ones.

The Buddha didn't like any of these standard Hindu ideas and explicitly argued against them throughout the Pali Tripitika scriptures. In the Aggana Sutta (which, you'll recall, I had my student Boramy read earlier), Buddha critiques the traditional caste story that Brahmins were born of God's mouth while the subservient caste, the Sudras, were born from his lowly feet. Buddha counters this long-standing prejudice and deflates the mystification by pointing out that all the Brahmins, warriors, craftsmen, and servants he knows were all born the exact same way— from their mother's womb! He follows up this dose of egalitarian common sense by pointing out that since virtue and vice are easily witnessed in all the castes, not just the Brahmin priestly class, there is no real ground for saying that one caste is inherently better than another. Open your eyes, he suggests, and you will find Brahmin scumbags and Untouchable saints; therefore, a higher law of value (ethical goodness) should trump the old hierarchy.

But the Buddha saved most of his critical acumen for a career-long sustained attack on the Hindu idea of the soul. His motivation was not to be some nihilistic killjoy, but to break the romantic obsession with eternal unseen realities that Indian culture had embraced—the kind of romanticism that, in scriptural form, led Hindu gods to pronounce that killing is okay because this mortal life is only illusion anyway.

In the case of Om Radsady, the assassinated politician, Hindu doctrine would assert that his eternal soul, his atman, has either gone on to be reincarnated in another mortal body or finally attained freedom from the physical wheel of becoming, leaving behind the realm of birth and death to join God (Brahman) in perfect blissful happiness. This second option is pretty close to the scenario that as an altar boy I heard uttered many times by Catholic priests at funeral services. Of course, in the West the final union with God is more like a union between lovers; that is to say, you and God become really close, but your soul still maintains its individuality. You and God and the other souls just hang out a lot together in heaven. Whereas, in Hinduism the individual soul actually merges with the godhead (Brahman), disappearing like drops of rain into the ocean. Still, both accounts, East and West, maintain that you're going to be really happy after the mortal coil is shed. In fact, you're going to find perfect joy forever and ever, amen.

The Buddha finds all this buoyant brightness rather suspicious. Like a proto-Wittgenstein, he thinks that language has gone on holiday. What does it mean to be perfectly happy? In the Potthapada Sutta (Digha Nikaya), Buddha recalls a debate he had with some "philosophers and Brahmins" who believed that "the soul is perfectly happy and healthy after death." The Buddha says, "I asked them whether, so far as they knew it or perceived it, the human world was perfectly happy, and they answered: 'No.' Then I asked them: 'Moreover, can you maintain that you yourselves for a whole night, or for a whole day, or even for half a night or day, have ever been perfectly happy?' And they answered: 'No.' Then I said to them: 'Further, do you know a way or a method by which you can realize a state that is altogether happy?' And still to that question they answered: 'No.' And then I said: 'Sirs, have you ever heard the voices of heavenly beings who had realized rebirth in a perfectly happy world, saying: 'There is a right path, a true path, which is in human capacity to follow, a path to the world of unfailing bliss, for we ourselves by following it have come to this world of bliss?' They still answered: 'No.'" The Buddha concludes from this Socratic questioning that, while their mouths are moving and words are coming out, these philosophers and Brahmins are really speaking nonsense. He says that people who dedicate themselves to an incoherent doctrine of eternal paradise are like carpenters who build staircases for mansions that they've never seen and for which they have no dimensions or measurements. In other words, they labor, but their misunderstanding renders the work absurd.

This epistemic argument is compelling, but the real point is the metaphysical one. Why can't we be perfectly happy? Why can't we even be happy for more than a few hours? The answer is anicca, that happiness is inherently impermanent. Like all other feelings, happiness comes and goes, and like all other things in the world, it cannot last. Treating a moment as if it were a thing to be possessed ad infinitum is a kind of regular human tendency and a regular human lunacy.

In the same way that paradise crumbles upon further inspection, so too the Buddha thinks that atman is nowhere to be found except in the literary inventions of Hinduism and the confused heads of its followers. Buddhism, contrary to all dualistic theories, asserts that we are not made up of two metaphysically different parts, permanent spirit and impermanent body. Buddhism breaks with most religions East and West by recognizing that man is a finite tangle of qualities, all of which eventually exhaust themselves, and that no part, conscious or otherwise, carries on independently. Remember that all humans, according to Buddha, are composed of the five aggregates (khandas): body (rupa), feeling (vedana), perception (sanna), dispositions or volitional tendencies (sankhara), and consciousness (vinnana). If the Buddha were standing around in the battlefield setting of the Bhagavad Gita, he would certainly chime in and object to Krishna's irresponsible claim that a permanent soul resides in Arjuna and his enemies. Show me this permanent entity, the Buddha would demand. Is the body permanent? Are feelings permanent? What about perceptions, or dispositions, or even consciousness? Buddha examines all the elements of the human being, finds that they are all manifestly ephemeral, and finds no additional permanent entity or soul amid the tangle of human faculties. There is no ghost in the machine.

Take Steve Asma as an example. All the dimensions of who I am—my taste for single-malt scotch, my hopes to be a good father, my expanding love handles, my moral sensibility, my memory of my grandmother—all these, even an exhaustive list, can be explained and accounted for by body, feeling, perception, disposition, and consciousness. And none of them are eternal or "miraculous" or "from a divine realm" or otherwise "spooky." In this conviction, Buddhism shares much with contemporary science, which also treats the soul question with skepticism and agnosticism. But while many contemporaries would still hold out for the chance of some spiritual ether lurking in the gaps between the scientific explanations— some soul substance, perhaps, skulking about in the brain—the Buddha just washes his hands of this clinging fascination and moves on to dispatch the very idea of self-identity.

Maybe there's no soul inside me, but at least there's a *me* inside me. Right? Not really. Here's where Buddhism gets really sticky. Getting rid of the soul is something that one may or may not agree with, but at least everyone understands the basic point. Getting rid of the *self* is a more demanding trail to follow.

Philosophers from all sides of the globe have puzzled over the nature of self-consciousness and agency. Every act of knowing or doing implies a knower or doer. When I weigh two choices, for example, or when I inspect an object, I do so from some centralized point of view (subjectivity). But it seems impossible to inspect this subjective point itself. It is impossible to grab hold of the "I" because as soon as you've placed it before your mind's eye, you have already moved it to become the mind's eye. It sees everything else but can never see itself. Nonetheless, it is the felt locus of our agency in the world, the thing with which we most identify. "I think, therefore I am," is Descartes' famous proof that my essential being is my mind and that it acts as the "commander in chief" of my whole physio-chemical vessel. It is also assumed to be the locus of my personality. Then Descartes, and most everybody else, attached other more religious properties to this immaterial mind, like the idea that it is immortal. This conflation of self and soul was also going on throughout Indian philosophy.

Theravada Buddhism, however, does not privilege the mind in the same way that Western philosophy and Vedantic philosophy do. It does not separate the mind out from the body, treat it as an independent thing, and give it special powers like everlasting life. Buddhism treats mind as an interdependent piece of the whole developing person; the human personality is a striving, growing composite thing, not a transcendental entity that eventually moves on to achieve perfect happiness. Buddhism rejects not only the idea of an immortal soul but also the humbler idea that a centralized immaterial person lives inside the body and runs the show. There is no essential "me" that persists throughout all the changes of my feelings, perceptions, streaming conscious thoughts, and so on; there is only a loose confederation of experiences that can be called "Steve."

In the Vajira Sutta (Samyutta Nikaya), the Buddhist nun Vajira is confronted by Mara, the personification of death, and is asked to describe her essential self. She responds by saying that there is no such being within her. Describing herself as a heap of five aggregates, she says,

> *Why now do you assume "a being"?*
> *Mara, have you grasped a view?*
> *This is a heap of sheer constructions:*
> *Here no being is found.*

> *Just as, with an assemblage of parts,*
> *The word "chariot" is used,*
> *So, when the aggregates are present,*
> *There's the convention "a being."*

> *It's only dukkha that comes to be,*
> *Dukkha that stands and falls away.*
> *Nothing but dukkha comes to be,*
> *Nothing but dukkha ceases.*

Here Vajira likens the identification of a human person (whether it be Vajira or Steve or Om Radsady) to the identification of a chariot. In this simile (repeated again in the Milindapanha), she is pointing out that "chariot" is only a word that describes a combination of wheels and ropes and wood and metal. And if you searched these parts over, you would never find some other thing called a "chariot" hidden in them. The name is just a convention that brings a virtual unity to a real multiplicity of constituents, like the word "Europe."

Buddhist philosophy is creeping now into rather unfamiliar territory. Countless times a day I feel like I'm in control of my actions and decisions and operate as a personal agent who acts from a free-will point of command. I feel consolidated into one person. So what is Buddha talking about?

The Buddha looks at this whole mess of tangled concepts like soul, self, person, mind, and body, and he says the real issue here is that we all have a sense of conscious *identity*, but we have mistakenly come to believe that this *awareness* is an actual *thing*. The truth, when you reflect on it, is that this self-awareness actually moves about a lot, migrating around the activities that you happen to be engaged in at any one time. The "I" itself is just a formal requirement of experience (an interpretive point of view), but it has no actual content. The Buddha says, in the Potthapada Sutta, that people experience self-awareness in three ways, that there are three domains of personal identity. Sometimes we identify ourselves with our *material body*, as in the process of physical exercise. But the real parts underneath this "person" are material ingredients like earth, air, fire, and water (the four elements of the ancient world). Other times we identify ourselves with our *mental* lives, as when we lie in bed and plan our next day's schedule or even enjoy a sunset. But underneath this "person" we find only a bundle of sensory and intellectual stimulations. We also sometimes identify ourselves with unadulterated *consciousness*, as in the case of pure mathematical contemplations or jhana meditations. But even here there is no true, persisting, essential self or person. The Buddha says that if you want to talk about a "self," then you have to admit that each manifestation of it bears no resemblance to the other manifestations. What's the true self? Answer: whichever one is activated at the time you ask.

The self is a movable awareness that emerges in the three functional modes of subjectivity: material, mental, and pure consciousness. For example, where is the real "Steve" when I'm doing a Boolean algebra calculation? In this case, the self resides in the activity of consciousness. But if, while I'm contemplating math, you suddenly stab me with a pointed stick, then the real "Steve" will quickly shift to the material body domain. Each new activity—indeed, each new moment—brings a new self. The Buddha says, "The past personality that I had was real to me at the time when I had it; and at that time the others were unreal. So also in the other two cases: the one that was operating at the time was real and the other two were unreal. When any of the three modes of personality is operating, then it does not come under the category of either of the other two. Personality is identified according to the mode which is operating."

Now we are into the mysterious heart of Buddhism. We have arrived at the edge of a very dark forest, and inside it lies the "higher" teachings of the Buddha known as the Abhidhamma. The Abhidhamma (literally, "higher teaching") refers to both the encyclopedia-sized scriptures that make up the "third basket" of Buddhist texts (together with the Suttas and the Vinaya, they compose the Tripitika) and the elaborate philosophical doctrine contained in those scriptures. Westerners in general know virtually nothing about this vast literature and the demanding ideas contained therein, and truth be told, the staggering majority of Eastern Buddhists don't know much about it either.

The Abhidhamma is territory that few practicing Buddhists need to visit. Buddhism recognizes that *praxis* is entirely possible when *theory* remains at a minimum. But there are philosophical types out there, after all, and they should have their path too. In the same way that you'd want to give a natural-born athlete a track to sprint on, so too the Buddha gives natural-born philosophers the Abhidhamma to exercise their minds upon.

Theravada legend holds that the Buddha actually transmitted the Abhidhamma teachings during his lifetime. The Pali Commentaries, written long after the Buddha's parinibbana, undoubtedly record the embellished oral traditions that slowly evolved in the popular imagination. According to the commentaries, the Buddha taught the entire Abhidhamma (seven books altogether—one of them alone is over two thousand pages!) during a three-month rains retreat. (All monks are expected to take up a three-month residence, coinciding with monsoon season, from mid-July to mid-October to study and meditate in retreat communities.) But he actually taught this full message to an assembly of *devas* (gods) in the Tavatinsa heaven, because mere humans are unable to sit still long enough in meditation to receive the deep, and apparently relentless, lessons. Legend has it that the Buddha would return to the human realm every day to go on alms-patrol; he did have to eat, after all. During these nutritional refueling stops, the Buddha summarized the heavenly lessons for his human pupil Sariputta. According to tradition, it was Sariputta who then wrote down the master's teachings and gave us the Abhidhamma. Scholars, though, claim that the seven books of the Abhidhamma were slowly compiled during the three great Buddhist councils in India, reaching some final codification during the first century B.C.E.

The Abhidhamma picks up where the Sutta doctrine of no-self leaves off. If it is true that there is no true essential self—a persistent subject that receives or collects our experiences into one personality—then some radically new way of describing experience is necessary. Even the deep grammar of our language breaks things up into subjects and objects that undergo changes, but technically that is not how reality is composed. Buddha, along with Heraclitus, is one of the first process philosophers— one of the first people to turn our commonsense thinking on its head by claiming that becoming is primordial and being is derivative. Our everyday view is that there are persistent beings or entities in the world (subjects like Steve and objects like this desk) and that these relatively stable things undergo changes or motions (becoming). Buddhism says, no, there is first the flux or stream of becoming and we just conventionally pick out waves of evanescent motion and treat them as independent substantial beings—we reify a restless flow. If that is true, then true philosophy cannot express a simple observation like "I see the scary brown dog running across the street." Notice how many problems there are with this sentence if there are no such things as "subjects" and "objects." First of all, I can't even say "I" legitimately, let alone "dog" or "street." I have to break down my experience into its rawest components and then redescribe the event without appeal to "substances." This is the main mission of the Abhidhamma.

The raw components or elements of all experience are referred to in the Abhidhamma as *dhammas*—which is extremely confusing since this term was already being used in the Suttas to mean "the teaching of the Buddha." Here in the Abhidhamma it's best to translate *dhamma* as "element of reality," and there are four: *rupa* (body), *cetasika* (mental factors), *citta* (consciousness), and *nibbana* (the unconditioned). These are further subdivided, and it takes an anal-retentive accountant's brain to keep the dhammas straight. For example, there are something like twenty-eight forms of body and fifty-two kinds of mental factors (including feelings, perceptions, and volitions), one consciousness, and one nibbana. The Abhidhamma doctrine is like an early atomic theory of the basic building blocks of experience, but unlike Democritus and contemporary material-ist theories, it includes consciousness and even feelings in the composi-tion of these fundamental particles.

The Abhidhamma breaks down our everyday experience into these constituent parts (or momentary functions) and then reveals an elabo-rate system of relations between them, expressing this map of classifica-tions as an analytical grid or matrix (*matika*). As an example of how the Abhidhamma method retranslates experience into the five aggregates, imagine drinking a good glass of wine. Whereas the average person would say something like, "I am pleased with this pinot noir," the Abhidhamma-style retranslation (avoiding substance lingo) would be

> In association with this momentary series of material dhammas [rupa], which constitute a deep red fluid, there is a simultaneous series of feel-ing dhammas [vedana] of a pleasant kind. The pleasantness is strong in force, but moments of sweetness are accompanied by moments of tartness. These same feelings are contemporaneous with perception dhammas [sanna] that recognize the tasty fluid of happiness as some-thing conventionally called wine, and this identification is simultaneous with volitional dhammas [sankhara] that both reflect a past pleasure in wine and affirm a future desire to taste it again. [It's in this volitional part of us that the craving can sneak in if we're not vigilant.] Finally, the entire bundle or cluster of momentary experiences has a conscious dhamma [vinnana] dimension that brings the events under the um-brella of awareness.

Notice that I didn't say "I" or "me" anywhere in this description, and I even avoided talking about the wine as though it was a real substantial thing. There is a field of awareness, but everything is de-centered. And if this wasn't enough, the Abhidhamma usually breaks down this aggregate experience level even further, coding each moment with categories such as "wholesome," "unwholesome," and "neutral." The purpose of all this is to show, in painstaking detail, how there can be thought thinking itself without a *thinker*, speech without a speaker, suffering without a sufferer, deeds without a doer, and so on.

A "matrix" of elemental-functional relations is literally what is provided in the Dhammasangani, or the first book of Abhidhamma, but "matrix" is also an apt metaphor. Just as in the famous *Matrix* movie trilogy—where the enlightened person, Neo, can see the myriad ones and zeros that make up the real code of experience, the causal level beneath the phenomenological level—so too a Buddhist philosopher trained in Abhidhamma can see the elements of reality beneath the substances of our daily experience. Unlike the conventional world of people, planets, and everything in between, the element dhammas are the most real things, albeit momentary, in the Buddhist metaphysic. They are said to have *svabhava*—an "essential nature" that is their defining character and identity. Like Democritus's "atoms," the dhammas are themselves irreducible.

Much of the philosophical Buddhism that Western people recognize today—like the Tibetan and Mahayana stress on "emptiness" (*sunyata*)—originates as a response to this Abhidhamma doctrine. In fact, it is from the debate around this dhamma (elements) doctrine that one can see the earliest forms of Mahayana evolving. Early Mahayanists like Nagarjuna (actually claimed later by both the Mahayana and Hinayana traditions) stressed the idea that all things are "empty," lacking inherent independent existence (svabhava). Emptiness has come to be a catchphrase in contemporary Buddhology, but few today understand that it is just a reemphasis of the original anatta teachings because later philosophers of Abhidhamma had begun to talk of dhamma elements as if they were permanent or at least "essentialist" entities—a big no-no in Buddhist ontology. The famous Perfection of Wisdom Sutras, so popular among Mahayanists, stress the emptiness of dhamma elements (*dhamma-sunyata*).

The Mahayana development is a very complicated historical story and not of much interest to us here. What is important about Abhi-dhamma doctrine, however, is that it is a "master science" of all things—one that attempts to systematize the connections between every possible being in the universe. Tall order? Certainly, but the taxonomy is pretty impressive. There are a finite number of ways that a physical thing can exist (have qualitative properties), and the same is true of consciousness, feeling, and the rest. Notice this is not an attempt to catalog the contents of all thoughts, and so on, but just a general outline of the direction or orientation of thoughts. (Some thoughts, for instance, are about physical objects, while other thoughts are about thoughts themselves.) In addi-tion, the matrix lays out the logical "value" possibilities to everything (healthy, unhealthy, neutral), and it just keeps spinning this huge web of relations. The ideal result is that every experience can, if you know what you're doing, find its home in the map of reality. That means that to know one thing well is to know all things, because the smallest moment of ex-perience contains within it all the chains of dependent relations. This moment, right now, is a microcosm of all moments. That is why meditat-ing on a Buddha statue or a candle flame or whatever is not about "relax-ing" or relieving stress (as Western yuppies have adapted it) but about finding a microcosmic entrance into the macrocosm. Anything will do as a point of entry—even meditating on a political assassination.

Venerable Nyanaponika Thera explains, in his *Abhidhamma Studies*, that "a single act of penetrative understanding starting from a limited object may acquire such intensity, width, and depth as to either lead to, or effectively prepare for, liberating insight." This is an important point about real Buddhism, and it is frequently misunderstood. Meditation is not an experiential encounter with a transcendental reality that is outside this world (though many Hindu and Christian mystics disagree). Bud-dhist transcendence is a direct grasp of the overwhelming sublime now. And the only way to truly have this realization is to forfeit your ego-centered view of things so that a truly de-centered view of things can manifest.

*   *   *

The Buddhist idea that "I" don't really exist may seem to come from outer space, but it's actually consistent with the latest advances in cognitive science. Cognitive theorists like Paul Churchland have developed compelling neuro-computational models of the brain that demonstrate higher-level problem-solving and even learning (two cognitive properties previously attributed to self and soul). The computer processes information by means of simple unconscious neural network PDPs (parallel distributed processors), and the power of these processors is so amazing that they are already starting to appear in our consumer electronics. The field of artificial intelligence (AI) has been revolutionized by the fact that a computer programmer can stack a chain of very simple on-off (binary) commands into a hierarchic order and then sit back and watch as a computer brain solves various puzzles through trial and error. If this is how the brain works, it suggests that information processing and very sophisticated activities can be managed and learned when no "self" or "soul" or even consciousness is there to do the directing. Many cognitive scientists are starting to demote the role of consciousness itself in the larger scheme of mental functioning, demonstrating that most of our intellectual moves can be relegated to the same kind of automatic working that we've long recognized in the autonomic systems.

In addition, other theorists, like Daniel Dennett and Susan Blackmore, make a persuasive argument, similar to the Buddha's, that the self is a fiction produced in us through the concomitant actions of our biological faculties. They completely abandon the language and metaphysics of self and prefer to think of self-identity as a "center of narrative gravity" that *feels* like a persistent entity but is really just the pooling of repeated experiential patterns and reflexive representations. Who you are really has more to do with the stories that get replayed in your mind (the representational system) and create an autobiography for you. This model, like the Buddha's, rejects the idea of a "substance self" that persists throughout one's life history and views the self as a function of brain substance—a useful function for organizing experiences that was selected over evolutionary history.

*   *   *

How the hell does Buddhism start out with advice about overcoming your desire and end up here in cognitive science? Believe it or not, the dhamma is all connected. It gets confusing when you're tracking the labyrinthine arguments, but when you step back you see that the Buddha has exactly the same agenda in mind when he critiques both the soul and the self. And even the Abhidhamma with its thousands of pages of obscure and intricate taxonomies of experience has the same agenda. The Buddha has to methodically deconstruct the popular assumptions of a persisting ego because they are the root confusions that cause selfishness. The realization of anatta is the greatest antidote to ego-centrism. When you realize that the body is not *mine*, and feelings are not *mine*, and disposition, perception, and even consciousness are not *mine*, then you turn away from your usual attempts to satisfy them (because they are inherently empty) and become free from craving. This is how you attain release from suffering. Anatta eliminates our tendency to pursue our own profit at the expense of other beings. There is no permanent self to serve and fret over, so compassion replaces narcissism.

For my Western students, many of these ideas seem depressing at first. Anatta is like a bitter pill that ruins the sweet and familiar flavors of the eternal happiness banquet. They see it as a cruel creed. Why should we rob Om Radsady's family, for example, of the comforting idea that he lives on in perfect happiness somewhere?

It might appear uncharitable to deny the soul, but here is where Buddhism shows an even more profound charity than simply asserting Radsady's individual immortality. Buddhism says there is no Radsady because he is you, and he is me, and his suffering must be acknowledged, appropriated, and made meaningful by all other beings. To say that Om Radsady is "empty" (sunyata) or anatta is not to make the nihilistic claim that he is meaningless or that he is nothing. It signifies that he exists, but not like you thought he existed. He does not exist as a persistent, independent essence—that's the illusion we usually cling to. Instead, he is part of a web of dependencies that make up the constantly undulating field of becoming.

This sounds strange at first, but we already accept an equally challenging idea from physics, which says that the hard wooden table in front of me is really a swirling mass of atomic particles and void. So too in Buddhism, the beings that seem to be individual, independent substances give way, on further analysis, to become interconnecting torrents and tributaries of energy. Each being is every other being, in the sense that Om Radsady and I are just momentary "slices" of the intersecting streams of body, feeling, perception, disposition, and consciousness. In my case, the aggregates are still bubbling and coursing, but sooner than later they will "extinguish" (nibbana) just as Om Radsady's did. He, like everyone else, is a burning flame, to use a common Buddhist metaphor. When the fuel is exhausted and the flame goes out, it is absurd to think that the flame has gone someplace else. In denying his and my own individuality and permanence, I eliminate whatever separates us and acknowledge that wherever there is suffering, I must be it and change it. And also wherever there is joy, I, in an awakened state, am a participant in it. Ultimately, for Buddhism, reality is more like a "field" of being that gets punctuated by momentary waves that we call individuals.

The idea that we're all made up of continuous energy sounds like some insipid New Age palliative, and it makes me cringe. I can hear my friend Chaminda laughing and rolling his eyes. But unlike the New Age attempts to merge physics and Eastern thought, real Buddhism is not interested in finding new "justifications" for telepathy, clairvoyance, psychic readings, séances, and the usual mystical fantasies. If the metaphysical idea that "we are all one" leads to anything other than *compassion* (the lesson the Buddha drew), then, as good Buddhists, we should just chuck the whole idea. The real measure of the dhamma is its ability to liberate us and engender compassion. So if the metaphysical ideas don't aid that goal, then, like the once useful raft, we should set them down. That's part of the thinking behind Zen Buddhism's famous koan "If you meet the Buddha on the road, kill him." The idea is to remember that Buddhism (the Buddha) is a "method" for attaining freedom, but if you get too hung up on the method (spending all your time, for example, trying to master the metaphysics of the Abhidhamma if you're a philosophical type, or turning Buddha into a deity if you're a submissive type, or massaging auras and energy flows if you're a New Age type), then you'll actually foil your own liberation. Killing the Buddha is a dramatic symbol for the proper prioritization of effort.

For Buddha, realizing that "we are all one" is a perspective shift in which reality is rethought as "fields of causal chains" rather than as independent substances. Unlike the New Age view, this perspective is not about getting new superpowers over the energies or manipulating the secret forces to your benefit. Not only is that agenda just more clinging and distraction, but it betrays the real means of changing the world. You're not supposed to meditate in order to persuade the universe to be nicer to you, and you don't improve the world by using mediums and crystals to channel energies. You improve the world by seeing that the guy down the street is really just like you and so you go help him.

In the end, what matters most is compassion. All the theory and heavy philosophy of anatta is great if you've got that kind of twisted disposition (alas, I do), but one can certainly find the heart of Buddhism independently of its head. The American pragmatist William James, for example, believed that "*feeling* is the deeper source of religion, and that philosophic and theological formulas are secondary products, like translations of a text into another tongue."

After I saw Om Radsady get shot to death, I had the natural reaction of self-examination. Were my priorities straight? After all, it easily could have been me or someone I love lying on the floor of that restaurant. I remembered that Gotama, the pre-Buddha, had felt a powerful wake-up call after he saw a dead man outside the palace gates. The tragedy of Om Radsady reminded me of the old adage "here today, gone tomorrow," which, when you think about it, pretty much sums up the Buddhist emphasis on anicca (impermanence).

I thought about my own attachments. Like other people in my age bracket, I found my priorities heavily weighted on matters of professional career success. I'd written a few books already and had some measure of professional accomplishment. I knew that I craved (tanha) more of it. Every writer is guilty of imagining best-seller fame, or at the very least literary longevity. I myself occasionally paged through a hundred-year-old book in the library and paused to wonder if someone would do the same with one of my books a century from now. There's nothing wrong with this desire when it remains occasional and inspirational, and I make no apologies for having it. It's not too different from the craving of my arts and media students back in Chicago who desperately want to be on TV, or in the movies, or on the stage, or at least on the radio. But it can slowly tilt the direction of your life away from this present moment and the riches it contains.

Seeing a man get shot to death makes one very aware of the preciousness of the present moment, and it also flips over the fame-game to expose its empty underside. Om Radsady was dead, and Phnom Penh mourned him, but nobody back home cared or noticed. In most cases, he didn't even get a mention in Western newspapers. It reminded me that obscurity is the destiny of all of us. All things must pass. Move your perspective from historical time (a mere blink) to evolutionary time or cosmic time and you'll see that no one will be spared from the consuming wheel of obscurity. In the same way that some Theravada Buddhists reminded themselves of their own impermanence by meditating on rotting corpses, I performed a meditation on my own inevitable vanishing.

Despite my illusions to the contrary, no one will read my books or know my name a hundred years from now. If for some strange reason I'm wrong about this, just add another hundred years to the example and my point will be recognized. I'm not important in the long run—no one really is. I'm only important in the short run, in the here and now. Radsady made me think about my son, who was not yet born. I wondered if one day my son would read one of my books. Maybe, but he's never going to be impressed or feel more loved or give more love because I was professionally successful, or because I met the president, nor even if I *became* the president. All that will matter to him is here and now and whether I can go to the soccer game or we can go fishing. This is the wake-up call. When the Buddha was asked whether he was a holy man, he replied simply, "I am awake." I wished I could stay awake to the present.

None of my friends or family or even colleagues back home knew who Om Radsady was. In their world, he neither came nor went. And if it had been *me* sitting at that lunch table, if it had been me who was shot, I would be as unimportant to Cambodians as Radsady was to Chicagoans. You can labor hard for immortality and fame and recognition, but even if you make a big splash on the global consciousness (with your role in a movie, with your bangin' CD release, with your political victory, with your best-seller book success), in the end you will eventually become just a footnote, and after that you will slip from the record of history and time altogether, finally evaporating like billions and billions of our predecessors. While this realization may seem deflationary at first, it proves to be rather inspiring after the ego-bruises fade away. Because now all motivation and purpose and rationale have to go to the work itself rather than to the "success"—to the journey rather than the destination. Since only the *now* really exists and obscurity awaits on either side of it, I resolved that I should try to live more deeply in the life I had—not the life I craved.

Since I've flinched my way through a platitude like "it's the journey, not the destination," I might as well open the floodgates on the others. Write books in order to learn something, not to gain ersatz immortality. Play your musical instrument as if it's the last time you'll touch it. Tend your garden like there's no tomorrow. Love like you've never been hurt. Dance like no one is watching. Oh brother. This treacly pap makes me a little nauseous, but it actually does have a good point. It's a point that is at once painfully obvious yet always forgotten. Letting go of the future, of the lust for fame, of transcendental meaning, and of the myriad "validations" that come through external recognition—letting go of all that allows you to find and create the local meaning of the here and now, which is the only thing that exists anyway. I hope, for my son's sake, that I can find a way to do that.

One of the best ways to actualize the no-self doctrine in your life is to give that life in service—a mundane but powerful gift that most parents understand perfectly well. When you become someone's parent, you pick up something that you can never really put down again. You don't have to go to Cambodia or India or Tibet to shift from the me-and-mine perspective to the no-self perspective. You only have to dedicate yourself to something or someone. To serve is to lose your self. And according to Buddhism, serving your child, or your elderly parent, or your lover, is far better than trying to serve God. After all, even if there *is* a perfect being, he certainly doesn't need your help in the way these people do.

Seven

LESSONS TO BRING HOME
Transcendental Everydayness

When it was finally time to leave Southeast Asia and come home to Chicago, I felt a mixture of anticipation and loss. I wanted to come home to take care of my soon-to-be-born son and his very pregnant mother, but I had also come to feel at home in this strange and mysterious part of the world.

Before I left for the West, I went on one last travel spree. Cut free from the grueling teaching schedule and with a little money left over from my self-imposed pauper's budget, I managed, in just a matter of weeks to retrace certain routes and add new ones. I returned briefly to Vietnam, where some academic friends of mine invited me to dinner with the renowned poet Nguyen Duy. We sat on the Mekong River, in Ho Chi Minh City, eating fresh shrimp and drinking rice wine with pickled cobras floating in the bottle. Mr. Nguyen, who started writing during his days in the trenches of the war, graciously shared beautiful miniature poems with us. One of them, titled "Respectfully to Ms. Beauty," translated:

Respectfully to the innocent Ms. Beauty
Xuy Van fakes her insanity,
Who knows when she will reveal her intelligence
Joy is close to sadness
Early morning is close to sunset in human life.

I couldn't be sure of Mr. Nguyen's intended meaning for this little verse, but I knew that Xuy Van was a famous character in *cheo*, Vietnamese popular opera. She feigns madness in order to escape her husband and then pursues wealth and fame. I felt that Mr. Nguyen was communicating something about the slippery rapport between appearance and reality. It was a philosopher's theme if ever there was one. We know that Xuy Van wasn't really insane. Is Ms. Beauty really innocent? Is the quiet American really quiet? And while the appearances of joy and sadness, or morning and sunset, are very distinct and different, the reality is that they are two sides of a coin. Polar opposites are caught in a dance where no one else can ever cut in. This all struck me as rather Buddhist in its holism and its skepticism. I had come to see many incongruities between appearances and realities while living in Southeast Asia. I wondered if Southeast Asians had also seen me as a puzzle of appearances and realities.

During this short tour in Vietnam, I wrangled an interview with a Pure Land Mahayana monk (no small feat under the watchful eye of the Communist censors); I witnessed the haunting chants of the strange Cao Dai devotees (the syncretic religion that blends Catholicism, Buddhism, Confucianism, Islam, Taoism, and secular science); had a claustrophobic freak-out in the tiny Cu-Chi tunnels (famous during the war for housing North Vietnamese soldiers in a network of underground passageways); enjoyed really good air conditioning for the first time in months; ate my weight in cheap, delicious *pho* (Vietnamese soup); and had the best goddamn foot massage of my life.

Shortly afterward, I found myself back in Bangkok, Thailand, visiting the giant reclining Buddha at Wat Pho. While there, I managed to take in the famous Calypso transvestite cabaret, where tourists flock to see diminutive Thai men sing and dance as women after their elaborate "sex reassignment surgeries." I also did some hard bargaining for Buddha amulets in the chaotic markets; witnessed the indescribable "pussy ping-pong" at the live sex shows, and did some peaceful sitting meditation at Wat Maha That.

Everywhere I went during those last few weeks I was surrounded by panic-stricken almond eyes that peered suspiciously over white surgical masks. It was the height of the SARS epidemic then, and people were dying in Southeast and Far East Asia. It was a very eerie experience to sit on a bus or puddle-jumper plane while all the passengers wore white masks over their faces. The ominous and unsettling experience of living in the hot zone of a deadly respiratory disease made me eager to return home. But in the end, I decided to say good-bye to Southeast Asia from the jewel of Khmer civilization, the Angkor Wat ruins.

Angkor Wat, which means "city of temples," is the generic shorthand name that's used to designate a cluster of jaw-dropping temples located in northwestern Cambodia, and the name also applies to a specific Vishnu temple that was built by Suryarvarman II (1112–52 C.E.). Angkor Wat is considered to be one of the modern "wonders of the world," and that is definitely not an exaggeration. You would be hard-pressed to visit a place more aesthetically beautiful and more spiritually inspiring. I think it's fair to say that architecture doesn't get any more sublime than the Angkor temples.

The nearly twenty temples were built between the ninth and fourteenth centuries, and they reflect not only the powerful and massive Khmer empire of the time but also the fairly quick cultural transition from Hinduism to Mahayana Buddhism to Theravada Buddhism. Angkor Wat proper is a temple devoted to the Hindu god Vishnu, for example, but in walking distance is the equally magnificent Angkor Thom temple, which was built by the celebrated Khmer king Jayavarman VII. Built less than one hundred years after Angkor Wat, the temple is devoted to Buddha, particularly Mahayana's Avalokiteshvara. But very quickly after this flash of royal Mahayana, Theravada Buddhism swept the entire region (Burma, Siam, Laos, and Cambodia) like a wildfire. By the time the Chinese envoy Zhou Daguan filed his report on Khmer culture in the late thirteenth century, he was already noticing the prevalence of Theravada temples; containing "no bells, cymbals, flags, or platforms," they were much more austere than the Mahayana temples. All of these ideological layers are here at the Angkor site, as are glimpses, through relief carvings, into the daily activities of court life and the chronicles of great military campaigns.

I had been to the temples several times in the past, and this time I decided to spend a little time in my favorite spots. After passing by the bridge of fifty-four gods and fifty-four demons, entering through the South Gate of Angkor Thom, I walked the long stretch of thick forest. Monkeys accompanied me through this incredibly peaceful corridor of tall banyan and coconut trees. This straight path leading to the Bayon monument, where two hundred giant sculpted Buddha faces peacefully await, is the kind of place where you might like to have your cremated ashes spread around.

One of my favorite temples is Preah Khan, which means "Sacred Sword." Part of its magic lies in the fact that very few people go there—I have spent whole mornings at the temple without seeing anyone. I had a palpable feeling of connection with the ancient past while climbing around the crumbling sandstone and laterite. Besides its aesthetic beauty, Preah Khan, built by Jayavarman VII for his father, symbolizes religious tolerance and pluralism. The central sanctuary of the temple was dedicated to Buddha, but the western sector was for the Hindu cult of Vishnu and the northern wing was for Shiva. In addition, the southern section was given over to ancestor worship. All the living spiritual options were gathered harmoniously at Preah Khan.

On my last trip there, I was approached by a young boy as I arrived at the garuda guardian statues. His English was excellent, and he launched into a relentless tour-guide pitch that eventually melted my resistance. After we negotiated the two-dollar price, he became very formal and announced to me, "My name is Bo, I am twelve years old, and I will be your guide this morning!" He then moved us methodically through a tour that he had observed and memorized by years of hanging on the coattails of licensed tour groups. He was a brilliant fount of information, but whenever I asked questions that went beyond the rehearsed script, he grew agitated and dismissive. He and I were the only people on the grounds that morning, and a gentle rain accompanied us through the open-roofed ruins.

I never let on that I had been to Preah Khan before and that I already knew the information. After Bo had shown me the phallic lingam-yoni altar (the carnality of which he didn't seem to grasp), the reclining Vishnu relief sculpture, and all the rest, we ended up outside the southern enclosure wall. Walking casually on the sand trail, surrounded by jungle, Bo asked for more money to help him pay for school. This is a very common appeal in Cambodia, and there is no reason to doubt its veracity. Around 43 percent of rural Cambodians live under the poverty line, and these poor families must make tough decisions about paying for registration, uniforms, books, pencils, paper, food, and transportation. Frequently a family can afford to send only one of its several children to school, and invariably it turns out to be a male.

Bo told me that he had to pay off the temple police (who were definitely on the take) so he could stay and offer his tour-guide services. He also got a regular shakedown from older kids who would simply beat him up and steal his profits. I handed him five dollars. He looked around furtively and crammed it into his pants. After we said our good-byes, he bolted back the way we had come. When I rounded the corner to leave, I bumped into two older boys, maybe sixteen years old.

"Hey, mistah, you Australian or American?" one of the boys asked me.

"American," I replied.

"America number one!" he smiled, holding up his forefinger. "Hey, how much money you give my little friend Bo?"

I knew these were the bullies that would eventually roll my guide for his profits. So I thought at first to deny the payment altogether, but then realized that they may have seen the exchange.

"Oh, I gave him four thousand riel," I lied. It's the equivalent of one dollar. They were utterly incredulous, but at least it gave Bo some chance of keeping a little profit after their inevitable rake-off.

I spent the afternoon at the incomparable Ta Phrom temple. Ta Phrom, a Buddhist structure, is the "spouse" temple of Preah Khan because it was made by King Jayavarman VII for his mother. But Ta Phrom stands out from all other structures because the Cambodian government and the Franco-Khmer restoration teams have chosen to leave the entire site in its overgrown, dilapidated, original state of discovery. It looks today just as it did when the French explorer Henri Mouhot (1826–61) "rediscovered" the Angkor ruins in the 1850s. The temple is crumbling and being absorbed back into the jungle in a manner that is both beautiful and frightening. The giant banyan trees are spilling, at glacial speed, over the tops of the temple walls, wrapping around pillars, and pouring into the nooks and crannies between the bricks. Teratological rhizomorphic tentacles grow over the ruins and each other in thick ancient layers. Green creeping vines bubble up out of every crevice and embrace the collapsing sandstone architecture. In the 1930s, H. W. Ponder, in *Cambodian Glory*, described Ta Phrom beautifully:

> Everywhere around you, you see Nature in its dual role of destroyer and consoler; strangling on the one hand, and healing on the other; no sooner splitting the carved stones asunder than she dresses their wounds with cool, velvety mosses, and binds them with her most delicate tendrils; a conflict of moods so contradictory and feminine as to prove once more—if proof were needed—how well "Dame" Nature merits her feminine title!

Here, more strongly than anywhere else in Southeast Asia and possibly the world, one really experiences the Buddhist doctrine of impermanence (anicca). If there can be a geographical manifestation of the metaphysical doctrine of impermanence, then Ta Phrom is it. In the

Sanna Sutta (Anguttara Nikaya, VII.46), Buddha explains how the awareness of impermanence or inconstancy helps us. "When a monk's awareness often remains steeped in the perception of inconstancy (anicca), his mind shrinks away from gains, offerings, and fame, bends away, pulls back, and is not drawn in, and either equanimity or loathing take a stance. Just as a cock's feather or a piece of tendon, when thrown into a fire, shrinks away, bends away, pulls back, and is not drawn in."

Wandering around Ta Phrom, you realize that no empire will last, no structure will persist, no attempt at immortality will succeed. But it is an agreeable realization, not angst-ridden. At Ta Phrom, you simultaneously perceive the disintegration of all grand gestures and the poignant beauty of the small present moment. I sat on a giant fallen brick, the sun splashing through a sieve of tree leaves, and pondered the lessons of my entire journey.

I stumbled and fumbled to articulate, to myself, my new perspective. If I could summarize the complex transformation that I felt, I would have to characterize my new viewpoint as "transcendental everydayness." It's a rather inelegant, mongrel phrase, but it accurately conveys the philosophy.

For too long, people like me have had no good way of expressing their sense of the spiritual—their sense of the deep profundity of nature, or the inspirational power of art, or the bittersweetness of the human condition. As soon as I say "spiritual," I am immediately given only two vocabularies with which to undergird my feelings of being "connected to something larger": traditional theism or equally disappointing New Age metaphysical theories about energy and mystical vibes and all the rest. For many people like myself, neither of these options seems compelling. I'm not alone. In 2004 the University of Chicago's National Opinion Research Center reported some major shifts in the religious landscape of America, and chief among the changes was a jump in the past decade (from 8 percent to 14 percent—double the number of Jews and Muslims combined) of people who claim to be spiritual but do not affiliate with a specific religion. Unfortunately, both the devotees of "God the Father" and "May-the-Force-be-with-you" mystical energy have tried to convince

us that the only alternative to their ghostly metaphysics is a cold, materi-
alistic nihilism of meaningless atoms whirling in the void. The lame
parameters of those options have been installed by, and are reinforced by,
ideologues who stand to profit from the simplistic dichotomy. But Buddhism offers a Middle Way—a spiritualism that does not require us to,
as Martin Luther urged, "tear the eyes out of our reason."

What does it mean to be "transcendental" without religion and without magical mysticism? We need to rethink the term while still
preserving its recognizable meaning. To transcend means to go beyond
some limit, but that activity need not be connected to a supernatural
metaphysics. If I have an ecstatic experience (from the Latin *ex stasis*, to
go out of one's place), I do not transcend to an unworldly divine realm. I
transcend my usual egoistic perspective and see things in a fresh way (in
a "disinterested" way, to use an old Enlightenment term). Religion may
give me this unselfish perspective, this sense of awe and reverence. But so
does art, nature, and human heroism. Since there is no distinction between the hidden and the manifest in Buddhism, one only needs to
attend (in a mindful way) to a bit of mundane experience to let the sublime aspect shine through.

Aldous Huxley expresses this idea that I'm calling transcendental
everydayness in his novel *Point Counterpoint*. One of the characters says,

> The whole story of the universe is implicit in any part of it. The medita-
> tive eye can look through any single object and see, as through a window,
> the entire cosmos. Make the smell of roast duck in an old kitchen di-
> aphanous and you will have a glimpse of everything, from the spiral
> nebulae to Mozart's music and the stigmata of St. Francis of Assisi. The
> artistic problem is to produce diaphanousness in spots so as to reveal
> only the most humanly significant of distant vistas behind the near fa-
> miliar object.

The transcendent is not something that lives beyond the here and
now, not something that we will meet in the future after death. It is the
sense of connection that comes suddenly in the middle of a card game

with your father; or the terrible yank on your heartstrings when you hear the stories of heroism during the 9/11 tragedy; or the moment you realize that your whole family is sitting around the dinner table for the first time in years; or the shock of unexpectedly pouring out a beautiful solo on your saxophone; or the perfectly brewed cup of coffee on a crisp early morning; or the full sweaty weight of your lover's body on top of you; or the breathless awe of watching the sun set from the top of Angkor Wat temple.

Going to a profoundly religious area like Southeast Asia, one naturally expects depth—and one gets it. But the spiritual depth is not always where you expect to find it. Monks smoking cigarettes and hustling tourists for money at Angkor Wat made my skin crawl, but the quiet pride and gentle humor of my kindhearted friend Kimvan, who lost most of his family to violence, or the way my grizzled hotel owner saved a baby who had been abandoned in the street and adopted him as his own—these experiences showed me a kind of human dignity and care that can be witnessed more readily where people have lost a great deal.

In addition to these dramatic experiences, I felt a new appreciation for the simple mundane things too. But I won't idealize my own awareness of a transcendental everyday too much. Even though its appreciation is something sought after by Buddhism, I have to confess that my own awareness of the everyday routines of life was not boosted by meditation or philosophy. I paid closer attention to everything because I always felt like I was tripping on some hallucinogenic drug. And that's because Southeast Asia really is an exotic place for a midwestern American. The atmosphere is so thick with unfamiliarity that I couldn't help but be rapt in infantlike wonder all the time. I'd sit down at a sidewalk food stand, and the proprietor might come sit next to me smiling and introducing family members, while an elephant lumbered by slowly, and a man with no legs or lower torso rolled up on a cart and took my shoes off for shining, and a snack plate of barbecued insects appeared on the table, followed by an amazing fish dish served inside a halved coconut, and then the streets might literally flood in minutes with monsoon rains, leaving motos and cyclos to wobble slowly through the muddy streets. I was forced to focus on everything because everything seemed to require it—I had to practice mindfulness by necessity. But even though my mindfulness was almost coerced by the exotic environment of Southeast Asia, I did carry some of that appreciation back to my less exotic life in Chicago.

The pursuit of happiness is perhaps the greatest motivation for all human beings, but Americans tend to see happiness entirely in the future tense. As an American, I think I'm driven by, even tormented by, the future more than other people. Not only does consumer culture dangle the promise of material satisfactions in front of me every day, but I am also influenced more subtly by the dominant and founding ideology of Christian eschatology. The pilgrims saw themselves on a mission of manifest destiny to create a new city of God in America, and the Protestant work ethic made us strive to attain the future goal of perfect happiness and divine union. Messianic religions and end-time religions will definitely train your eye on the future, and if you mix that orientation with the gospel of prosperity, then the present looks paltry next to the future. Everything good is just about to happen, is just around the corner. That is a human condition certainly, but an acute condition for Americans.

David Brooks, in his book *On Paradise Drive*, gives us an insightful look at our American obsession with the future. Noting the American ethos as seen by Europeans, for example, Brooks gives us a perceptive sketch through the eyes of the Spanish philosopher George Santayana. Santayana claimed that Americans live life with two worlds in their heads: the real world and the imagined ideal world. In the mind's eye, this ideal world seeps over into the real world and the result is a character who is "more attached to what might or should be than to what already is." Santayana says of the American, "His enthusiasm for the future is profound."

> At the same time, the American is imaginative; for where life is intense, imagination is intense also. Were he not imaginative he would not live so much in the future. But his imagination is practical and the future it

forecasts is immediate; it works with the clearest and least ambiguous terms known to his experience, in terms of number, measure, contrivance, economy and speed. He is an idealist working on matter. . . . All his life he jumps into the train after it has started and jumps out before it has stopped.

*   *   *

One of the great lessons that I learned living in the land of the tattered Buddha is the value of slowing down a little. I don't want to sound like some knee-jerk Thoreau type who just thinks the simple life of Southeast Asia is inherently better than the hustle and bustle of the American rat race. Things are relative. If Americans need to slow down and live in the present a little more, maybe Southeast Asians should speed up and live a bit more in the future. (It's taken Cambodians twenty-five years just to start a war crimes tribunal for the Khmer Rouge atrocities.) All I know is that the future mania that I've inherited as an American has given me more than just anxiety—it has also motivated many of the worthy accomplishments of my life. If that imaginative energy that Santayana describes can be harnessed for something more than consumerism and the aggrandizement of the ego, then it is also the greatest engine for art, science, and social justice.

Unfortunately, most of the Americans I know are filled with nervous unease because they are increasingly striving to realize a future that tortures them with its carrot-stick impossibility. Not only is the ideal future unachievable because it can't ever exist in the present by definition, but the American future is also unachievable because it defines satisfactions and successes in terms of pleasures and products that are inherently ephemeral. The Harvard psychologist Daniel Gilbert and his colleagues have shown that pleasures always prove to be less intense and more fleeting than people predict. He calls this gap between our predicted pleasures and the actual experiences the "impact bias." And this impact bias leads us to what Gilbert calls "miswanting"—an endless error that starts from our dissatisfaction at the quick pleasure-fade and then moves rapidly to successions of novel pleasures (jewelry, cars, shoes, bigger houses, and so on).

Contrary to Americans and others who chase after the future and dissect the past, Buddhists affirm the present over everything. When people asked the Buddha why his followers were so joyful and healthy when they lived so simply, he replied, "They do not repent the past, nor do they brood over the future. They live in the present. Therefore they are radiant. By brooding over the future and repenting the past, fools dry up like green reeds cut down [in the sun]" (Samyutta Nikaya).

The tanha (craving) that we all experience and that serves as the main culprit in human suffering is a natural but ruinous tendency to reify impermanent realities, be they pleasures, or future goals, or even idealized versions of ourselves or our lovers. For Americans, one of the major lessons of Buddhist sati (mindfulness) and panna (wisdom) is that we must stop seeing ourselves as incomplete and in need of completion by external realities, like that ideal soul mate, that coveted promotion, that audience applause, that new car, and all the other *things* and "extreme experiences" that mass media is selling us. Don't get me wrong, there's nothing bad about aspiration and ambition. But for one thing, ambition can be like heroin, and for another thing, it can fix upon everything from the stupid to the sublime. To aspire to nibbana (enlightenment) is to fix upon the sublime, to aspire to increase the bling-bling, well . . .

As a college professor, I spend a lot of time with young Americans who are at that intoxicating and frightening phase of life—when they are making tough decisions about who they want to be when they grow up. It is a watershed moment (one of many) when dreams and reality make brutally intimate contact. It's a wonderful time of self-development, but if you ever want to see the meeting of dreams and reality go completely off the rails, then watch the tryouts for *American Idol*. To my sick mind, this amateur pop-singer competition is some of the most cruelly funny stuff you'll ever see on TV. I actually stop watching the show as soon as the talent pool has been reduced to the capable, because then the mesmerizing train wreck is over. Never will you see a more patently obvious display of distorted self-perception than when you witness thousands of young Americans stand and confidently deliver such devastating a cappella disasters. And in the few years that the show has been on the air and become a national obsession, I've had several of my students audition to become the next American Idol. I bring it up here because it demonstrates how Buddhism can both enhance experience and protect against suffering, even in our nation of Disney, Vegas, and Hollywood.

One of my students, who actually had a strong voice and made it through several *American Idol* cuts, was also a good-humored, prudent, and insightful twenty-one-year-old regular guy. He was in my Introduction to Philosophy course, and when he returned from his brush with fame, he regaled us with stories that only confirmed (albeit with behind-the-scenes élan) what any viewer can readily witness: young men and women with no clue about their paucity of talent, subjecting themselves to humiliating judgment, responding with an even more amazing rebellious rejection of reality and reaffirmation of their own inflated self-appraisal, all topped off with tears and histrionics of disappointment. All of which would be terribly depressing to watch unless of course you're me—who has to laugh to keep from crying. My student, who took a very Buddhist approach to the whole affair, remained detached and laid-back enough to actually enjoy the whole experience. He met a few interesting people, got some girls' phone numbers, sang his heart out, accepted both accolades and eventual elimination with grace, and came home with good stories and memories of an odd adventure. The vast majority of his young associates, however, were practically suicidal with despair. Their craving for fame was so overwhelming, coupled with their astounding myopia regarding their own skills, that my student could not believe it. Tens of thousands of kids line up in cities all around the country, and record-breaking millions more crowd around the cathode tube at home, in order to taste some little morsel of fame and adulation—even if it's just a vicarious taste for viewers. Most people don't seem to notice the obscene amount of craving and attachment in all this. Alas, the dukkha (suffering) is real and ridiculous.

Buddhism offers a way to train and discipline the mind so that it can enjoy pleasures but not be imprisoned by them. I think that, through a natural disposition (rather than from formal training), my student managed to have a very mindful experience of this *American Idol* circus, which is a little microcosm of America. The mindful person can experience joy but simultaneously understand its sublime emptiness or impermanence (and the same with pain). Buddhism is a psychological state of peace and a philosophical grasp of reality that gives the practitioner the savvy to handle even the Ring of Gyges.

Remember, from chapter 1, that the ring of invisibility is a thought experiment that asks how a person can stay ethical when absolute power and absolute hedonism are hers for the taking. Buddhism blows out (nibbana) the three flames of lobha (greed), dosa (hate), and moha (delusion), and with those three extinguished, even the ring cannot corrupt a person. Furthermore, this freedom or nirvana is attainable now, not in some future state. In the Anguttara Nikaya, the Buddha says, "If lust, anger, and delusion are given up, man aims neither at his own ruin nor at the ruin of others, and he experiences no mental pain and grief. This is *nibbana* visible in this life, immediate, inviting, attractive, and comprehensible to the wise."

Westerners are frequently confused about Buddhist nibbana, and it doesn't help that Hinduism uses the same word for something different. Scholars and popularizers have been correcting people for about a century now—explaining that nibbana is not "heaven," so we should have that lesson down by now. But even a 2003 BBC documentary film, *The Life of the Buddha*, begins with the erroneous definition of nirvana as "the everlasting bliss we all dream of." Think back to the explicit arguments of the Potthapada Sutta and you'll see that such a definition is not only divergent from the Buddha's actual teachings but downright contradictory. And yet it persists unchecked, mostly because confused Tibetan Buddhism (a mere 6 percent of the total 400 million Buddhists) continues to be taken for the dhamma in the West. Since nothing is everlasting in Buddhism, we know that nirvana is not heaven or everlasting bliss.

It remains to be emphasized that nibbana is a multi-use term in Buddhism. Sometimes it's used to mean a dramatic culmination of freedom that occurs to bhikkhus after years of solitary practice, but more commonly and more important for Americans, it's used to describe a cooling or an absence of craving (and consequently a cessation of suffering). Nibbana in this sense is something that I think Americans (including myself) can increase through effort and benefit from tremendously. There is nothing abstract or mysterious about cooling off our boiling manic dispositions. Buddhadasa Bhikkhu, for example, points out that everyone has a few moments of nibbana in the morning after a restful sleep. "When you awaken, you usually continue in this state of calm, even while talking, thinking, or doing anything at all. You are usually not possessed by love, hate, greed, anger, passion, or the feeling of 'me and mine.'" Mindful Buddhists can keep much of that negative egotism at bay throughout the day, while the rest of us quickly become filled with poisonous feelings. Riding public transportation to work, I'm usually ready to kill somebody by 9:00 A.M., and my other cravings are in full swing by lunchtime—not so good on the enlightenment meter.

But this chain of irritations, leading to suffering, is a domino effect that can be halted. The Buddha calls this causal chain paticca samuppada, or "dependent arising." Each experience and each phenomenon is dependent on something else for its existence. My existence depended on my parents, just as my son's depended on his parents. But since Buddhism is primarily a science of the mind, it also articulates the dominoes of psychological experience. According to the Buddha, tanha (craving) is dependent on (and would not arise without) vedana (sensation). In other words, the craving would not begin unless we first had sensual pleasures that we wanted to pursue or sensual pains that we wanted to avoid. But sensation itself is dependent upon *phassa* (contact), or the meeting of sensory objects with our sensory equipment (the physiological root of conscious sensation). The Buddha continues this causal analysis, tracing where each step comes from and where each steps leads, considering metaphysical realities together with psychological realities. Eventually, he concludes with twelve causal steps, and the total circle of relations is called paticca samuppada. If, through practice, you can cut one of the links, then the linkages that follow on to suffering can be dropped.

Here is where the practical art of liberation and the philosophical insight of transcendental everydayness came together for me. Overcoming craving is achieved by living more mindfully in the present (the transcendental everyday), and in some paradoxical way, you actually get what you most want by not wanting it anymore. In other words, Buddhism taught me the oblique pursuit of happiness.

What we most want from life is happiness, so we set out to pursue it. This makes perfect sense on the face of it. The problem is that happiness is universally confused with "pleasures," and then we're all off to chase gratifications. The basic assumption is that when we get that one last thing—the tank-sized SUV, the customized guitar, the trophy wife, the Gucci bag—or attain that one culminating gratification, we will finally be satisfied and fulfilled. We'll finally be who we wanted to be. But we are doomed, like a modern-day King Midas, to ruin every true happiness we have by touching it with our insatiable obsession. The life of hedonism cannot find its own termination—it's a fire burning inexorably across an infinite tinder field.

Buddhism teaches us to see the beauty in this present moment or activity rather than the payoff pleasure that comes at the end of an activity. In this way, you stop pursuing happiness and actually become happy. What you should pursue instead of gratifications are activities that engage your creativity, or your mental faculties, or your physical powers. If you want to be happy, don't work on being happy—work on learning to play a musical instrument, study karate, take up small-engine repair, gardening, or calligraphy, learn a language, paint a house, or try your hand at a soufflé. If you can keep your ego-consciousness from seeping in and turning these wonderful activities into manic fixations, then happiness (not always pleasure) will emerge out of the focused, careful activity itself. A state of well-being and peacefulness comes forth as a by-product of your mindful activity because you have (perhaps only temporarily) dissolved the ego by distracting and luring it into a busy immersion with the minutiae of your chosen activity. This is the oblique pursuit of happiness.

There is another important virtue to this oblique approach. Parodies of Buddhist detachment often picture isolated navel-gazers who are removed from society, living in caves or communes or what have you. But in fact, abandoning your cravings will totally change your friendships for the better as well. Most of us who are chasing our egoistic drives tend to have "utility" friendships. We picture ourselves as dedicated to the wellbeing and success of our friends, but more often than not we surround ourselves with people who can be of use to us. If the utility is mutual, then it's considered a solid friendship. There's nothing wrong with this, because everybody needs these kinds of relationships. But cultivating and maintaining deep friendships in a culture of "me and mine" is very difficult. More enduring and deeper friendships, the ones beyond utility, happen when we forget about ourselves. So, contrary to the stereotype of the Buddhist loner, a little detachment goes a long way to enhance true friendships. If I take myself out of the equation temporarily, then I can make it possible not only to serve my friend when she needs help but also to enjoy that service and not feel "used." Many people believe that they can only let their guard down and be selfless with another person *after* significant trust has been built up. No one wants to be a doormat. But of course the only way to build that trust is by little acts of selflessness.

In addition to the individual psychological benefits of Buddhism, I learned a great deal about the social relations of Theravada culture. I lived in a world where the family dynamics, the gender relations, and the political structures were all very different from those in America.

Southeast Asian cultures, which seem "backward" from the arrogant viewpoint of so many in the West, in fact have many valuable social lessons to teach us.

The Buddha is often interpreted as an otherworldly philosopher, but in fact he gave plenty of temporal advice for people who want to get along better with their spouse, their employer, their parents and children, and their friends. His Sigalovada Sutta, or "Code of Lay Ethics," which is widely known and followed throughout Theravada countries, charts out how husbands and wives should treat each other, as well as children and parents, employers and workers, teachers and students, and friends. Buddha asks us to envision a social map with the four directional points of east, west, north, and south, but also a third-dimensional axis moving through the middle of the map. The eastern point represents the relationship of parents and children, the western point is the relationship between husbands and wives, the northern point represents friends, the southern point is teachers and students, the nadir of the central axis represents workers and employers, and the zenith symbolizes spiritual leaders. The Buddha gives five pieces of advice to each pair of relations. For example, parents should relate to their children by restraining them from doing evil, encouraging them to do good, training them for a profession, arranging a suitable marriage, and leaving them an inheritance. Whereas sons and daughters must relate to their parents by supporting them in old age, fulfilling their duties, keeping the family traditions, making themselves worthy of an inheritance, and honoring departed relatives. In the western region of the social map, a husband should respect his wife, be courteous toward her, be faithful to her, hand over domestic authority to her, and provide her with adornment (jewelry, clothes, and so on). In response, a good wife is to perform her duties well, be hospitable to relations, be faithful, protect her husband's earnings, and be skillful and industrious.

By our "politically correct" standards, this map of social relations probably seems retrograde, but let me offer some modest praise for how and why the social system works well in Southeast Asia. I have no interest in suggesting that Americans turn back the clock and live with older social hierarchies, but in trying to abolish all hierarchies we have also thrown out the very helpful idea of a "division of labor." In my humble opinion, families tend to function better in Southeast Asia, not because they are patriarchal, but because there is a division of labor. Things would work equally well with a matriarchy or, preferably, an egalitarian division of labor. But things won't work and don't work when *every* function, task, decision, and authority in a family is up for debate, competition, rivalry, and opposition.

Let's take the "war of the sexes" as our primary example. Certainly the war of the sexes is familiar all over the globe, but the feminist movements of the West have not really shaped the landscape of Southeast Asia. The terrain is quite different there, but it would be too simplistic for us to denounce the difference as inferior. The West's rigorous individualism and dogmatism of independence have brought a mania for self-autonomy into every domain of human interaction, including the conjugal and other intimacies of our shared lives.

Contrary to the "love marriages" of the West, for example, the arranged marriages of the East are more successful—as measured by divorce rates anyway. The American divorce rate is something like 50 percent. We have to acknowledge the fact that in some countries it is women's economic reliance on men, not philosophy, that contributes strongly to the low divorce rates. But my informal research and experiences in cross-cultural relationships lead me to point out something about Asian women that most Westerners fail to perceive. Asian women are frequently pitied by Westerners, who see them as subservient, disempowered, and unliberated. What outsiders do not see is that in Asia husbands are allowed a slice of bravado so as to showboat the public face of power and authority, but women actually control most of the affairs of the private sphere, including the children, the house, and, significantly, the husband's wallet. The Buddha himself realizes that if you want a happy home, you better hand over your wallet to your wife—but the flip side is that she must be thrifty, not spendthrifty, with the income. This division of labor, which

Westerners fail to see, works well. It is hard to imagine American men and women submitting to such an arrangement, although it does happen sometimes. If two people are going to raise a family, then some division of labor is absolutely necessary. It doesn't matter which gender does which job, but it can't be an internal struggle. This was the Buddha's point when he charted the power-responsibility sharing system of the Sigalovada Sutta.

Spurred on by the economic empowerment of women, Western couples are constantly locked in a power struggle of "no-surrender." Many spouses have a hard time surrendering on any issue because they constantly fear exploitation and are trapped in opposing postures of self-validation. In a partnership, bowing is not breaking. It is compromise—something we have less and less of in America. The family dynamic has changed partly because the workforce has changed. But inside many homes (and the divorce rate bears this out), there are significant battles for territory. There are unhappy and unhealthy marriages in Asia, of course, but in the Theravadan world, where one doesn't even believe in a "self," ego protection seems minimized. The Buddha's lesson of paticca samuppada even applies here in the gender relations (as well as in family and work relations). The members of the marriage are not struggling to carve out their own independence—they are interdependent parts of a larger reality. And this underscores the fact that while marriage (and family) is still an important survival strategy in the developing world, this strategy no longer seems to be required in much of the developed world. Capital can make family expendable.

Americans can't go back in history to some old patriarchy in order to reestablish peaceful, harmonious homes and families, nor can they adopt a Southeast Asian way of doing things. But the idea of a family division of labor and power is a flexible and adaptable model. Living with the Buddhist version and seeing its benefits made me realize that Americans could do better on the business of family peace.

The "householder" (the economic center of the family) is traditionally male in Southeast Asia, but it doesn't have to be that way. Only the division of labor is necessary, not the gender assignments. And it is necessary primarily so that you and your mate can forget about it and get on with the difficulties of raising a family and surviving in a hostile and economically depressed condition. Life is hard enough without warfare and turf disputes inside the sanctuary of your own home.

The traditional American division of men in the workplace and women in the kitchen is happily over and done. I'm not sure, however, that we've been entirely successful in finding a new set of divisions, and of course this has to be worked out by individual couples and families. But we still seem to be in a postliberation power-grab moment. Most members of my generation are racing through relationships with the ease and frequency of underwear changes. Nothing and no one ever seems to be "enough" because we in the developed world live in a postfamily age. Economically, we don't *need* each other in the way Southeast Asians do, but psychologically speaking our needs may be greater than ever.

I returned to Chicago six weeks before my son was born. His devoted mother labored hard in the birthing room, while I held her hand and offered my useless Lamaze breath counts. Talk about an unequal division of labor! His mother pushed and struggled for eight hours, while I fetched ice chips for her to chew on and counted breath exercises. I thanked the Buddha that I was born a man. When my little boy finally made his grand entrance on Father's Day, he was so quiet and pensive right out of the womb that the nurse called in a special pediatrician to examine him. Finally, much to our relief, the doctor announced that he was healthy as an ox, but simply "a quiet, shy little guy." That day was certainly the last day that he was quiet or shy, and he has been running me ragged with his infinite energy ever since.

The day after my son was born, a woman turned to me in the hospital elevator and, seeing me awkwardly juggle this fragile newcomer, said wryly, "Your life is not your own anymore."

"Oh, it never really was," I replied, smiling back. She looked confused, but smiled back at my sleep-deprived weirdness. I didn't have the time—or the faculties for that matter—to tell her about my recent journey through Southeast Asia. Even if I did have the time then, I doubt that I could give full voice to the intricate lessons I learned in those many months overseas. I could only dumbly sense that my newborn son was somehow the culmination of my recent and exotic education in Cambodia, Laos, Thailand, and Vietnam. To express this in a less opaque way, I had an inarticulate sense that my first child had completed a perspective change or paradigm shift for me that had begun in the jungle temples of Angkor Wat and the seedy back alleys of Bangkok and Phnom Penh. The Buddhists of Southeast Asia characterize this difficult perspective change as the movement from "me and mine" to emptiness and "no-self."

Living in Southeast Asia and teaching in Cambodia was a transformative experience that goes beyond measure. There is no way to "sum it up." I'm sure I'll be processing it for years to come. Since I left, I have stayed in contact with my students, some of whom have recently been hired as researchers at the Buddhist Institute. They ask me to send pictures of my son through e-mail, and they keep me posted about their Buddhist research. I am extremely proud of their accomplishments, and I feel fortunate to have met such strong, modest young people of dignity and character. The downside of coming to know them so well is that many of my American students now seem irreversibly spoiled to me.

My American students have their own charms, and they're fundamentally good kids. But I see them differently now. My Khmer students have lived very dangerous lives compared to my American students. The Khmers have struggled with poverty, corruption, violence, and disease in ways that none of my American students have experienced. But they did not see themselves as victims; they were too proud and hopeful for that, and frankly, they were too busy working on helping their families survive and also getting an education to stop for self-pity and complaining. They did not spend their time complaining that something was owed to them. They just worked hard to achieve their goals. My American students, in contrast, who have never tasted such struggle, are phenomenally articulate about their perceived victimization. Indeed, over the past twenty-five years high school and college students have perfected the curriculum of whining and blame-placing. All of my American students are sanctimoniously clear about the ways in which "someone else" has robbed them of their dazzling potential. They write clever essays about "negative media representation," they form clubs to complain that it's society's fault that they're fat, and they feel victimized by every imaginable prejudice, but they never notice how remarkably lucky they are. Americans wrap themselves in a cloak of victimization that looks pathetic and pusillanimous after you've spent time with real victims. It makes me hope that one day all colleges will require that students spend a year abroad in a developing country.

Since my American students don't know enough to feel fortunate, then I'll try to make up the difference by feeling truly blessed. One of the major lessons I learned on my journey was that I could, with some effort, live more deeply in my own life—not the life I was craving but the life I actually had. I could be more present, aware, compassionate, and responsive within the web of connections that already interlaced through me. I fail at this project every day, but I have also learned to be patient with myself.

Like many other searching Americans, I had turned the exotic spiritualism of a faraway land into a holy grail of sorts, and I had to journey there to discover the exotic, mysterious, and transcendental qualities of my own Chicago life. Whether in Bangkok, Angkor Wat, or Chicago, the mundane becomes transcendental because every moment and event of our lives can take us out of ourselves and connect us to the larger web of being simply by our attending to it with mindfulness. We tend to think of the spiritual as something that takes place in exotic places like Cambodia, but we must remember that even Wisconsin is exotic to a Khmer villager, because "exotic" by definition means "the place you're not at." The real trick is seeing the exotic and the transcendent where you are.

Notes and Further Reading

Introduction

The translations of the Buddha's teachings are from the Pali scriptures. I have leaned heavily on the established and excellent Pali translators gathered at the Access to Insight website (www.accesstoinsight.org/index. html), which has been a library of Pali translations since 1993. Translations of the texts quoted here are by the following renowned scholars: Bhikkhu Bodhi, former president of the Buddhist Publication Society in Kandy, Sri Lanka; Thanissaro Bhikkhu (Ajaan Geoff), Acharya Buddharakkhita, Bhikkhu Khantipalo, Nyanaponika Thera, and Soma Thera.

In writing this book, I practiced something that, for lack of a better term, I call "philosophical journalism." I tried, as a participant-observer, to ferret out some of the daily cultural expressions and beliefs of Theravada Buddhism and also to keep one eye on the philosophical scriptural tenets and traditions. Of course, in addition to this unique sort of journalism, I had the benefit of many excellent scholarly books and articles on the history and culture of Southeast Asia, as well as some very fine newspaper reporting. The following list, while certainly not exhaustive or definitive, includes some general area-studies books that I benefited from tremendously. I offer them as recommendations to fellow neophytes—a group with whom I still identify strongly.

For surveys of Southeast Asian history and culture, one would do well to study *The Cambridge History of Southeast Asia*, volume 2, part 2, *From World War II to the Present*, edited by Nicholas Tarling (Cambridge University Press, 1999); D. R. SarDesai, *Southeast Asia: Past and Present*, 5th edition (Westview Press, 2004); Charles F. Keyes, *The Golden Peninsula: Culture and Adaptation in Mainland Southeast Asia*, Shaps Library of Asian Studies (reprint, University of Hawaii Press, 1995); George Coedès, *The Indianized States of Southeast Asia* (Australian National University Press, 1975); and Robert C. Lester, *Theravada Buddhism in Southeast Asia* (Ann Arbor: University of Michigan Press, 1973).

The following texts are focused more specifically on Thailand and Cambodia, and they provided me with much-needed context for my own work: David K. Wyatt, *Thailand: A Short History*, 2nd edition (Yale University Press, 2003); David K. Wyatt, *Studies in Thai History: Collected Articles* (reprint, Silkworm Books, 1999); Pasuk Phongpaichit and Chris Baker, *Thailand: Economy and Politics*, 2nd edition (Oxford University Press, 2002); Henry Kamm, *Cambodia: Report from a Stricken Land* (Arcade, 1999); and Usha Welaratna and James M. Freeman, *Beyond the Killing Fields: Voices of Nine Cambodian Survivors in America* (Stanford University Press, 1994). The writings of David Chandler are absolutely crucial for understanding Cambodian history; particularly helpful to me were: *A History of Cambodia*, 2nd edition (Silkworm Books, 1996); *Brother Number One: A Political Biography of Pol Pot*, revised edition (Westview Press, 1999); and *Voices from S-21: Terror and History in Pol Pot's Secret Prison*, 2nd edition (University of California Press, 1999). See also François Ponchaud, *The Cathedral of the Rice Paddy: 450 Years of History of the Church in Cambodia*, translated from the French by Nancy Pignarre and the Bishop Salas Cambodian Catholic Center (Le Sarment, Fayard, 1990); Ponchaud's seminal *Cambodia Year Zero*, translated from the French by Nancy Amphoux (Allen Lane, 1978); *Cambodian Culture Since 1975: Homeland and Exile*, edited by May Ebihara, Carol A. Mortland, and Judy Ledgerwood (Cornell University Press, 1994); and Grant Curtis, *Cambodia Reborn? The*

Transition to Democracy and Development (Brookings Institution Press, 1998).

The data for the 1993 Columbia University survey regarding American awareness of Southeast Asia are taken from the preface to Donald Swearer's excellent study, *The Buddhist World of Southeast Asia* (State University of New York Press, 1995).

Chapter 1

I have drawn many facts regarding the burning of the Thai embassy in 2003 from the *Phnom Penh Post* (January 31–February 13, 2003). That particular issue, headlining "Mobs Go Berserk in Anti-Thai Frenzy," is rich with additional information. I benefited particularly from Robert Carmichael and Michael Coren's article "'Deplorable Incident' Ruins Thai-Khmer Relations." Information on Piseth Pilika, Prime Minister Hun Sen's alleged lover, is drawn from Kevin Doyle, "Controversial Piseth Pilika Booklet Sold Out," *Cambodian Daily* (February 1–2, 2003). The quote from the opposition leader Sam Rainsey on the CPP's poor handling of the anti-Thai riots is taken from Lor Chanara and Kevin Doyle, "Lawmakers Lay Riot Blame with Hun Sen," *Cambodian Daily* (February 1–2, 2003).

Additional information on the draconian antidrug record of Thailand's prime minister, Thaksin Shinawatra, is taken from Raymond Bonner, "Thailand Tiptoes in Step with the American Anti-Terror Effort," *New York Times* (June 7, 2003). Statistics regarding the use and abuse of *yama* (methamphetamine) are drawn from Jessica Frommer, "Battle Plan to Combat Yama Drug Craze," *Phnom Penh Post* (volume 12, number 25, 2003). Factual information on the shooting of the Khmer singer Touch Srey Nich and her mother was taken from Cheang Sokha and Caroline Huot, "Actress Shot After Journalist Slain," *Phnom Penh Post* (October 24–November 6, 2003).

Prostitution in Southeast Asia is a very complex issue. My treatment of it has been informed by many communications with NGO workers in

Southeast Asia. Some facts included here are drawn from the press release of the Asia Pacific Women's Consultation on Prostitution, held in Bangkok in February 1997. The figures for 2002 on the percentages of local versus foreign sex customers in Southeast Asia are taken from Thomas M. Steinfatt, Simon Baker, and Allan Beesey, "Measuring the Number of Trafficked Women in Cambodia: 2002," a paper presented at the conference "The Human Rights Challenge of Globalization in Asia-Pacific-U.S." (Globalization Research Center, University of Hawaii at Manoa, Honolulu, Hawaii, November 13–15, 2002). Some information on the relationship between prostitution and traditional Southeast Asian patriarchy is drawn from Tanh-dam Truong, *Sex, Money, and Morality: Prostitution and Tourism in Southeast Asia* (Zed Books, 1990). Unfortunately, Truong's weak understanding of Theravada Buddhism undercuts her analysis in places. The Janet Ashby quote and some of the factual information regarding the Svay Pak brothel are taken from Caroline Green, "Notorious 'K11' Closed Yet Again—Driving Prostitution into the Shadows," *Phnom Penh Post* (February 14–27, 2003). The quote originally from the Microsoft CD-ROM encyclopedia referring to Bangkok as a flesh trade center is reprinted in Niels Mulder, *Thai Images: The Culture of the Public World* (Silkworm Books, Chaing Mai, 1997, p. 196).

The story and analysis of the Buddha's Kutadanta Sutta and Cakkavatti Sutta is found in Elizabeth J. Harris, "Violence and Disruption in Society: A Study of Early Buddhist Texts," *Dialogue* (new series, volume 17, 1990), published by the Ecumenical Institute for Study and Dialogue, Colombo, Sri Lanka. These same Buddhist scriptures are nicely discussed in chapter 8 of Walpola Rahula, *What the Buddha Taught*, revised edition (Grove Press, 1974).

Chapter 2

In addition to personal communications with Khmer people about animism and neak ta spirits, I benefited tremendously from chapter 3 of Ian

Harris, *Cambodian Buddhism: Its History and Practice* (University of Hawaii Press, 2004). My discussion of bray spirits and their symbiosis with Theravada Buddhism draws on Ang Choulean, "Animism in Popular Buddhism in Cambodia," *Asian Folklore Studies* (volume 47, number 1, 1988). Additional information about the complex relations between Buddhism, animism, and Brahminism was gleaned from Stephanie Gee and Cheang Bopha, "Bouddhisme, brahmanisme, et animisme: Coexistence ou syncretisme?" *Cambodge Soir* (December 5, 2002), and Stephanie Gee's entire 2002 series for *Cambodge Soir* in honor of the Buddhist World Summit is highly instructive. Some of my discussion of boran Buddhism, particularly the connection to the Three Worlds cosmology and the discussion of Venerable Duang Phang, is informed by John Marston's paper, "Reconstructing 'Ancient' Cambodian Buddhism," presented at the seventeenth annual Center for Southeast Asian Studies (CSEAS) conference, "Religion, Civil Society, and NGOs in Southeast Asia" (Berkeley, University of California, February 12, 2000). Information on Mongkut's creation of the Thammayut order and the Three Worlds cosmology is derived from Swearer's *Buddhist World of Southeast Asia*.

The Tibetan practice of suffocating yaks is discussed in chapter 2 of Lee Feigon, *Demystifying Tibet* (Ivan R. Dee, 1996). Additional information on the tooth relic that traveled from China to Thailand was taken from *People's Daily* (December 16, 2002).

Some of the facts regarding the disease outbreak in Ratanakiri Province and the animistic responses are drawn from Seth Mydans, "In Cambodian Forest, Battling Besieging Spirits," *New York Times* (May 11, 2003). The full story of the Khmer brothers who murdered their neighbors can be found in Chris Tenove, "That Old Black Magic," *Globe and Mail* (August 9, 2003).

The Albert Einstein quote regarding Buddhism is taken from *Albert Einstein: The Human Side*, edited by Helen Dukas and Banesh Hoffman (Princeton University Press, 1954).

Chapter 3

My discussion of the 2003 "disciplinary order" of the Ministry of Cults and Religions against proselytizing is informed by Porter Barron and Kuch Naren, "Spread the Word," *Cambodian Daily* (March 8–9, 2003). The story of the sixteenth-century Portuguese missionary Gaspar da Cruz is from chapter 5 of Chandler's *History of Cambodia*. The quotes from Steven M. Ellis of the Cambodian Baptist Convention are taken from www.newchurches.com, a website devoted to "church planting for the new millennium." My quotations from the letters of the Committee of Twenty Pagodas are taken from Caroline Green and Lon Nara, "Christian Groups Described as 'Second Pol Pot,'" *Phnom Penh Post* (November 13, 2002). Additional facts about the growth of Mormonism in Cambodia are drawn from Liam Cochrane, "When the Saints Go Marching In: Missionaries in Cambodia," *Phnom Penh Post* (November 21–December 4, 2003). The quote from Father Ponchaud criticizing Mormon conversions comes from the same article.

The quote from Leo Strauss on democracy is taken from the introduction to his book *City and Man* (University of Chicago Press, 2004). The quote from H. L. Mencken on liberty is from a letter to Ernest Boyd reprinted in *Letters of H. L. Mencken*, edited by Guy J. Forgue (Knopf, 1961).

Information on U.S. aid to Cambodian NGOs and the quote from the director of Cambodia's National Mother and Child Health Center are taken from Emily Watts, "U.S. Aid Rules Alarm NGOs," *Phnom Penh Post* (January 16–29, 2004). The quote from S. C. Dube and the quote from Peter Gyallay-Pap regarding the multiple functions of the traditional Theravada wats are both taken from Gyallay-Pap's helpful article, "Buddhism as a Factor of Culture and Development in Cambodia," *Cambodia Report*, a publication of the Center for Advanced Study (volume 2, number 2, March–April 1996). I supplemented the conversation about "losing face" with information from Trevor Ling's excellent book, *Buddhism, Imperialism, and War: Burma and Thailand in Modern History* (Unwin Hyman, 1979).

Maha Ghosananda's parable about the dragon can be found in his book *Step by Step* (Parallax Press, 1992). Emperor Asoka's edict on religious toleration is quoted from chapter 1 of Rahula, *What the Buddha Taught*.

My discussion of Thich Quang Duc's 1963 self-immolation is informed by Sallie King, "Thich Nhat Hahn and the Unified Buddhist Church of Vietnam: Non-Dualism in Action," in *Engaged Buddhism: Buddhist Liberation Movements in Asia*, edited by Christopher S. Queen and Sallie B. King (State University of New York Press, 1996). Thich Nhat Hanh's simile of flowers and garbage is from his public dharma talk at Loyola University, Chicago, on August 23, 2003. The quote from David Halberstam regarding the self-immolation of Thich Quang Duc is taken from his *The Making of a Quagmire: America and Vietnam During the Kennedy Era*, revised edition (McGraw-Hill, 1987).

Chapter 4

The analysis of mindfulness of feelings and the analogy of "scientifically" observing one's own feelings is from Rahula, *What the Buddha Taught*. The reproductions of the corpse images from the Chaiya manuscripts and the analytical commentary is found in Buddhadasa Bikkhu, *Teaching Dhamma by Pictures* (Social Science Association Press of Thailand, 1968).

The numbers of American plastic surgery procedures for 1989 and 2001 are taken from Susan Bordo, "The Empire of Images in Our World of Bodies," *Chronicle of Higher Education* (December 19, 2003). The discussion of the psychologist Barry Schwartz's findings on the relation between freedom of choice and happiness is drawn from his article "The Tyranny of Choice," *Chronicle of Higher Education* (January 23, 2004).

My discussion of Hernando De Soto's theories is informed by his book *The Mystery of Capital: Why Capitalism Triumphs in the West and Fails Everywhere Else*, reprint edition (Basic Books, 2003).

Chapter 5

David Chandler's work on the S-21 torture chamber is unparalleled. Much of my own understanding has been shaped by his "S-21: The Wheel of History and the Pathology of Terror in Democratic Kampuchea," in *Cambodia Emerges from the Past*, edited by Judy Ledgerwood (Center for Southeast Asian Studies, Northern Illinois University, 2002). Also see Chandler's *Voices from S-21*. The story of S-21 survivor Bou Meng is detailed in Lon Nara, "S-21 Survivor's Reported Demise Much Exaggerated," *Phnom Penh Post* (January 31–February 13, 2003). John Marston's research on the uses and abuses of the word *Angkar* can be found in his "Democratic Kampuchea and the Idea of Modernity," in Ledgerwood, *Cambodia Emerges from the Past*.

The quoted interview with Venerable Tep Vong can be found at the website of the Documentation Center of Cambodia, www.dccam.org. Much of my discussion of karma as it relates to HIV/AIDS is indebted to the excellent thesis work of my student Mech Samphors. Her 2004 thesis, "*Kamma* as a Concept in Addressing HIV/AIDS," was presented to the Faculty of Social Sciences and Humanities, Royal University of Phnom Penh and should be available through the Ministry of Education or the Buddhist Institute, Phnom Penh, Cambodia. The quote from Venerable Tep Vong on AIDS is cited in Samphors's thesis.

After my friend Chaminda introduced me to the important work of Buddhadasa Bhikkhu, I read several of his books, including *Heartwood of the Bodhi Tree: The Buddha's Teachings on Voidness*, edited by Santikaro Bhikkhu (Wisdom Publications, 1994); *Practical Dependent Origination* (Dhamma Study and Practice Group, 1992); *Me and Mine* (State University of New York, 1989); and *Dhammic Socialism*, edited by Donald Swearer (Komol Kimtong Foundation, 1986). Some of my biographical information on Buddhadasa is drawn from Santikaro Bhikkhu, "Buddhadasa Bhikkhu: Life and Society Through the Natural Eyes of Voidness," in *Engaged Buddhism: Buddhist Liberation Movements in Asia*, edited by Christopher S. Queen and Sallie B. King (State University of New York

Press, 1996), and also from personal communication with Santikaro Bhikkhu. The quote from Donald Swearer regarding Buddhadasa's critique of *tham pun* is taken from Swearer's introduction to *Me and Mine*.

Chapter 6

Additional facts about Maha Ghosananda and his quotes about the dhammayietra are gleaned from Bob Maat, Liz Bernstein, and Yeshua Moser, "A Moment of Peace, a Glimmer of Hope," *Primary Point* (volume 10, number 2, Fall–Winter 1993), and Maha's introduction to his *Step by Step* (Parallax Press, 1992).

More information on Om Radsady's murder can be found throughout the *Cambodian Daily* starting February 19, 2003, and continuing into March and April. Similarly, the *Phnom Penh Post* contains two months of articles relating to the assassination. The quote from Prince Ranariddh concerning Radsady's murder is taken from Susan Font, "Jailbreak Renews Focus on Radsady Murder," *Phnom Penh Post* (September 24–October 9, 2003).

The Einstein quote on compassion is from a letter he wrote in 1950 to a rabbi. It is included in *Mathematical Circles Adieu: A Fourth Collection of Mathematical Stories and Anecdotes*, edited by Howard W. Eves (Prindle, Weber & Schmidt, 1977).

The Abhidhamma pitaka is deep and murky territory. Some good translations and commentaries were crucial for my own understanding. In particular, see Buddhaghosa's famous *Visuddhimagga*, recently published by the Buddhist Publication Society and Pariyatti Press as *Path of Purification: Visuddhimagga* (2003). Also see Venerable Nyanaponika, Thera's *Abhidhamma Studies* (Wisdom Publications, 1998), and *A Comprehensive Manual of Abhidhamma* (Abhidhammattha Sangaha), edited by Bhikkhu Bodhi (Buddhist Publication Society and Pariyatti Press, 1999). Contemporary scientific "no-self" theories can be found in the writings of cognitive scientists and philosophers such as Daniel Dennett, *Consciousness Explained* (Back Bay Books, 1992), and *Brainchildren: Essays on*

Designing Minds (Bradford Books, 1998). Also see Susan Blackmore, *The Meme Machine* (Oxford University Press, 2000), and Paul Churchland, *The Engine of Reason, The Seat of the Soul: A Philosophical Journey into the Brain* (Bradford Books, 1996). There is a good example of abhidhammic analysis (eating an apple) in chapter 10 of Alex Skilton's helpful book *A Concise History of Buddhism* (Windhorse Publications, 1994). My own example is inspired by Skilton's description. The quote from Venerable Nyanaponika Thera is from his book *Abhidhamma Studies*. The quote from William James is from *Varieties of Religious Experience*, reprint edition (Touchstone, 1997).

Chapter 7

The quote from Aldous Huxley on glimpsing "everything" through the smell of roast duck is from his novel *Point Counterpoint*, reprint edition (Dalkey Archive Press, 1996). The quote from Zhou Daguan and the historical sketch of the Angkor period is drawn from Chandler, *History of Cambodia*. The quotation from H. W. Ponder on Ta Phrom temple is taken from Dawn Rooney, *Angkor* (Odyssey, 2002). Facts about the difficulties of getting an education for rural Cambodians were drawn from *Cambodia: An Oxfam Country Profile* (Oxfam, 2001).

The information regarding Daniel Gilbert's psychological studies on happiness is taken from Jon Gertner, "The Futile Pursuit of Happiness," *New York Times Magazine* (September 7, 2003).

The Buddhadasa quote concerning "early morning nibbana" is from chapter 8 of his book *Me and Mine*. The quotes from George Santayana and David Brooks's related discussions of the future-looking American ethos are found in chapter 4 of Brooks's *On Paradise Drive* (Simon & Schuster, 2004).

Glossary

Abhidhamma (Pali), refers to the third division (pitika) of the Pali scriptures. Literally means the "higher" (abhi) teaching (dhamma). These texts are particularly philosophical compared to the more narrative sutta scriptures.

Anatta (Pali), no-soul, or no-self. The anti-essentialist doctrine at the heart of Buddhism.

Anicca (Pali), impermanence.

Atman (Sanskrit), soul, self, ego. Sometimes used generically to mean "permanent essence." This Hindu idea was the Buddha's bête noire.

Barang (Khmer), foreigner.

Bhikkhu (Pali), Buddhist monk.

Bhikkhuni (Pali), Buddhist nun.

Boran (Khmer), a mystical, supernatural form of Buddhism, practiced in rural areas.

Brahman (Sanskrit), the Hindu term for God or the supreme ultimate being.

Bray (Khmer), a powerful spirit, said to be the ghost of one who dies violently or painfully, like a woman in childbirth.

Deva (Sanskrit), usually a supernatural being, god, or deity that often occupies a parallel dimension, occasionally interacting with our human dimension. Also used as an honorific title.

Dhamma (Pali), the Buddha's teachings, or the truth, or the way. In later Abhidhamma scriptures the term takes on a different metaphysical meaning, something like "element of reality."

Dhammaraja (Pali), a just ruler, a good Buddhist king.

Dharma (Sanskrit). *See* Dhamma.

Dukkha (Pali), unsatisfactoriness, suffering.

Farang (Thai), foreigner.

Hinayana, literally "smaller vehicle," a derogatory term applied by later Northern Buddhists (Mahayanists) to older orthodox schools of Buddhism.

Jai yen (Thai), a phrase that means "cool your heart," usually said to calm another person from losing their temper, from losing face.

Jhana (Pali), also transliterated as "dhyana," a trance state of meditation.

Kamma (Pali), literally means "action," but usually means the law of action that rewards good actions with good consequences and bad actions with bad consequences.

Karma (Sanskrit). *See* Kamma.

Khanda (Pali), a faculty, component, or aggregate present in all living beings. There are five khandas altogether: body, sensation, perception, volition, and consciousness.

Kru (Khmer), a shaman or sorcerer who can negotiate with the animistic powers.

Ksatriya (Pali), the second caste of the Indian caste system, usually composed of warriors and royals. The caste of the historical Buddha, Gotama Siddhattha.

Magga (Pali), path, way.

Mahanikay (Pali) a mainstream moderate monastic order within Theravada Buddhism (dating back to the Mahavihara period in Sri Lanka).

Mahayana, literally the "greater vehicle" (as opposed to Hinayana), used to designate later schools of Buddhism, including forms now practiced in China, Korea, Japan, Vietnam, and Tibet.

Neak ta (Khmer), a genus of popular tutelary spirits that inhabit geo-

graphical places in Cambodia. A specific animistic being that is sometimes integrated with, sometimes antagonistic with, Buddhist beliefs.

Nibbana (Pali), literally "blowing out" cravings. The ultimate goal of
Buddhism. A peaceful state of extinguished desires.

Nirvana (Sanskrit). *See* Nibbana.

Panna (Pali), wisdom.

Parami (Pali), literally "perfection," but informally "superhuman power."

Parinibbana (Pali), final passing away or extinguishing of an enlightened
being.

Paticca Samuppada (Pali), dependent arising or conditioned causality.
The metaphysical/ethical doctrine that every event has a cause (no
uncaused causes) and that there is a distinct sequence of causes leading to and from human suffering. With proper insight into these
causes, one can work to become free of them (nibbana).

Punna (Pali), acts of merit-making that eventually lead to good consequences.

Rupa (Pali), body or matter (one of the five aggregates, khandas).

Samadhi (Pali), concentration.

Samsara (Pali), literally "to come again and again," the doctrine of rebirth.

Sangha (Pali), the community of Buddhist monks.

Sankhara (Sanskrit), volition (one of the five khandas).

Sanna (Pali), perception (one of the five khandas).

Sati (Pali), mindfulness.

Sila (Pali), moral virtue (expressed in the Five Precepts and also as part
of the Eight-fold Path).

Sunyata (Sanskrit), also **Sunnata** (Pali), literally means "emptiness." A
prevalent Buddhist doctrine of the emptiness (impermanence) of all
phenomena. An alternate way of expressing the anatta doctrine and
the doctrine of paticca-samuppada. The rejection of essentialism and
transcendentalism.

Suttas (Pali), literally "threads." Generally used to designate the threads
of discourse contained in the narrative teachings (for laypeople) of

the Theravada Pali scriptures (the other two baskets (pitika) of the Tipitika are the Vinaya, or monks' rules, and the Abhidhamma). Most understanding of Buddhism, both East and West, comes through the suttas.

Tanha (Pali), craving, thirst, desire.

Thammayut (Pali), literally "adherence to the dhamma." A stringent monastic order of Theravada established in Thailand around 1833—during the reforms implemented by Mongkut (1804–68), the son of King Rama II, who became a monk shortly before his father's death and became king of Thailand in 1851. Thammayut spread to Cambodia and Laos.

Theravada (Pali), literally "doctrine of the elders." The oldest surviving form of Buddhism and only remaining school of Hinayana. It is practiced in Sri Lanka, Myanmar, Thailand, Laos, and Cambodia.

Tipitika (Pali), the Pali language Buddhist scriptures, considered to be the oldest and purest documentation of the dhamma.

Vajrayana, literally the "diamond vehicle" or path. It is the Tibetan subspecies of Buddhism that exists in the genus of Mahayana Buddhism.

Vedana (Pali), sensation/feeling (one of the five khandas).

Vihar (Pali), the spiritual center of a Buddhist temple complex.

Vinnana (Pali), consciousness (one of the five khandas).

Vipassana (Pali), insight through meditation.

Wat, a Theravada Buddhist temple.

Acknowledgments

This book was written during an especially tumultuous time in my life. I am extremely grateful to my family for their openhearted support. My parents and brothers were pillars of strength, and my extended family offered much-needed sanctuary. Thanks to Ed, Carol, Dave, Elaine, Garrison, Maddy, Dan, Lynn, and Keaton.

I owe a debt of gratitude to my friends who stuck by me through tough weather: Peter Altenberg, Brian Wingert, Jim Christopulos, Tom Greif, Kyle and Ann Olson, Amy Weisbrot, Anna Seifert, Aaron Gigliotti, Teresa Prados-Torreira, Dominic Pacyga, Ben Dauer, Bob Long, Baheej Khleif, and Susan Anderson-Khleif.

I have been fortunate to enjoy the support of Columbia College Chicago. Particular thanks go to provost Steve Kapelke, dean Cheryl Johnson-Odim, director of the Center for Teaching Excellence David Krause, and troubleshooter extraordinaire Oscar Valdez.

Many professional colleagues and friends have aided my work generally, and I'd like to recognize Annuska Derks, Michael Shermer, Alex Kafka, Erik Davis, Judy Ledgerwood, David Kalupahana, Stephanie Gee, Charles Foran, Yann Martel, Jennifer Lieto, Zung Dao, Sheryl Fullerton,

Herman Stark, Micki Leventhal, and Dawn Larsen. This book has been improved by the careful attention of Eric Brandt, Kris Ashley, and Lisa Zuniga at HarperSanFrancisco. Their encouragement was instrumental in the parturition of my book. Of course, I take full responsibility for the remaining shortcomings.

I was privileged to work with many wonderful people in Southeast Asia, some of whom I count as good friends. Chief among these friends is Peter Gyallay-Pap, whose goodwill and expertise proved to be crucial. Much gratitude is also owed to Heng Kimvan, Hean Sokhom, Heng Joli, Chaminda Rajapakse, Neth Barom, Bhikkhu K. Sovanratana, and Venerable Say Amnann. My friend Pierrot Hostettler and his fine crew at L'Oasis Little Hotel (in Kapko Market) always made me feel at home. Practice on that guitar, Pierrot!

With great admiration, I wish to acknowledge the following inspirational people: Pong Pheakdey Boramy, Sok Ra, Chor Chanthyda, Than Bunly, Aing Sokroeun, Chea Bunnary, Yin Sombo, Ham Samnom, Chheat Sreang, and Seng Hokmeng. Very special thanks to my friends Mech Samphors and Hel Rithy.

Last on my list, but first in my feelings of gratitude, is my mercurial Manchu Wen Rong Jin, who gave me a beautiful son. Together, let us make him proud.

I dedicate this book and myself to Julien.